Philadelphia Merchants on Western Waters

Philadelphia Merchants on Western Waters

Commerce and Empire in the Riverine West, 1750–1803

KIM M. GRUENWALD

Johns Hopkins University Press
Baltimore

Printed in the United States of America on acid-free paper

2 4 6 8 9 7 5 3 1

Johns Hopkins University Press
2715 North Charles Street
Baltimore, Maryland 21218
www.press.jhu.edu

Library of Congress Cataloging-in-Publication Data is available.
A catalog record for this book is available from the British Library.

ISBN 978-1-4214-5215-9 (hardcover)
ISBN 978-1-4214-5216-6 (ebook)

Special discounts are available for bulk purchases of this book. For more information, please contact Special Sales at specialsales@jh.edu.

EU GPSR Authorized Representative
LOGOS EUROPE, 9 rue Nicolas Poussin, 17000, La Rochelle, France
E-mail: Contact@logoseurope.eu

For Jill

CONTENTS

ACKNOWLEDGMENTS

A number of institutions helped make this book possible. The Kent State University Research Council has granted me either a faculty professional improvement leave or an academic year research and creative activity appointment to work on the manuscript for a semester free from teaching duties on a few occasions. The College of Arts and Sciences at Kent State University awarded me a substantial grant through an A&S Research Advance Incentive Award in the spring of 2013. I spent a very productive month following the course of the Ohio and Mississippi Rivers by car, stopping at various archives along the way thanks to their support. I received short-term fellowships from the Program in Early American Economy & Society at the Library Company of Philadelphia in 2003 and 2015, respectively. I came to love spending time in the City of Brotherly Love while doing research at the Library Company and the Historical Society of Pennsylvania next door, as well as attending talks at the McNeil Center for Early American Studies while living in the Cassatt House. The Library Company kindly let me stay there during another summer visit when they had a room free. Philadelphia is truly a walking city that hosts a wonderful scholarly community—I consider it my research home.

I made the largest strides toward completing this project when I presented my work at a conference titled "Zones and Lines, Water and Land: New Conversations on Borders" in 2019, convened by Rachel Herrmann of Cardiff University and Jessica Choppin Roney of Temple University. After hosting a series of meetings on this topic, they edited a forthcoming book that pulls together the work of those who participated and others. Their comments on my chapter have been both invaluable and wonderfully insightful. I am also tremendously grateful to the pair of anonymous reviewers at Johns Hopkins University Press, who gave me just the feedback I needed to clarify my argument. Barry Beer, a now-retired colleague here at Kent State, read an early draft, and my old mentor at the University of Colorado, Fred Anderson, read a later draft and sent me helpful comments. Everyone at Johns Hopkins University Press has been wonderful, and I thank them for guiding me along every step of the way.

Seth Rainey from Kent State University's Geography Department created the maps for me. Discussions with Emily Hager Kasecamp as I directed her dissertation helped shape my characterization of Samuel Wharton. Another of my doctoral students, Stephanie Jannenga, served as my research assistant one semester. Colleagues at the History Department have provided good fellowship, and I especially enjoyed the semester during which Ann Heiss and I met for lunch each week to discuss our projects. Back in Colorado, I've been lucky to have such a supportive family, especially my mother, my sister, and my niece, as well as my aunt and uncle in Boston. Thanks to them for their love and encouragement over the years. I feel like my friend Jill Beer acted as the midwife to this project, and it is to her that I dedicate this book. I can't thank her enough.

Philadelphia Merchants on Western Waters

Introduction

In the eighteenth century, as a general rule, the Mississippi and Ohio Rivers rose in late fall thanks to rain and in the spring thanks to melting snow. As an army officer, Thomas Hutchins had made a detailed study of the western waters. He sent Thomas Jefferson the following report on February 11, 1784: "The periodical flood commence[s]" on the Wabash and Illinois Rivers in early February, with the Ohio River beginning to rise in March unless the winter was mild. "The Missouri begins to rise early in February, and the upper Mississippi early in March." The flood on the Ohio River might come on suddenly or gradually depending on the weather, and it could last from six to eight weeks. The Upper Mississippi ran high for a couple weeks longer than that, and the water ran high on the Lower Mississippi "between four and five months, that is, from January to July." When descending the Mississippi River during the spring floods, boats encountered "eddies or counter-currents, which always run in the bends, close to the banks of the river, with nearly equal velocity against the stream, and assist the ascending boats." The current's rate ran five miles an hour in the spring but only about two miles an hour later in summer and early fall, when the river ran low. Boats had to make their way around sand banks, islands, and shoals, making the faster sections "more dangerous than in the spring." Merchandise sent from New Orleans to Illinois in spring or fall covered a distance of 950 miles, requiring eighteen to twenty men rowing a 40-ton boat for eight to ten weeks. In consequence, most people who went downstream on the western waters made the trip during the same short window, creating gluts in the market by the time they reached the Gulf Coast. Goods could come upriver as far as Natchez, but for the most part the vast majority of cargo went downstream only. People walked home, one way or another—either up the Natchez Trace or west from an eastern port after a sea voyage to the Atlantic coast from New Orleans.[1]

During the second half of the eighteenth century, Philadelphia merchants wanted to expand their commercial networks into the interior of North America, but to do so, they would need to know that they had the right to navigate and trade on western rivers. This study explores the central role rivers played in the establishment and growth of the United States at a time when Philadelphia assumed the role of North America's most important port. Reliance on western waters to expand into the interior meant that there was no way for rivals to avoid each other—the rivers brought them together whether they liked it or not. Before the American Revolution, one empire controlled one bank of the Ohio or Mississippi, while another controlled the opposite bank. The first roads to Pittsburgh gave Philadelphia merchants a head start during and after the Seven Years' War, as merchants sought to corner the fur trade in Illinois and slave owners of all nations sought flour from the farmers of eastern Pennsylvania. In the 1790s, Philadelphia helped lay the groundwork for the Louisiana Purchase by opening up trade in New Orleans. The experiences of Philadelphia merchants on western waters are at the heart of how and why Americans finally established control over both banks of the Ohio and Mississippi Rivers in 1803 to claim a region that had eluded European empires as the first step toward creating an American empire of their own.

The popular image of North American colonies growing in isolation from Europe has long been debunked by scholars of the Atlantic World. The Atlantic World of colonial America had relied on merchants extending their networks from the coast to the fall line of rivers, providing access to a backcountry that stretched from New England to the Lower South. As for the Lower Mississippi, both France and Spain hoped the region would protect their other territories from the British, while the British sought trade in exchange for Spanish specie, as well as setting their sights on the rich lands of West Florida. During the opening years of the nineteenth century, the Lewis and Clark Expedition headed up the Missouri River to explore the Louisiana Purchase—after all, utilizing rivers to gain access to the interior of North America had worked for a half century. However, Lewis and Clark failed to discover any northwest passage to the Pacific Ocean. Americans would expand instead across the plains on foot or horseback, by wagon, and eventually by railroad. In between that colonial Atlantic

World and the world of overland trails in the trans-Mississippi West lay a world where life and livelihoods centered on rivers. What has long been referred to by historians as the trans-Appalachian West would be better served by understanding both the region and the era of its settlement as "the Riverine West."

As Philadelphia merchants engaged in commerce on the international world of the western waters of the interior of North America, their story reveals what happened when the Atlantic World made landfall and then surged along western waters, before giving way to the beginning of a new continental empire in 1803, when one nation at last controlled both banks of the Ohio and Mississippi Rivers. Philadelphia merchants forged commercial connections in the Riverine West while moving downstream along the most efficient route for goods to travel, and they had to share that journey with peoples of all nations because rivals claimed opposite banks. They sought to harness the downstream power of interior rivers from the Ohio's headwaters to New Orleans during the second half of the eighteenth century, providing flour to the hungry port that sat at the key exit point for shipments from the interior of the continent. In the process, Philadelphia merchants took part in extinguishing Native American land titles, expanding slavery up the Mississippi River, and claiming a continental empire for the new United States. Their letter books, journals, ledgers, and other business records allow us to track the movement and networks of people and goods that would integrate East and West along the western waters between Pittsburgh and New Orleans.

Two firms in particular stand out. The firm of Baynton, Wharton & Morgan left behind extensive records from a time when Philadelphia was a colonial port before the American Revolution, perhaps because the Wharton family was an influential one. The firm made the greatest investment in trade down the Ohio River in the 1760s. After the American Revolution, the firm of Reed & Forde was among the first to trade extensively with Spanish New Orleans in the years before Pinckney's Treaty opened up the port for all. Their records may have survived because they had made claims against the federal government over spoiled flour that took decades to settle. Reed and Forde were not particularly wealthy or influential in Philadelphia itself, but they were extremely active, with a wide range of connections that open a window into the commercial world of western rivers.

The events chronicled here all played out in an era when people could travel no faster than the current of a river, and they made their way downstream out in the open for anyone on shore to see. The distant horizon wouldn't have been as important as scanning what awaited them around the next bend. Trees lined the banks, making the rivers corridors on which everyone might find the clearest path to their destination. It was an intimate setting with face-to-face meetings in boats, as well as stops on shore to exchange news or a meal when a settlement came into view. When people descended rivers, they couldn't take a detour to avoid others like they might on the ocean or when they crossed the plains. People received goods that came downriver from the Ohio's headwaters and sent their own crops downriver to the Gulf Coast. Because the Ohio ran low in both the summer and winter, shipments of flour arrived in New Orleans at roughly the same time in the spring and fall, creating gluts that lowered prices. But the rivers were the artery of travel for everyone west of the Appalachian Mountains, and avoiding fellow travelers would be impossible.

The story of the Riverine West begins with the emergence of Philadelphia as the most important port in North America. In 1750, Philadelphia's merchants primarily traded with England and other English colonies in North America and the West Indies. The Seven Years' War brought a flood of bills of exchange and a host of new trading opportunities. Afterward, as colonists, the merchants transformed the port and expanded its hinterland to the west while seeking land grants beyond the Appalachian Mountains from the king. When the colonies declared independence, Philadelphia became a national port and, for a time, the new nation's capital. As citizens of this new nation, a new generation of merchants sought to connect East and West along the Ohio and Mississippi Rivers and corner the market on land warrants issued by states attempting to raise money to pay war debts.[2] Two generations of commercial plans came to fruition with the Louisiana Purchase. The merchants who made those plans and their role in integrating the Riverine West into a new American empire are the focus of this study.

Extending Philadelphia's hinterland into the heart of North America meant utilizing western waters. England, France, and Spain were all well established in the Western Hemisphere; Native Americans had been allying with one European empire or another for well over a century; and the slave trade was in full swing by 1750. After nibbling away at the continent by way of the St. Lawrence River, the Atlantic coast, and the Gulf Coast, Europeans set their sights on the interior by way of the Ohio and Mississippi Rivers. All manner of human interaction along those riverbanks would follow.

According to an early chronicler, Native Americans on the Upper Mississippi called it Metchasippi, or Father of Rivers. The Mississippi's headwaters are in present-day Minnesota, and the river flows over 2,000 miles to a delta on the Gulf of Mexico. Tributaries bring water to it from over two-thirds of the land south of the Great Lakes between the Appalachian and Rocky Mountains. Whoever controls its course controls much of the flow of people and goods in North America. The Ohio River is a little less than half as long and is the Mississippi River's largest tributary. The Ohio begins where the Allegheny and Monongahela Rivers come together in Pittsburgh, Pennsylvania. The Northwest Ordinance made the river an official boundary between slave and free states, but merchants and farmers on the northern and southern banks created a region referred to as the Western Country in the era before steamboats. Economically speaking, the river's drainage supported some crops that could be profitably produced with slave labor; thus, it wasn't only as a border that the Ohio becomes part of the story of slavery in North America (see figs. I.1 and I.2).[3]

During the second half of the eighteenth century, the Ohio and Mississippi Valleys were not simple frontiers—the "meeting place[s] of peoples" without clear boundaries; rather, they were what historians Jeremy Adelman and Stephen Aron labeled *borderlands*—"the contested boundaries between colonial domains."[4] Each empire had its own concerns—the French wanted to extend the fur trade down the Mississippi River to the Gulf of Mexico, while the Spanish wished to protect their assets to the south. The British wanted to capture the fur trade by creating their own alliances with Native Americans, while Native Americans wanted to trade with whoever gave them the best prices without encroaching on their territory. During the eighteenth century, the opposite banks of the Ohio and Mississippi Rivers were often claimed by rivals. After the British exiled the French from the Ohio Valley, Shawnee Indians wanted to protect their hunting grounds south of the river. The Spanish controlled territory west of the Mississippi River, while first the French and then the English took control of the eastern bank. Getting along meant trade, and trade meant access to rivers. Europeans, colonists, and Native Americans eyed each other warily and traded with each other even while trying to press their advantage.

Doing business in the borderlands involved trying to establish connections to other interested parties in places that might be under the control of a different empire in the future. Pensacola on the Gulf Coast might have changed hands the most often: the Spanish controlled the area in the late sixteenth and early seventeenth centuries, the French took over for a few years in 1719, but the Spanish soon reasserted their claim until the end of the Seven Years' War. The settlement served as the capital of British West Florida from that point until 1781, when the Spanish captured it during the American Revolution and managed to hang on to it until 1819. The French established New Orleans in 1718; the Spanish took over in 1763 but then ceded it back to the French for a

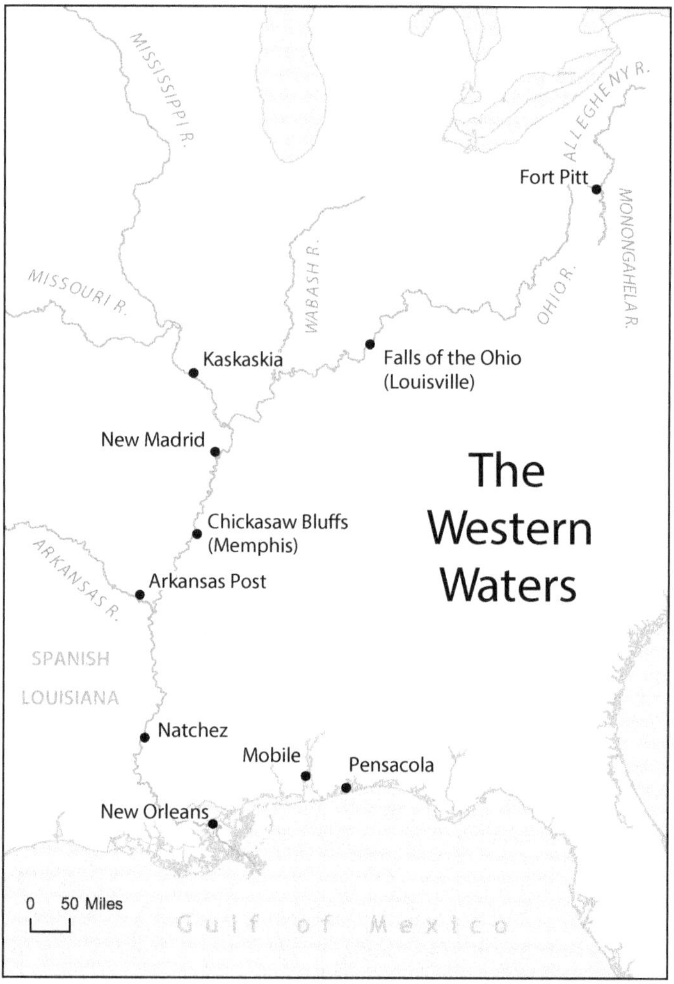

Figure I.1. Map of the western waters in the eighteenth century. © Seth Rainey

short time, before the United States purchased Louisiana and its all-important port in 1803. The history of Illinois looks stable by comparison: the French settled in there in 1673, until ceding it to the British in 1763, and then it became part of the new United States in 1783. Havana, Cuba, grew as a Spanish settlement in the seventeenth century; Great Britain captured it in 1762 but traded it for Florida a year later, and it remained under Spanish control until nearly the end of the nineteenth century.

Recent scholars have begun reimagining how the history of such contested spaces fits into the larger narrative of the eighteenth century. Traditionally, schol-

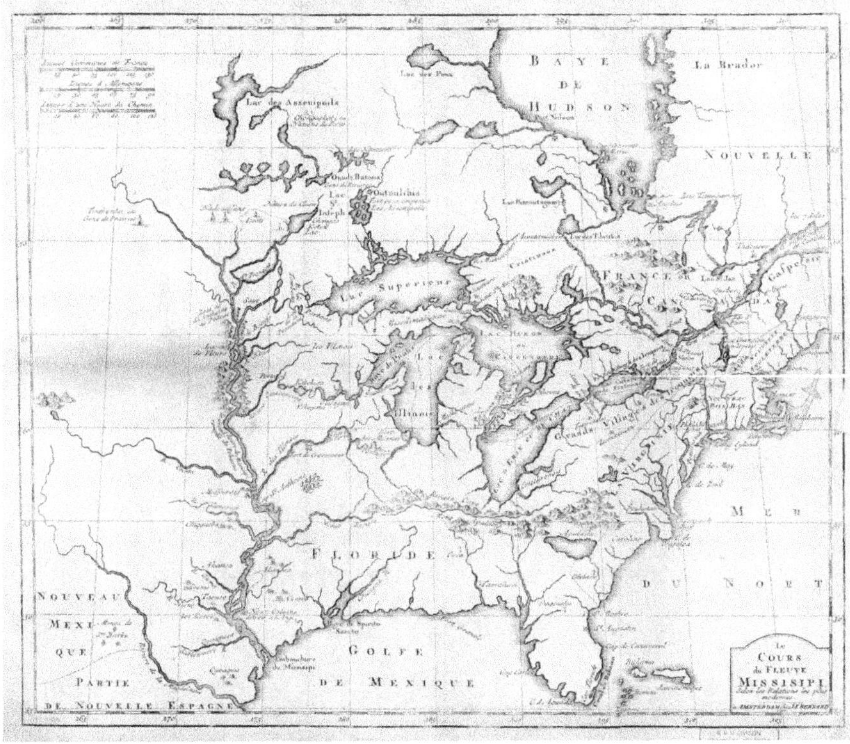

Figure I.2. The western waters in 1737. Jean Frederic Bernard, *Le cours du fleuve Missisip selon les relations les plus modernes.* Courtesy of the Library of Congress

ars situated the history of the trans-Appalachian frontier between the colonial frontier of the eighteenth century and the trans-Mississippi frontier of the first half of the nineteenth century. In the 1890s, Frederick Jackson Turner introduced the idea of the frontier in North America as a moving line of settlement that came in waves: fur traders, pioneers, farmers, and men of commerce. Europeans did battle with the wilderness and all who lived there, becoming Americans in the process. Key themes included individualism and self-sufficiency. The "new western historians" of the 1980s challenged Turner's thesis, focusing on communities and the role of the federal government, among other things. They also focused on the frontier as a place rather than a process, and for many of them that place was west of the Mississippi River. But another path opened by scholars involved comparative frontiers, which they defined as zones of "cultural interaction" or "intercultural penetration," a definition that applied well to the trans-Appalachian frontier. Rather than proffering a story of the "conquest" of North America, these scholars concentrated on "accommodations" between various peoples to tell a more complex story.[5]

A new generation of scholars would use these themes to tie the history of the Ohio and Mississippi Rivers to the wider field of Atlantic history. Historian Paul Mapp focused on the interaction between empires, studying the interior of North America and adding the Pacific Ocean to the mix between 1713 and 1763. Mapp noted that explorers from all nations continued to look for a northwest passage that did not exist, while other European powers wanted to stop the flow of specie to Spain from the western coast of South America. Mapp explored what Europeans misunderstood about North America and how it affected their calculations during the decades leading up to and through the Seven Years' War. By the end of the conflict, France had given up on their plans for the interior of North America, while England's plans grew. Spain focused on using the Lower Mississippi to defend other holdings, and Native Americans lost a crucial ally they had utilized to make demands of the British.[6]

As for the war and its aftermath, historian François Furstenberg dubbed the era from 1754 to 1815 "the Long War for the West." Furstenberg sifted through the various viewpoints and strategies of the English, French, Spanish, and Native Americans as all sought to control the region. As the only outlet for trade beyond the mountains at that time, he labeled New Orleans a "hot spot" and focal point of many plans. Going beyond the usual reason scholars of American history peg 1789 as a turning point, Furstenberg explored the impact of the French Revolution on westerners clamoring for more from the new federal government. Furstenberg showed that, far from being an isolated frontier, the Ohio and Mississippi Valleys were a key stage upon which the "sweeping forces of imperialism and global warfare" played out from the Seven Years' War through the fall of Napoleon.[7]

The most recent scholarship puts rivers even more squarely at the center of the narrative. Historian Susan Sleeper-Smith focuses her attention on the world of Native American women in the Ohio Valley in the eighteenth century, while historian Jacob F. Lee characterizes Native American tribes in the Mississippi Valley as "Masters of the Middle Waters." Historian Susan Gaunt Stearns has proposed a different way to periodize the Riverine West after the American Revolution, by highlighting three key diplomatic events. First, the Spanish created a crisis for the new United States by closing the Mississippi River to trade in 1784; second, the reopening of the river to trade through Pinckney's Treaty in 1795 forever changed the relationship between East and West; and third, with the purchase of Louisiana in 1803, the United States controlled the entire course of the Mississippi River at last. Stearns concentrates much of her analysis on the western settlers in Kentucky and Natchez, who pushed hardest for the United States to take control of the Mississippi River.[8]

In the end, the Riverine West became part of the United States. Historian Eric Hinderaker wrote of "elusive empires" in the eighteenth-century Ohio Valley under French and English rule, while Paul Mapp characterized the interior of North America as the "elusive West" prior to the Seven Years' War.[9] But control of the region did not elude the new nation. Rather than colonies, newly independent Americans established territories that became states, and they crested the mountains in large numbers as they eagerly sought land of their own. The course of the Ohio and Mississippi Rivers, among others, dictated most of the early settlement patterns, as well as the direction in which goods would flow. Philadelphia merchants were among the first to use those rivers to make sure that the region remained connected to the Eastern Seaboard and the Atlantic World. Who did they encounter on those rivers, how did they interact with them, and how did they build the commercial connections that laid the groundwork for the diplomacy that followed?

Merchants were often at the forefront of western expansion, not following settlers as Turner often portrayed them. "Towns were the spearheads of the frontier," argued Richard Wade.[10] Recent historians like David Hancock who analyze the role of merchants and trade in the early modern world have shifted the focus from markets, hierarchy, and state institutions to the study of personal relationships and individual decisions. Hancock posited that successful entrepreneurs were people who shared three traits and talents: "a willingness to shoulder uncertainty and risk, management, and creative opportunism."[11] The people he studied did not care as much about changing international boundaries as they did about expanding their commercial networks. Taking advantage of local opportunities, the distributors of Madeira wine created a decentralized, networked, and self-organized world. But when those networks made landfall, extending along a continent's rivers, did that trend toward favoring networks over boundaries hold true—did Philadelphia merchants act the same way? In a study comparing the mercantile communities of Philadelphia and Liverpool, Sheryllyne Haggerty focused on how merchants managed information, risk, credit, and their reputations. Traditionally, she wrote, property was among the safest of investments. But what happened when the pursuit of property in the form of unsettled western lands became a major source of investment for Philadelphia merchants? The heart of Hancock's and Haggerty's studies, as well as mine, is the creation of commercial connections.[12]

The world of eighteenth-century merchants, including those of the Riverine West, was one of partners and associates. Most firms were made up of a pair, but three partners were not out of the ordinary. In a world without instant communication, partnerships allowed firms to act in two or more places at once. Baynton, Wharton & Morgan stretched from Philadelphia west to Illinois and east to London after the Seven Years' War. After the American Revolution, the firm of Reed & Forde typically had one man heading west through Pennsylvania and then down the Ohio and Mississippi Rivers from Pittsburgh to New Orleans, while the other remained back home in Philadelphia. Daniel W. Coxe and Daniel Clark Jr. didn't even reside in the same city (Philadelphia and New Orleans, respectively) when they sought to corner the market in Spanish New Orleans in the 1790s. There were richer men in Philadelphia, many of them bankers and investors and political figures, but businessmen like George Morgan, John Reed, Standish Forde, and Daniel W. Coxe actually traveled on western waters to deal with opportunities there firsthand. They were the ones truly responsible for expanding commercial networks from Philadelphia to Illinois and New Orleans and back by way of the Atlantic.

Throughout the tussle over territory, Philadelphia merchants made their presence felt at the scene of the action. Baynton, Wharton & Morgan competed with David Franks & Company for influence in Illinois after the Seven Years' War. Oliver Pollock first visited the West Indies and New Orleans as an agent of the Philadelphia firm Willing & Morris before settling in New Orleans and acting as an American agent during the American Revolution. Reed & Forde dispatched many of the first American ships to trade in New Orleans in the early 1790s. Coxe & Clarke set up the most direct link between Philadelphia and New Orleans. All these men had to find a way to do their business in places not firmly under first British and later American control.[13]

Historian Jacob Price called merchants of the early modern world the "ringmasters" who established and coordinated the economic infrastructure of commercial paper, clearinghouses, and insurance. Before banks became common, merchants were the ones extending credit. Rather than focusing on amassing capital, they kept their wealth flowing through accounts receivable, debt, warehouses, and shares in ships. During the second half of the eighteenth century, American merchants acquired nearly all their manufactured goods from Europe, and the processing they engaged in utilized simple mills to turn wheat to flour, corn to whiskey, or logs to planks. They regularly transferred and discounted English bills of exchange, making them the true negotiable instruments of business.[14] The letter books, account books, ledgers, and other records of Baynton, Wharton & Morgan; Reed & Forde; and Coxe & Clark, among others, reveal the flow of goods and the building of networks. Their travel accounts unveil a truly international world in the West.

It is no accident that the merchants best known for their ventures west came from Philadelphia. Boston merchants had made their port the most important during the seventeenth century by exporting fish, shingles, and barrel staves to England and the West Indies. In the 1750s, Southerners created land companies, but they lagged behind the North in terms of commercial networks. New Yorkers engaged more in the coastal trade early on and did not come into their own until the nineteenth century. During the eighteenth century, Philadelphians concentrated on provisions for southern Europe, the West Indies, and New Orleans. As a port, Philadelphia would be the most affected by the Seven Years' War thanks to commercial paper spent by the British Army. During and after the Revolution, as the new nation's capital, many banking, insurance, and land schemes originated there.[15] The evolving strategies and choices made by Philadelphia merchants are the story of the expansion of English settlement across the Appalachian Mountains. Philadelphia merchants forged the widest Atlantic World ties, from their European suppliers to the Ohio and Mississippi Rivers to the Gulf Coast, as the North American British colonies sought to expand over the Appalachian Mountains and then as the new United States sought to establish a continental empire.

Examining the correspondence of Philadelphia merchants and tracing their connections through their business records reveals a few key themes. First, they often wrote about land. Samuel Wharton intended to set up a new colony in the West and drew up plans for how land would be distributed and society governed. George Morgan had a comprehensive plan for a colony on the Mississippi River a quarter of a century later, but by that time a new kind of land speculation had begun. John Reed and Standish Forde bought and tried to sell hundreds of thousands of acres by way of land warrants issued by states like Pennsylvania and Virginia. They invested in mills as well, but they had no plans to be in charge of a new society in the West; instead, the region would be part of the new United States. Land speculation in North America did not simply change course from colonial land companies to speculation by individuals through the General Land Office in the 1790s. There was a transition period, and Philadelphia merchants were in the thick of it.

That interest in land also meant that Philadelphia merchants took part in an important turning point in the relationship between Native Americans and Europeans and their descendants. After the American Revolution, fur traders crossed the Mississippi to the plains and beyond as the development of towns and manufacturing began in earnest in the West beyond the Appalachian Mountains. Newly independent Americans wanted Native American territory rather than trade. Baynton, Wharton & Morgan had taken a much greater interest in the fur trade than Reed & Forde did two decades later. Shifting priorities and the loss of European allies meant that Native Americans faced new challenges after the war.[16]

Another important development Philadelphia merchants took part in involved directly contributing to the growth of the slave economy on the Lower Mississippi River by selling flour in New Orleans. New flour markets provided incentives, and their access to it gave them an advantage over other eastern ports. Philadelphia merchants also imported slaves to Illinois. Flour from Pennsylvania, Illinois, and the Ohio Valley allowed staple crops, harvested by slaves, to flourish in the Riverine West. Philadelphia merchants also did business regularly in the West Indies. The expansion of slavery is at the heart of this story.

The half century of commercial expansion along the Ohio and Mississippi Rivers from 1750 to 1803 represents a riverine world different from the Atlantic World of the East Coast before it and the expansion by overland trail across the plains after. Philadelphia merchants wanted to integrate the interior of North America into the Atlantic World, first as British subjects and then as citizens of a new republic. The British could provide a wide variety of manufactured goods not available from the French or Spanish, but the Spanish eagerly paid with specie. Native Americans and the French were the first to create commercial links at the most likely spots in the Riverine West, and Americans followed their lead. New Orleans had to be supplied from outside the region with flour, and that's what Philadelphia merchants brought to the table—they were eager to trade for both furs and specie. Empires usually hold things together with armies, while merchants hold things together with commercial networks. In the Riverine West, those loyal to British, French, or Spanish empires met to do business—they crossed boundaries on a regular basis and sometimes even traded one imperial loyalty for another. Philadelphia merchants created commercial networks that bound East and West together and provided the foundation for the new nation's continental empire.

The study of Philadelphia merchants on western waters is divided into two parts. Part I, "Colonial Port," explores the intersection of acquiring territory and creating new commercial networks as merchants worked the imperial land grant game and established trade with Native Americans in the Ohio Valley and Illinois to the north and along the Gulf Coast to the south. The story begins with Philadelphia pulled into imperial rivalries in the West thanks to the Seven Years' War. At the war's end, some American merchants wanted to capture the fur trade in Illinois, while others saw value in establishing trade on the Lower Mississippi. George Morgan set off for Illinois and encountered people of various backgrounds as he traveled on the Ohio and Mississippi Rivers. The same merchants who were trying to overcome obstacles to trade along western waterways also pushed for royal land grants. As subjects of a king, they tried to work Great Britain's mercantile and land grant systems to their own advantage.

Part II, "National Port," traces the intersection of acquiring territory and creating new commercial networks, which involved speculating in land warrants and trading staples along western rivers and in New Orleans. After declaring independence, the new states used land sales to make money in the North, while those along the Gulf Coast had choices to make about who to back in the war. Merchants would find it tough to make their western plans work because hegemony over western waters remained in doubt when the war ended, and competition intensified over who would control the Lower Mississippi and New Orleans. But after Pinckney's Treaty, Americans flooded into the southern port with all manner of commercial schemes, and the new United States made the biggest land purchase of them all—Louisiana—in 1803. As citizens of a new nation, Americans made the Ohio and Mississippi Valleys their own.

PART ONE

COLONIAL PORT

Philadelphia merchants sought to expand the port's hinterland west after the Seven Years' War. Rivalry between European powers along the Ohio and Mississippi Rivers had been ongoing since the early eighteenth century. When war finally broke out in 1754, it shook up the merchants' world in Philadelphia and brought a flood of commercial paper into the city. Three men came together to establish the firm that made the biggest splash in trade to the west shortly after the war ended—John Baynton, Samuel Wharton, and George Morgan. France and Spain had a head start west of the Appalachian Mountains during the first half of the eighteenth century, and the Seven Years' War positioned Philadelphia as the port that would give England their entry into the West in the decades that followed.

The first moves made by Baynton, Wharton & Morgan involved trying to capture the fur trade in Illinois. As they descended the rivers with their goods, they discovered an international world at a time when rival European empires and Native American alliances controlled opposite banks. George Morgan served as the firm's representative there, and he had a tough time negotiating with French settlers, Spanish officials, and British officers. At the same time, other Philadelphia merchants explored their options on the Lower Mississippi and on the Gulf Coast. In the aftermath of the Treaty of Paris, Philadelphia merchants had to contend with shifting boundaries in North America as their plans bumped up against those of England, France, Spain, and various Native American alliances.

Philadelphia merchants wanted to do much more than corner the market on western commerce; they also plunged into land speculation schemes, with all the resources they could assemble. Samuel Wharton served as the firm's representative in London, taking the tried-and-true path of trying to gain the favor of the king while rivals nipped at his heels. In addition to competition from other Philadelphia firms, rivalry between colonies proved important as well when the actions of Lord Dunmore of Virginia led to violence. Philadelphia merchants also speculated in lands in West Florida. The last of the land speculators who sought to use the imperial system to chase land grants lost their bids for colonies of their own when their fellow Americans declared independence, and a new kind of land speculation would begin during the Revolutionary War.

An Imperial War

George Morgan is the Philadelphia merchant whose career provides the clearest lens through which we can view the role western rivers played in the expansion of the British empire and in the establishment of the empire of the new United States. Morgan's mother died days after his birth in 1743, and his father died a few years later. But he was hardly without family, including one brother who became a physician and another who became a merchant like their father before them. In his youth, the merchants of the port of Philadelphia did business with England, southern Europe, Madeira, and the West Indies, as well as participating in a lively trade with other ports along the coast. Morgan apprenticed with men known to his older brother just as war broke out and everything changed. Those changes would make Philadelphia North America's largest and most important port for the next half century—an era that witnessed the birth of a new nation and its expansion over more than half of the continent.[1] Philadelphia's merchants would be at the forefront of the effort.

In the decades before the Seven Years' War, British and Spanish ports in North America were oriented toward the Atlantic Ocean. France had penetrated the most deeply into the interior of the continent by way of the St. Lawrence and Great Lakes. When the French established the port of New Orleans, intending to control the Mississippi River from Illinois to the Gulf of Mexico, they planted themselves between Spanish territory in Florida to the east and present-day New Mexico to the west. Eventually, British colonists began to push west of the Appalachian Mountains, sparking a war between Great Britain and France that began at the Ohio River's headwaters in 1754 and spread around the globe between 1756 and 1763. It would be because of that conflict that Philadelphia merchants first began extending their commercial networks to the western waters. Rivalry between European powers along the Ohio and Mississippi Rivers had been ongoing since the early eighteenth century, as all three imperial powers kept watch on their rivals and competed for alliances with various Native American groups, all the while importing slaves for labor. When war finally broke out in 1754, merchants in Philadelphia made the most of new opportunities to supply the British army west of the Appalachian Mountains. After serving first as an apprentice and then as a clerk, George Morgan used money inherited from his father to become a partner in the firm that was to make the biggest investment in trade to the west shortly after the war ended: Baynton, Wharton & Morgan.

The Seven Years' War grew out of long-standing rivalries between European empires that began along the margins of North America. The Spanish firmed up their northern buffer zone protecting Mexico after the Pueblo Revolt, spread west to the Pacific coast, and kept an eye on the British from their stronghold at St. Augustine. After first settling the Atlantic coast from Chesapeake Bay to the Hudson River, the English settled north of Spanish Florida, bringing in slaves and establishing relationships with the Creeks and Cherokees, as well as other Native American tribes. The French had made good use of rivers to expand the fur trade when René-Robert Cavelier, Sieur de La Salle, first explored the Mississippi in 1682, claimed the valley, and named it Louisiana. Settlements followed on the Gulf Coast, along the Mississippi, in Illinois, and at Detroit over the next quarter of a century. The colony of Louisiana came under control of the Company of the Indies in 1717; the French established New Orleans the next year and then built Fort Chartres in Illinois in 1720. The company relinquished control in 1731, and Louisiana remained a royal colony until the English and Spanish took over at the end of the Seven Years' War in 1763.

The placement of French settlements in the interior of North America testifies to the importance of western waters in the eighteenth century. Two of the Mississippi's tributaries, the Red and Arkansas Rivers, start their journeys deep in the heart of Spanish territory in present-day New Mexico and Colorado. Pointe Coupée, about two-thirds of the way to Natchez from New Orleans, guarded the mouth of the Red River, and Arkansas Post, a little over halfway to the settlements in Illinois, guarded passage along that river. As for the Missouri River, the farthest north of the Mississippi's three largest tributaries from the west and the one that penetrated the farthest into North America, Cahokia in Illinois at its mouth had been an important Native American trade center for centuries before the French established their own settlement there, with Kaskaskia and Fort Chartres farther south (see fig. 1.1).

Reports from Louisiana in the 1720s reveal key themes about early attempts to control the interior, including French relationships with Native Americans, their early interest in utilizing African slaves as labor, and their concerns about European rivals. In 1719, Jean Baptiste Bernard de la Harpe's mission included "entering into trade with the Spaniards at the province of Texas" and exploring "the western part of Louisiana." Using the term *nation*, he wrote of one Native American tribe that kept chickens and grew corn and beans. Farther upriver his party stayed overnight at Baton Rouge, named for red stakes that separated the deer- and buffalo-hunting territories of two local tribes. Next, they encountered larger settlements where they found Jesuit missionaries doing their work. As they made their way up the Red River, de la Harpe's men traded with one group for corn and another for meat. The men of a Caddoan village helped them cut logs, and he described another group thus: "formerly they were nomadic."[2] Some Native Americans in the region had adapted to the coming of Europeans and taken advantage of the trade they offered.

However, others lost control of their territory. With the deerskin trade expanding, the French built a storehouse at the site of present-day Natchez in 1714, where traders exchanged goods for skins. The next year, the governor of Louisiana passed down the Mississippi without stopping to speak with local leaders. Not long after this breech of alliance-affirming diplomatic protocol, a group of Natchez Indians killed four traders and stole goods from the storehouse. The French retaliated and executed six men. The two sides negotiated a truce, and the Natchez agreed to accept the presence of French troops and helped build Fort Rosalie in 1716. Unfortunately, the peace did not last long.[3]

With the French came influenza and smallpox, and the Natchez tribe lost about half of its population by the early 1720s. In the fall of 1722, a fight broke out over a debt, and several Native American men were killed in the fort itself. When the French commander declined to punish anyone, some of the younger warriors began raiding the settlers' stock. Negotiation again led to peace a year later, but the older Natchez were unhappy with the impact European settlement had had on their children. The Natchez Indians were farmers, as well as hunters, and they controlled the best area for crops on the Lower Mississippi thanks to

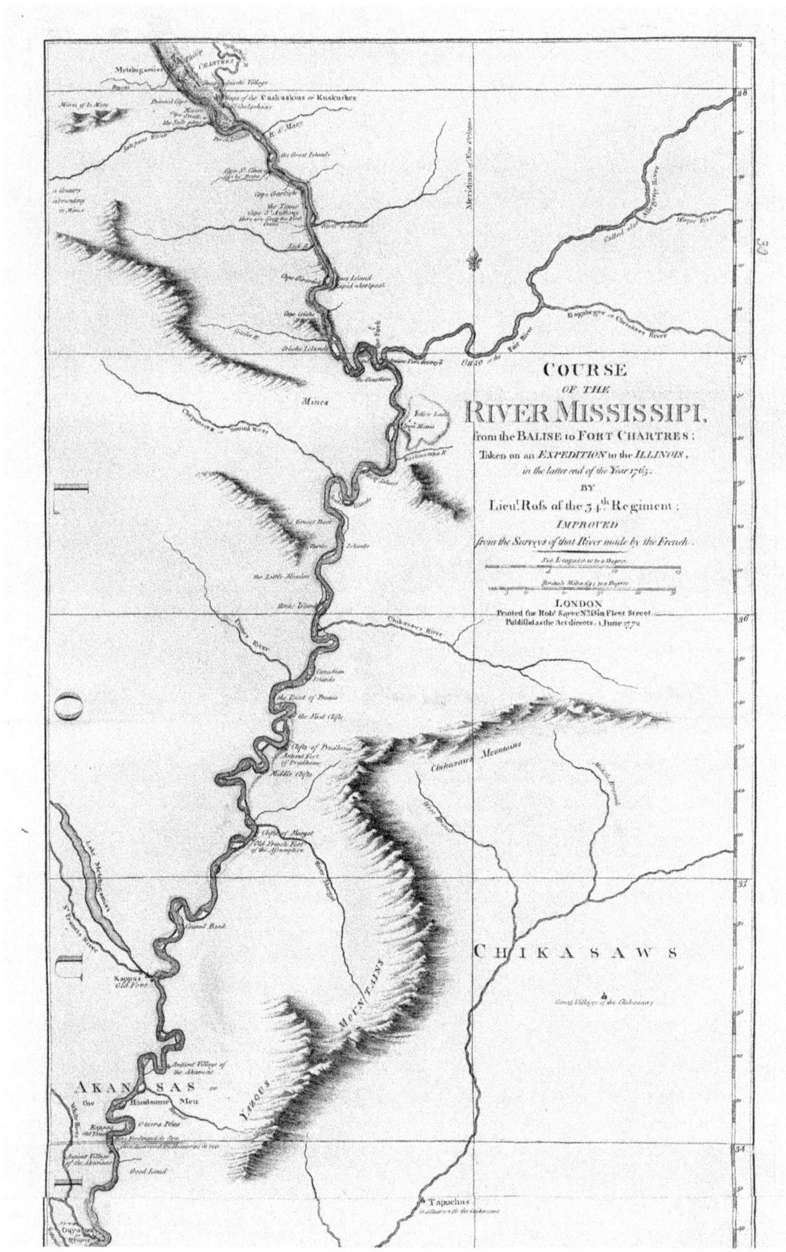

Figure 1.1. The course of the Mississippi River. *Left*: North; *Right*: South. Lieut. Ross and Robert Sayer, *Course of the River Mississipi from Balise to Fort Chartres; Taken on an Expedition to the Illinois, in the Latter End of the Year 1765.* Courtesy of the Library of Congress

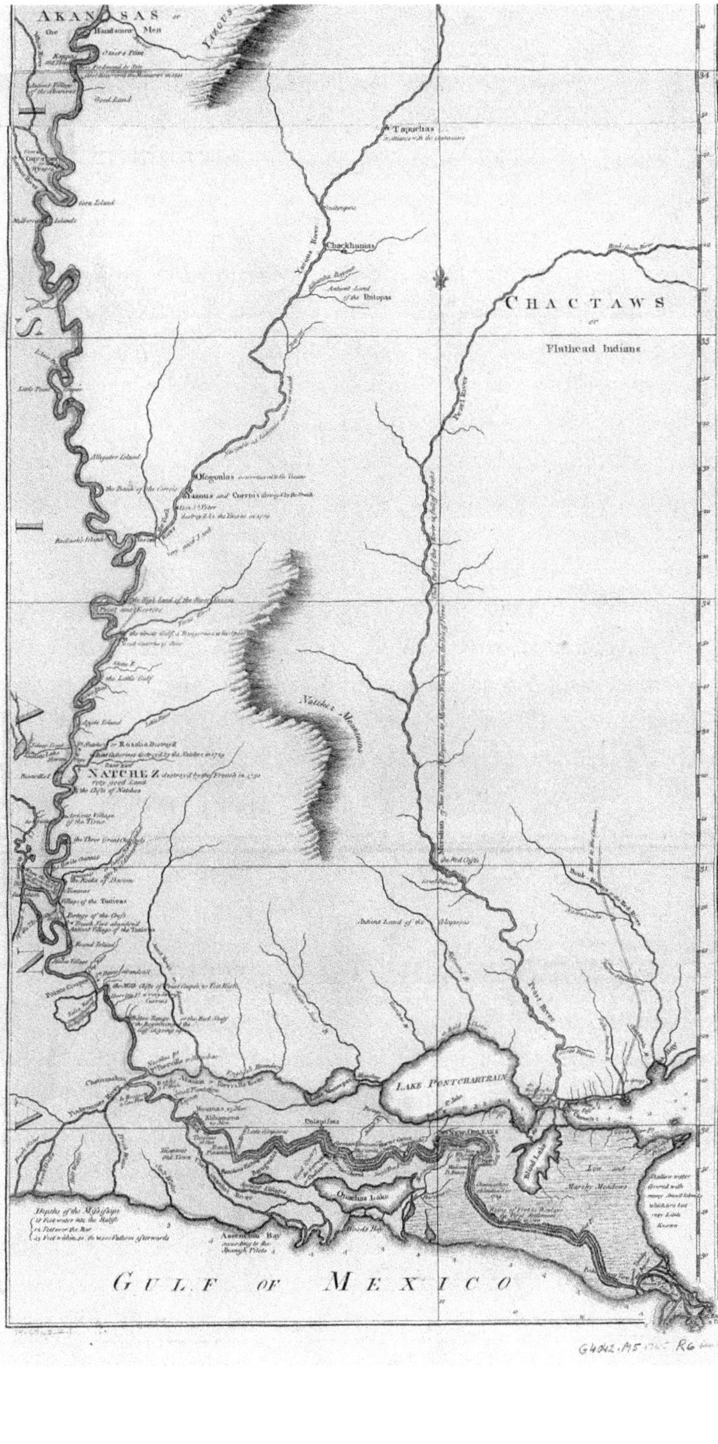
AKANSAS or
the Handsome Men
YAZOUS
Tapuchas
Chackhumas
Yazous River
Antient Land of the Ibitoupas
CHACTAWS
or
Flathead Indians
Ofogoulas
Yazous and Corroys
Alligator Island
Point aux Roches
Pearl River
NATCHEZ destroy'd by the French in 1730
very good Land
the Cliffs of Natchez
Natchez Mountains
Antient Village of the Tioux
the Three Great Cliffs
Village of the Tunicas
Portage of the Cross
Round Island
the Red Cliffs
Antient Land of the Colapissas
Pearl River
LAKE PONTCHARTRAIN
Chetimachas
Oumas
Ouachas Lake
Ascencion Bay
Woods Bay
Blind Lake
Low and Marshy Meadows
Shallow water
Depths of the Mississippi
GULF OF MEXICO

high ground. The Company of the Indies granted lands to settlers to grow tobacco in 1726, and this led to a large influx of both Europeans and slaves. A series of corrupt officials and the death of key Natchez men inclined toward negotiation led to a rise in tension as the decade wore on. The Natchez attacked the French in November of 1729, killing over two hundred men, women, and children and capturing three hundred slaves. The French allied with the Choctaw Indians and wiped out the Natchez the following spring, gaining control of a key, fertile stretch of the Mississippi Valley.[4]

Another early report on Louisiana, this one penned by a Company of the Indies official named Banet in 1724, focused on the second key theme: the central role slavery would play in the success of colonial schemes. As Banet traveled, he concluded that the most successful places had the most slaves. Banet was dismissive of a settlement named Tensas, populated by fifty to sixty families but no slaves, stating that they could do no more than subsist. The families were small, he wrote, two or three persons each—they would not be able to provide the labor needed to make the place flourish. He judged potential by the number of slaves in the settlements he described. Banet noted the best regions for growing mulberry trees (for silk), tobacco, and grains, and he wrote that insects ate grain planted near New Orleans as soon as sprouts appeared. He prized both the site of Natchitoches on the Red River and Mobile on the coast for their proximity to Spanish trade, as well as trade with Native Americans. Mobile also figured into plans to keep the English out.[5]

The slaves did not participate willingly in France's plans. In 1730 or 1731 there was nearly a slave revolt in New Orleans. How the French got wind of it is not clear. One story claims that a slave woman assaulted by a soldier told him that the French would not always have power over them. Another account states that a house servant warned her master. At any rate, officials investigated, torturing the overseer of the company's plantation, a slave called Samba, to try to make him talk, and then executed several other slaves. All accounts point to slaves who spoke the same language. One account stated that the slaves killed their masters at night and then turned the weapons they captured on the troops; another account stated that the slaves intended to burn down New Orleans during Sunday mass. The governor's report in 1731 exaggerated the danger of Indian conspiracies as well, leading some to conclude that the slaves and Indians acted together as allies. Though scholars cannot pin down the conspiracy to a single set of facts, it is clear that there was much unrest, and it worried the French. One scholar attributes the fall of the company to slave revolts on both sides of the Atlantic in the early 1730s.[6]

Despite such troubles, slavery spread. The Company of the Indies brought in over one thousand German settlers in 1721. According to a 1726 census, most were part of two-parent families and did not own slaves. Twenty years later that had changed: the 1746 census listed two hundred slaves on the German Coast, more than 20 miles north of New Orleans. Farmers grew tobacco and corn, as well as supplying New Orleans with vegetables and meat. Pointe Coupée lay northwest of Baton Rouge, and slaves supplied most of the labor there from very early on. Reports from the 1740s list both tobacco exports and runaway slaves. A tobacco planter named Philippe Haineaux left behind an estate in 1743 that consisted of six wooden huts, 30 feet long by 14 feet wide. He lived in one of the huts, ran a store out of another, and housed four slaves in the rest. A faded waste book left behind by an entrepreneur who set up shop in nearby Baton Rouge in 1748 bears witness to the growing slave economy, listing goods and debts, an adventure to Jamaica, and the sale of rice and dry goods.[7]

The last theme related to French expansion on western waters in the early eighteenth century concerned European rivals and maintaining control over the territory. In 1720, de la Harpe focused on trade and military matters. He wrote that the French needed to settle the area properly to keep the English out, take advantage of trade with Spanish colonies, and place themselves on New Spain's borders to ensure that the Spanish made no alliances against the French with anybody else. The Spanish traded in the region from East Texas through New Mexico, using the Rio Grande and Red Rivers, as well as pack trains. In fact, de la Harpe mentioned horses useful for ground transport often in his study, as wild horses roamed the area, proliferating freely, thanks to the Spanish. Soldiers would be necessary—he referred to Native Americans on the coast as warring nations and discussed other tribes as allies of the Spanish and potential allies of the French. De la Harpe didn't think much of swampy New Orleans and believed that New France should have its capital at Natchez, where wide prairies would yield grains and tobacco and France could keep in contact with settlements on the Red, Ouachita, Mississippi, and Missouri Rivers.[8]

The French chose other spots along the Mississippi to keep an eye on activity on the river and its tributaries. The French established Baton Rouge in 1721, where high ground kept the area from the flooding that plagued the rest of the Mississippi's course south to the coast. It seemed a safe place to build an early fort to keep track of movement on the river between New Orleans and Natchez. The French targeted the St. Francis River in present-day Arkansas, one tributary north of the Arkansas River itself, as an excellent place to hunt bears and buffalo for hides and meat to supply New Orleans and Canada. George Morgan and others described some of the Frenchmen they encountered in the West as hunters. The French were doing more than simply trading furs.[9]

The French intended farms on the Upper Mississippi to supply New Orleans with food because poor soil, humidity, and fungus destroyed wheat crops on the Lower Mississippi before they could be harvested. French settlements in Illinois stretched over 70 miles north of Kaskaskia to Cahokia. Kaskaskia began as a Jesuit mission and fur trade outpost in 1703, but by the 1730s the main job of the French settlements in Illinois was to supply the southern port with flour. In the early 1700s, fur traders married local Native Americans and settled down to grow wheat to export as flour to New Orleans after the closing of regional trading posts. French colonial officials in Louisiana supported these plans in the decades that followed. Between 1726 and 1752, the number of French in Illinois more than doubled, while the number of African slaves more than tripled; the number of Native American slaves outpaced the growing population of Europeans as well. Both Kaskaskia and Cahokia supported gristmills. During the 1730s, excellent harvests were the norm, though harvests were uneven in the decade that followed.[10]

An Illinois planter named Antoine Bienvenu helped establish trade between Illinois and New Orleans in the 1730s and 1740s. His father brought the family to Illinois to work for the company as a carpenter who helped build Fort Chartres. Bienvenu would inherit his father's tools along with land to establish himself in Illinois, later acquiring more capital by marrying well. Combining his skills as a craftsman with strategic land purchases, he ended up being the largest landowner in Illinois. To get his crops to market, Bienvenu made use of the French convoy system. The Company of the Indies organized the first convoys, which included over a hundred men: soldiers and their officers, slaves and indentured servants to row, and those who wanted to reach Illinois for their own reasons. Convoys were most vulnerable heading upstream when they hugged the banks and camped onshore at night. Coming back downstream, they stuck to the middle of the river and traveled fast. Convoys headed to Illinois in late spring, arriving a month or so before the end of the year, and didn't return until the next spring, though the trip to New Orleans took less than a month. The company first established a store at Fort Chartres and then a second at Kaskaskia. Royal officials set the prices, and wholesalers took over once the company disbanded.[11]

Historian Cecile Vidal concluded that most New Orleans merchants didn't really pursue trade in Illinois at that time; instead, it was independent businessmen from the north like Bienvenu who organized trade. Few had partners; most worked alone. They bought goods in New Orleans on one year's credit, transporting goods north with one convoy and sending payment south with the next. In terms of the flour trade, in 1746 officials in New Orleans gave Illinois flour preference over that from a Dutch ship that arrived in port. Some owned plantations in addition to their trade, and others just worked the transport business, though both sorts rented slaves as labor. Over the years under French rule, sixty-five men traded up and down the Mississippi, nearly three-quarters of them based in Kaskaskia, with smaller numbers at Fort Chartres and Cahokia.[12]

Lower Louisiana never fulfilled France's hopes for the colony on the Gulf Coast. A typical shipment from Bordeaux, France, to New Orleans would have included "soldiers, munitions, flaxseed, hemp, merchandise, flour, and brandy," and the ship would have returned with "lumber, pitch, tar, tobacco, and beaver skins."[13] But the fact of the matter was that French merchants would rather trade in the Caribbean than Louisiana because they couldn't find enough profitable goods to fill their holds for the return trip. There were plenty of risks involved in sending goods to New Orleans, including pirates from Jamaica who targeted commerce in Louisiana. In December of 1739, a ship under English colors captured another called *Le Comte de Maurepas* headed for New Orleans with goods for a merchant named Sieur Pery, who intended to sell the cargo wholesale. Only after damaging the French ship with cannon fire did the pirates inform the French that war had been declared and that they had orders to stop ships flying French and Spanish colors. They boarded the ship, took the captain's papers, and forced the crew to sail to Jamaica, avoiding the official outpost guarded by two English warships and slipping off to an out-of-the-way location to plunder the ship. Eventually they let the ship and crew go on its way after forcing the captain to sign a document written in English stating that the pirates had done no wrong. The French intended to complain to officials in Jamaica, but the pirates let it be known that they would not allow them to sail that way. The French ship, with its rigging and sails in tatters, arrived at the Mississippi River a couple of weeks later. There the French captain logged a formal complaint.[14]

But the French colony of Louisiana did serve to keep the English out of the interior of North America beyond the Appalachians during the opening decades of the eighteenth century. Historian John G. Clark argued that New Orleans should be considered in the context of the ongoing hostilities between France and England, which began with the ascension of William and Mary and ended with the defeat of Napoleon. He characterizes it as a "pawn" in the foreign policy game more than a real effort by France at establishing an economic powerhouse.

The settlement began as a French colony, giving them a whole different point of entry into North America, and the French intended to consolidate their hold over the middle of the continent along the Mississippi River. The Spanish took control of New Orleans for a time during the latter half of the eighteenth century and used it as a base for their own operations in the Gulf of Mexico and the seas to the south. Spanish gold and silver attracted Americans to the port.[15]

Europeans from various empires did make incursions into the territories of their rivals. In 1717 an official complained that the Spanish viceroy and governor had told him that the English couldn't cut logwood on Trist Island, in Campeche Bay on the Gulf Coast of Mexico. The official stated that the logwood trade was of "great importance to our Navigation & the American Colonies," arguing that although the Spanish had settled it first, they had abandoned it in 1667. The English had "thrice taken" the spot during hostilities at one time or another, and the current peace treaty placed the area in English hands. The colony of Virginia sent an expedition down the Ohio and Mississippi Rivers in 1742, ostensibly seeking Native Americans who had raided settlements in western Virginia. The men ended up being arrested by a French force composed of Europeans and others of African and Native American descent and taken to New Orleans. One man described a place where the government was tyrannical, the common people were poor and oppressed, local officials cheated planters, and the Catholic Church reigned triumphant. The people were poor, he wrote. In 1745, Chevalier Grenier tried to conduct trade while avoiding getting entangled in the affairs of the major empires that claimed to control trade in the Gulf and beyond. The wars of the mid-eighteenth century kept the port of New Orleans busier than ever. The War of Austrian Succession in the 1740s opened up trade between the Spanish and the French in the Caribbean as both made war with the English. The English weren't the only ones making forays into the territories of imperial rivals: Paul Mapp told the tale of two French traders from Illinois who showed up in Spanish New Mexico in 1752.[16]

Back in England, interested parties debated over expanding their reach beyond the Atlantic coast through either trade or settlement, and colonists set out to do both. There was plenty of tension between the English and Spanish in the Gulf of Mexico. The English had two different views about the lands west of the crest of the Appalachian Mountains. There wasn't much early interest in planting colonies beyond the coast, and those interested in North America's resources concentrated their energy on the fur trade and didn't want large numbers of settlers moving west, farther and farther away from Imperial control.

But as the eighteenth century wore on, new views emerged. Why not grow the colonial population? That could only lead to more markets and more consumption, the reasoning went. Manufacturers began to stress markets over access to raw materials as the best way to manage the colonies during and after the Seven Years' War. Some argued that perhaps they should even let Canada go to the north and let Guadalupe go to the south, concentrating instead on the lands south of the St. Lawrence and north of Florida. Many British officials feared that without the French presence the colonists would become more independent; thus, driving the other empires out of North America might be a mistake. The British were just getting to know the Ohio and Mississippi Valleys at midcentury and had begun to realize their value, even though they didn't really understand the geography of the region yet.[17]

A letter from Richard Carpenter, an American planter on the Mississippi River, to merchant John Collins back in Newport, Rhode Island, highlights the clash of three empires on the Lower Mississippi in 1744. Carpenter had managed to collect a variety of specie—milled dollars, doubloons, and Portuguese coins. He put some of the specie in the care of one Captain Barker, who was taking a load of lumber to Jamaica but would first stop at the cape to "defray expenses" and exchange the coins for gold on the planter's behalf. Carpenter warned Collins not to send cargo yet—the French governor of New Orleans had seized five or six English ships and jailed their crew. A postscript noted that the small sloop of a man named Nash had been seized—Nash lost 2,500 Spanish dollars, and he and his people had been jailed in New Orleans. English sloops of war in the area were looking to shut down French trade, and "the Spanyards keep such a close look out that there is no doing business about New Orleans."[18]

Two of the three key themes related to early European attempts to control the interior also apply to the Ohio River Valley: their evolving relationship with Native Americans, and concerns about the imperial ambitions of European rivals. As the French expanded along the St. Lawrence River and the shores of the Great Lakes, colonists focused on the fur trade even though officials back in France had hoped the colony would produce naval stores and other goods. Disease outbreaks and guns upset the balance of power between Iroquois and Algonquin tribes, and the Five Nations expanded their reach south to the Ohio River. Delawares, Shawnees, and others migrated away from the coast under pressure from the English, and the Five Nations' hold over them was tenuous at best. They considered the lands south of the Ohio as their hunting grounds, and violence broke out as Virginians made inroads into Kentucky. As they lost their hold on the lands to the south, the Shawnees and others hoped to make the Ohio River a boundary between European colonists to the south and their homes on the northern banks.[19]

As for the English, Virginia colonists began to covet lands on the Upper Ohio River in the 1740s. Traders from Pennsylvania also expressed interest in the region. An interesting letter from the fall of 1752 reveals the attitude of one French official toward Philadelphia traders in the West. Father Alexis De Guyenne wrote Pierre Vaudreuil that rumors ascribed to Englishmen "in that quarter" should be taken with a grain of salt. He characterized the men as Philadelphia Quakers, "people who think only of peltry" and "who scarcely recognize the government of England." Quakers were pacifists, he wrote, and they had proved their disinclination to participate in England's wars on previous occasions. De Guyenne didn't believe they'd have much luck settling lands "beyond their mountains" and allying with Native American tribes against the French.[20]

A pamphlet by one J. Payne published in 1756 lays out an English view of the French in North America that is far from complimentary. Payne stressed that the English had bought land from Native Americans, arguing that if the French made inroads with them, the French were making inroads on English claims in turn. He stated that Native Americans did not betray alliances—if the English dealt with the Native Americans fairly, they would be loyal. Payne had his sights set on more than the fur trade, hoping for metals, ores, iron, and even fossils. The French were treacherous and had been knocking on the back door, he wrote. Payne believed that most Englishmen didn't realize what they had in North America—rather than a barren, desolate place, it was chock-full of important natural resources. The French had discovered North America by accident, they drifted in from the sea in fishing boats, and now they were scheming to lay claim to what was rightfully England's, according to Payne.[21] He warned that the French built forts "behind our settlements," trying to control territory from the Great Lakes to the Gulf of Mexico.[22]

By the mid-eighteenth century, rivalries and trade between the French, the Spanish, the English, and various Native American tribes were already well established along the Ohio and Mississippi Rivers. Those doing the work to harvest resources already included African slaves. Virginian Lawrence Washington and others set up the Ohio Company with allies in London to petition the Crown for a land grant. The Crown supported them at first, hoping to counter the spread of France's influence in the Ohio Valley. But when the Ohio Company sent Lawrence Washington's half brother George to check on things at the Ohio's headwaters two years later, a violent encounter with the French and their

Native American allies sparked a war that would spread around the world in the years to come.

When war finally broke out in 1754, it shook up the merchants' world in Philadelphia. The influx of commercial paper led to flush times, but when the war shifted south to the Caribbean, business took a downturn. Some merchants expanded their business by supplying the army, and Fort Pitt became the center of British attempts to capture the fur trade. Pontiac's Rebellion put a damper on celebrations when the war ended, but Philadelphia's role as a port had expanded during the war, and that expansion would only accelerate thereafter.

During the first half of the eighteenth century, Philadelphia merchants relied mostly on Boston merchants for British goods, trading directly with the West Indies, but not so much with England itself. The Seven Years' War changed that. The British aimed to stake their claim to the Ohio Valley through Fort Pitt, and suddenly bills of exchange showed up in town on a regular basis. Imports to Philadelphia quadrupled between 1757 and 1760. Exchange rates fell, and English merchants lavishly extended credit to many. But the boom was short-lived, and when military operations shifted to the West Indies, a depression followed. Bringing troops to North America in the 1750s spurred trade; shifting the troops to the Caribbean in the early 1760s to battle the French led to losses (see fig. 1.2).[23]

The trials and tribulations of a young man named Daniel Clark make the rough transition clear. The first correspondence in Clark's letter book dates from the time when the influx of English goods was hitting its peak. He bought tobacco in Virginia and sugar and rum from the West Indies. From London he imported furniture, china, and leather, first from a merchant named William Neate and then from the firm of Mildred & Roberts. Clark hoped to sell £10,000 of goods per year, and in 1761 he informed Neate that he would be involved in "an Indian trade next spring." Later that year, however, he noted that he had sold only about a tenth of the £5,000 worth of goods he imported, and payments from customers totaled £20. Sales were "dull" by 1762, and "heavy sums" were owed to English merchants.[24]

Despite these growing pains, Philadelphia's role as a port had changed for good. Prices were rising for wheat and flour in Europe, and letters from the early 1760s mention unusually large wheat harvests in eastern Pennsylvania. The Seven Years' War opened up the insurance business in Philadelphia. Though one or two local brokers offered insurance by the 1740s, most shipowners preferred

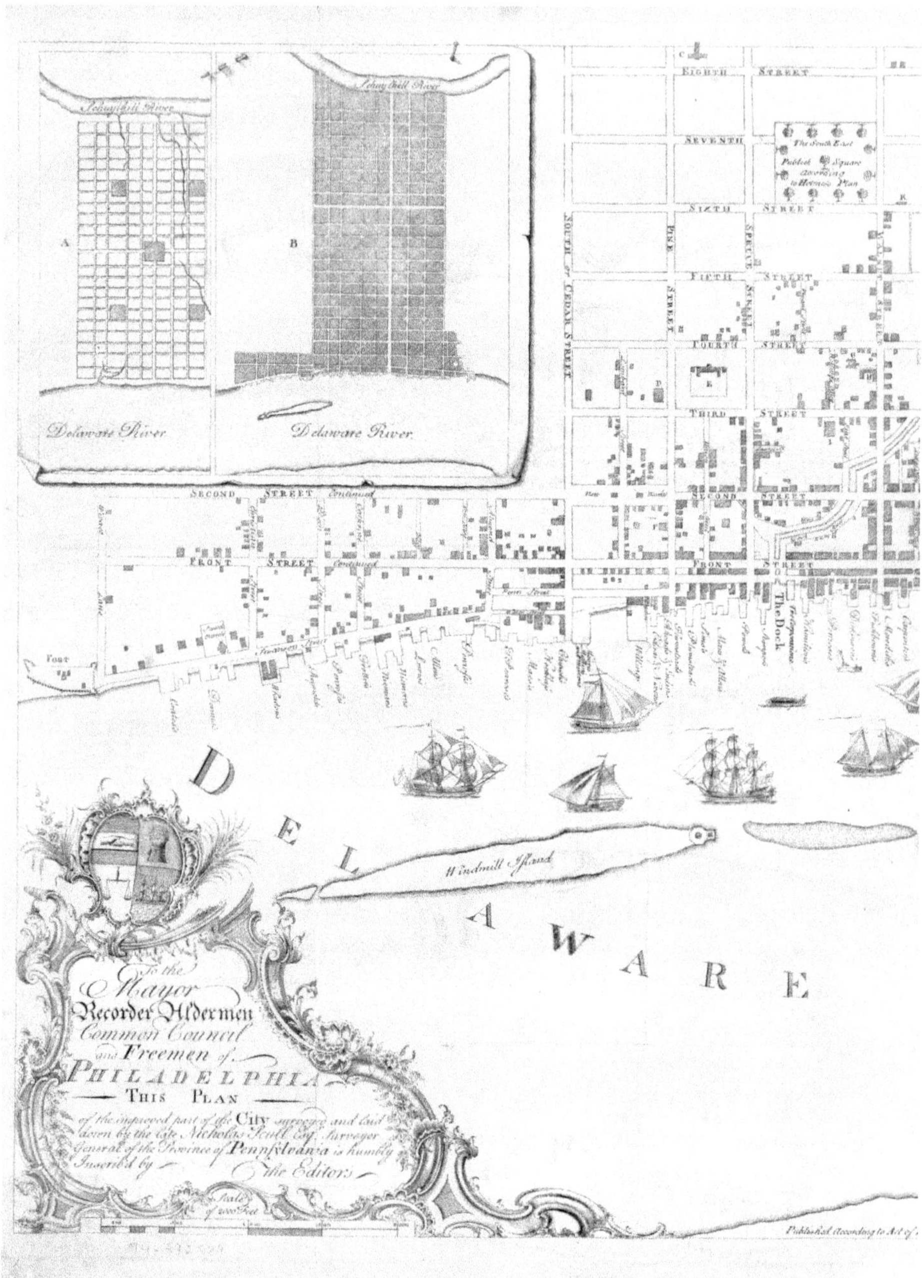

Figure 1.2. Philadelphia in 1762. The Whartons' pier is third from the left. Nicholas Scull, Matthew Clarkson, and Mary Biddle, *To the Mayor, Recorder, Aldermen, Common Council, and Freemen of Philadelphia This Plan of the Improved*

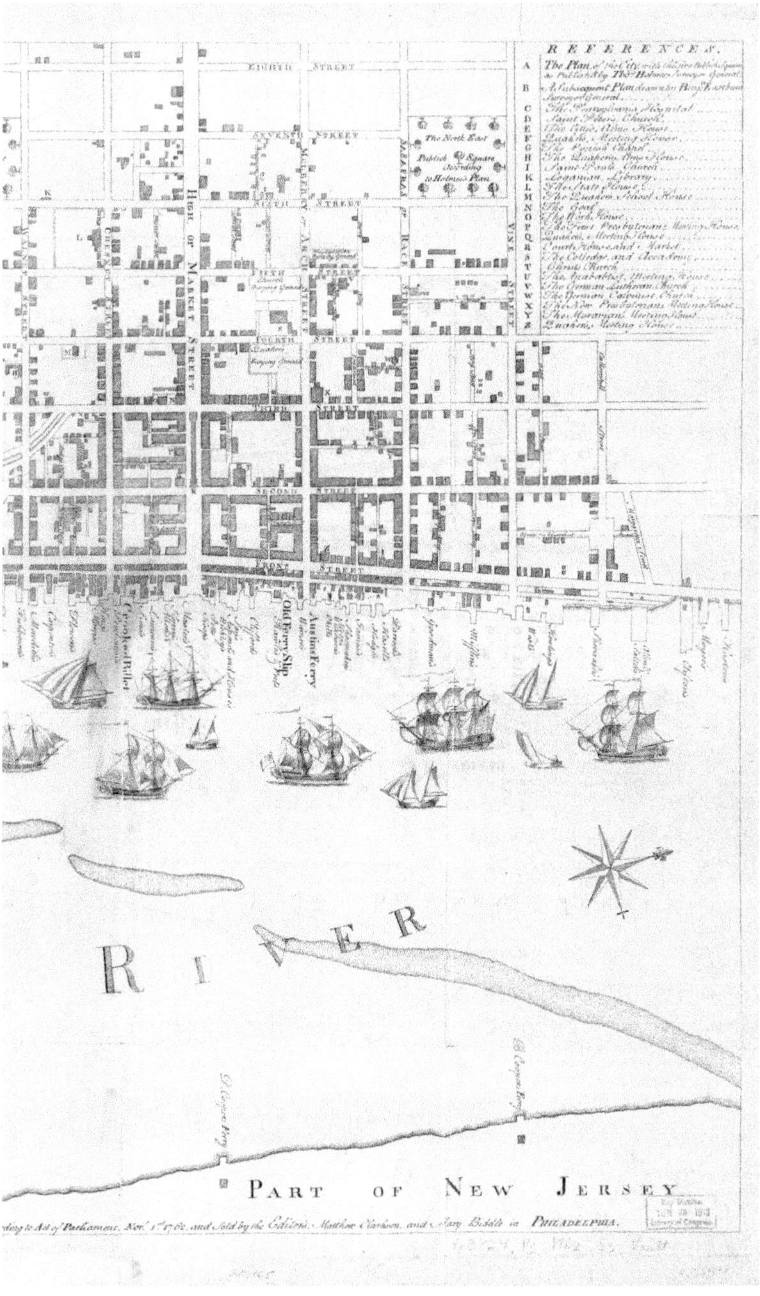

Part of the City Surveyed and Laid Down by the Late Nicholas Scull.
Courtesy of the Library of Congress

to buy their insurance from London. During the war, however, premiums rose because of new risks. The war also disrupted the transmission of news across the Atlantic. London insurers pulled back a bit because by the late 1750s the colonists actually had better information about Caribbean markets. By the 1760s, more and more Philadelphia merchants bought their insurance locally, one factor in the growth of Philadelphia's reputation as a major port. Philadelphia's hinterland expanded to the north and west as farmers without access to other ports sought the city's mills, bakers, and butchers. A lively rivalry arose with Baltimore over trade from the Susquehanna Valley, but for most consumers access to Philadelphia proved easier. Philadelphia surpassed Boston as North America's largest port during the second half of the eighteenth century. New York surpassed Boston as well, but it wouldn't pull ahead of Philadelphia until the early nineteenth century.[25]

The correspondence of merchant John Baynton provides a glimpse into the evolution of Philadelphia's business world. His father, Peter, had sold goods consigned to him in the 1720s, trading tobacco, butter, and bacon with merchants in New York and in turn selling iron, loaf sugar, and rum at home. Thirty years later, his son acted as a middleman, selling groceries that he bought from importers to shopkeepers.[26] Before the war, John Baynton specialized in the provisions trade. His journal entries from 1754 and 1755 are mostly filled with accounts of importing and selling wine, rum, and spirits. Though some Philadelphia merchants were pessimistic about the wine trade, it had a favorable trade balance. Baynton had some land dealings as well. He launched adventures to Jamaica and sent flour to Newfoundland, and business with men in Boston continued. At one point, Baynton sent goods to Barbados in partnership with Evan Morgan, his soon-to-be partner's older brother.[27]

Baynton's records also recount the spread of the insurance industry in Philadelphia. Insurance shows up in the journal of 1756 as premiums paid. In 1757, Baynton expanded both his insurance coverage and his shipments to Jamaica, including cargoes of flour, bread, pork, tallow, butter, starch, fish, and barrel staves. The insurance entries petered out rather quickly thereafter, and then in 1758 there were more entries for bills of exchange, with an even greater number the following year. Clearly the war changed how Baynton did business, given the few entries for wine by 1760.[28]

In November of 1758, John Baynton dissolved his partnership with William Bard and established a new partnership with Samuel Wharton. The Whartons were a Quaker merchant family, and the first Thomas Wharton arrived from England in the 1680s. His son Joseph was the father to brothers Thomas and

Samuel Wharton, and his son John was the father of Thomas Wharton Jr. Samuel was born in 1732. Baynton and Wharton wrote to Richard Neave in London, placing orders for the spring and fall of 1759. They expected Neave to buy part of a vessel to transport the goods in order to keep as many of the profits within their circle as possible, indicating that if the war ended before spring they would cancel their order. They ordered goods from other British merchants, asking them to send news of Neave's plans to buy a ship and telling them to send the goods to Neave. Baynton and Wharton had many customers in "the back parts" of Virginia, Maryland, and North Carolina and "the west parts" of Pennsylvania, who came for the winter's supply at the end of the summer and the spring's supply at the end of the winter.[29] One of the men they were supplying was George Clark. The Philadelphia firm wrote him: "We sincerely congratulate [you] upon regaining the country upon the Ohio—the acquisition we think with you, will increase much the trade of this province & expcially from the western frontier." Baynton and Wharton also did business with the Spanish during the Seven Years' War.[30]

The impact of the war was also on display in John Baynton's dealings with John Noble of Bristol in 1757. After one successful consignment had been dispatched, Baynton wrote that Noble's bills had proven to be safe, and he liked Noble's "candid manner." His firm could send flour and bread, as well as molasses. Bread prices had fallen after the "Carthagena Expedition," and they expected no naval expeditions during the summer of 1758. On land, however, Howe intended to take Fort Ticonderoga, which would "give [them] command of the lake." The American told the Englishman that he agreed that it was time for the empire to "restore [her] ancient glory," for the world had been mocking them. Baynton seemed confident of good times in the future.[31]

But three years later correspondence from John Noble contained news of glutted markets as ships arrived at the same time from many ports. Noble sold sugar for Baynton & Wharton at public auction. Bread and flour were cheap—Noble wrote that they could be obtained cheaper by buying them from Newfoundland than having them brought from America. French cargoes of dry goods were mentioned, as well as French sugar. In July Noble wrote about trade with Hispaniola—"the profit is too [e]nticing," despite the war, and the ships went directly to markets without going through America or Bristol first.[32]

A 1762 Baynton and Wharton letter book shows a firm still bound up in old-style trade with links among Philadelphia, London, and Jamaica. The Philadelphia firm was dealing in wine, sugar, and indigo and writing to suppliers about the New England trade, sending cargoes of fish. Rumors of peace with

France and war with Spain permeate the letters. Baynton and Wharton sent instructions to captains about gun placements and what to do if captured. They also wrote a number of letters about insurance. That year proved to be a very unsettled one, filled with anxiety about ships and markets. In April of 1762, Baynton & Wharton had a long exchange with the firm of McLeane & Field about acquiring white sugar. They wrote about purchasing "a parcel of negroes" to send to Jamaica. It's not clear what was going on, but at one point one of the islands surrendered more quickly than expected, and Baynton wrote that it had "injured our scheme." By the spring and summer of 1763 their attention turned elsewhere, as Noble began sending news about markets for peltry and beaver, deer, and bear skins.[33]

In December of 1763, the firm wrote to a would-be customer named Frederick Dansey, offering to supply him with flour, bread, beef, and pork. Baynton & Wharton indicated that Dansey could buy those commodities cheaper in Philadelphia than anywhere in America, boasting that "we have no rivals." The Philadelphia firm challenged Dansey to check the newspapers going back ten years—promising they would show that Philadelphia prices were better than New York's and currently Baynton & Wharton could ship provisions for 15 percent less than what Dansey would pay at that port. Baynton wrote that there were one hundred vessels waiting to depart with the harvest before the onset of winter. Bills of exchange were always welcome as payment because they were very useful in making remittances, and all the silver that came into their hands wound up being sent to Britain. The firm wanted Dansey to know that they had taken on a new partner and now went by the name of Baynton, Wharton & Morgan.[34]

John Baynton envisioned supplying backcountry settlers with goods, but the opening of Philadelphia's hinterland to the west really began with the supplying of the British army during the war. David Franks was one of the first merchants to take a chance on expanding his trade to the Ohio's headwaters. The commercial opportunities of Philadelphia attracted the first Jewish settlers in the mid-1730s. Nathan Levy established a business there, his nephew David Franks from New York joined him five years later, and other family members settled in London and Jamaica. Philadelphia on its own lacked a strong Jewish community for support but provided a necessary linchpin in the extended family's wide-ranging commercial network. Parliament's Plantation Act of 1740 was intended to make settling in British colonies more attractive, and for Jews it meant that they could become naturalized citizens after seven years with an oath that did not refer to "the true faith of a Christian." More than two dozen Jews followed over the next two decades, and many made a start through David Franks and his commercial contacts.[35]

David's father, Abraham, had settled in New York to represent the London family in the early 1700s, and David moved to Philadelphia in turn to do the same in 1741. In business with his uncle Nathan, the firm of Levy & Franks engaged in the usual import-export trade involving American raw materials, furs, and tobacco; British cloth and tools; and sugar and slaves from the West Indies. Franks forged ties with those involved in the Indian trade in Lancaster, about 80 miles west of Philadelphia, and his earliest land speculations were quite old-fashioned—commercial properties in town. Strong commercial and family ties ran between Lancaster and Philadelphia, and Franks partnered at one time or another with wealthy and connected men such as George Croghan, William Trent, and Robert Callender. Though Nathan Levy died in 1753, it was his uncle's connections that allowed David Franks to make his fortune during the war that followed.[36]

Franks first partnered with a man named William Plumsted, signing a contract to supply the British army in December of 1759. They were to send supply wagons and carriages to Fort Pitt. The next year they supplied Carlisle as well. Settled in the 1750s, the town provided the link between Philadelphia and the headwaters of the Ohio River. Wagons made the 100-mile journey there, and then traders loaded goods on packhorses for the 300-mile haul to Fort Pitt. They could travel west along either Braddock's Road through Fort Cumberland or Forbes Road by way of Bedford. Franks also reached agreements with a handful of other merchants to engage in the fur trade over the next nine years—an agreement that allowed any of them to engage in other business elsewhere. Shipping salted meat by wagon proved to be expensive, so the British had the partners supplement the supplies by driving live cattle and hogs as far west as Fort Pitt.[37]

The colony of Pennsylvania made Fort Pitt an official trading post in 1758. Private traders soon arrived as well, and they complained about regulations that favored the official store, while the official agents complained that the private traders undercut their prices. William Trent and Levi Levy established what became the largest store in 1760 as partners of Simon & Franks from Lancaster. Worries about the war kept tensions high, and floods proved to be a problem. As Pontiac's Rebellion got underway in 1763, only the fort remained—the rest of the settlement had been burned to the ground. Trade opened once again in

1764, and the two largest competitors were Baynton, Wharton & Morgan and Simon & Levy, which were closely aligned with the Gratz brothers out of Philadelphia.[38]

A trader named James Kenny provides two different snapshots of the action at Fort Pitt just a few years apart. In 1758, the Commissioner of Indian Affairs sent him there to take charge of supplies sent to Native American allies in the region. Kenny described a lively place where Indians from different nations visited daily and rumors abounded about French schemes and armed conflicts. Andrew Montour, a respected negotiator, passed through and troops departed on different missions from time to time. Kenny kept track of troops who went out looking for provisions and noted that courts of inquiry into their actions were not uncommon. News came from as far away as the mouth of the Mississippi, and Indian trader George Croghan made regular appearances as well. Most of the commerce involved skins, but Kenny traded lead as well.[39]

Officials sent Kenny west once more in 1761, this time to man a store stocked with supplies. When he arrived in May, he found "trade very dull" and reported that "our store has lost a great part of what it had." There was news of Native Americans in Mississippi "being set on" the English by the French. News came from Detroit as well. Kenny tried to convince allies that the English had their best interests at heart to a greater extent than the French. Some Native Americans had received credit from Trent & Levy, he wrote. A slave ran away to join a nearby Native American tribe in August. Dull trade was the rule that summer, and Kenny left in September. Things had quieted down at the Ohio's headwaters—for the time being.[40]

Trouble south of the Great Lakes made the victory seem less sweet when the war ended. In July of 1763, Philadelphia lawyer Benjamin Chew wrote to William Allen about the beginning of Pontiac's Rebellion. He wrote that Pontiac had taken everyone by surprise and that "all our Traders, above 100 in Number of this Province," were among the first casualties. The French had used goods for diplomacy in the Indian style; they understood that they were creating alliances. The British refused to do that, thinking of gifts as bribes. Native Americans felt like the British were treating them like conquered people instead of allies.[41] Merchants and trading networks were part of this story too. Peace generally reigned when trade flourished, but land hunger only led to war. Despite such an inauspicious beginning, interest in western trade and lands would only grow.

Philadelphia's emergence as the most important port in British North America began with the Seven Years' War. The British army made its way to the Upper

Ohio River by way of the city, freely spending money as it provisioned the troops. When it became clear that the British would be occupying the Illinois Country, Philadelphia merchants intended to build networks to Fort Pitt and beyond that had begun during the war. One firm in particular, that of Baynton, Wharton & Morgan, would take the deepest plunge.

In 1763, John Baynton and Samuel Wharton promoted a younger man who had apprenticed with them, George Morgan, and he, in turn, brought in some much-needed capital. Together this trio would straddle the worlds of commerce before and after the American Revolution. Morgan's career, more than that of any other, revealed the evolution of Philadelphia merchants on western waters during the second half of the eighteenth century. Born in 1743, Morgan took an apprenticeship with John Baynton in 1756 when he was thirteen years old. Over the next four years he took on the job of clerk and then bookkeeper. In 1762 he tried his own hand at adventuring, sending a shipment of goods to Havana. John Baynton and Samuel Wharton asked Morgan to join their partnership on more than one occasion. He had some property that had been left to him by his father, and the older men needed capital. Morgan resisted for a time, but they finally persuaded him with an offer of three-elevenths of the business profits and an equal share of land deals. Their ties to men like George Croghan and Richard Neave also persuaded the young man that he could do well in their company. Visions of supplying the British in the West while enriching themselves with the fur trade that would come their way as a result proved to be too good an opportunity to pass up. During the fall of 1763, Morgan traveled throughout New England, selling goods on commission. By the end of 1764, the firm was in good financial shape, and Morgan had married Baynton's daughter.[42]

The interior of the continent that drew the attention of Philadelphia merchants after the war had undergone many changes in a short time. As early as the spring of 1762, King Louis XV of France indicated a willingness to end the conflict but ended up signing a treaty that ceded Louisiana to Spain first. When Great Britain, France, and Spain finalized the Treaty of Paris in 1763, Spain took control of territory west of the Mississippi, including what was often called "the island of New Orleans," and the British took control of lands to the east, including East and West Florida along what is today the panhandle. Great Britain also gained possession of Canada, and a few Caribbean Islands changed hands as well. The Gulf Coast became more of a mishmash than ever. Great Britain decided to set up the new governor of West Florida at Pensacola, the old

Spanish port farthest east. West Florida also included the French settlements of Mobile and Natchez. The Spanish would impose its imperial structure over the French settlement of New Orleans, and of course various American Indians would have their own say. With the territorial shuffle and colonists turning their attention to the Ohio Valley, Native Americans adapted, pursuing their own alliances.

Conventional wisdom has long held that the Proclamation of 1763 garnered the first widespread discontent with new British policies that would lead to revolution, but more recent scholars have found that there were plenty of colonists who did not view it in such a negative light. Virginia land speculators thought that it would be temporary, and Philadelphians in particular saw it as a positive measure. Many Quaker politicians believed that frontiersmen stirred up too much trouble with Native Americans, and the massacre by the Paxton Boys in 1764 only confirmed that view. Perhaps the British policy would help quiet things in the West by preventing more settlement until a more robust plan could be put in place.[43] As for merchants like Baynton, Wharton, and Morgan, the proclamation cleared the way to their entry into the fur trade.

In the immediate aftermath of the war, new regulations frustrated Philadelphia merchants as Great Britain moved to take firmer control of their colonies in North America, now that their territory had doubled. Scholars disagree about some aspects of the history of Philadelphia's business cycle during the last half of the eighteenth century. Not so long ago, many characterized the 1760s as an economic downturn, but more recently others have written about a thriving trade with the West Indies at that time. Merchants were practical, one argues, and participating in the boycotts of 1765 and 1769 didn't harm their bottom line when the embargoes didn't include trade to the south. The embargo of 1774 proved to be a much tougher choice and took real commitment to the patriot cause because it cut off trade with the West Indies as well.[44] The experiences of George Morgan and his partners provide insight and show how their interests shifted west.

A Baynton, Wharton & Morgan letter book that begins in October of 1763 started off with a letter about new British customs duties, detailing how to avoid paying duty on rum from "his British Majesty's domain." They would only use ships of a certain size, and they seemed to have deals with collectors in a couple of different ports. Baynton wrote about sugarhouses in Philadelphia that operated during the war but had to cease manufacturing once their supply from the French dried up, even though the demand for rum remained high. Bills of exchange could always be found in Philadelphia but were best acquired in the fall as the ships were heading to Europe, and especially to Ireland, with flax seed and other cargo.[45]

John Baynton wrote to a few of his contacts about two men-of-war arriving in the harbor to enforce the new acts of Parliament. He thought that trade with Portugal, the Netherlands, Hamburg, and the Mediterranean was at risk. Rum, sugar, and molasses were all in high demand, but none but the wealthy could profit with duties so high. Baynton mentioned illicit trade and gentlemen of fortune. He debated the merits of British brandy versus West Indies rum with one correspondent and wrote that the same Catalonia wine Frenchmen in Louisiana railed against sold at a good profit in Philadelphia. The colonies of North America also seem to have been cut off from access to Bohea tea from continental Europe by the English presence in their harbor. The letter book also mentions the problems caused by loss of trade with the French.[46]

A merchant named Benjamin Marshall echoed Baynton's opinion of the message sent by the newly arrived ships. Marshall stated that their purpose was to stop "clandestine trade" with the Iberian Peninsula and the French West Indies. Pontiac's Rebellion had an impact as well, and Marshall wrote that there were more ships in the harbor that fall than he had ever seen, but they just sat with "people not knowing what to do with them." The next spring, disagreements between the "Quaker Party" and the "Presbyterian Party" put a damper on trade as well. A year after the British ships arrived, Marshall wrote that bills were scarce, cash even more so, and the men-of-war were "so strict that nothing can escape them." Trade had ground to a halt as many American merchants suspended payments.[47]

When it came to Baynton, Wharton & Morgan's business, the harshest aspects of the Revenue Act, better known as the Sugar Act, involved a new duty on imported wines and a ban on selling lumber outside of the British Empire a year later. New regulations included having a document signed by a customs official for "every item" in the hold. Philadelphia merchants had for the most part ignored the Molasses Act of 1733 and traded flour for molasses and rum from any of the Caribbean islands at will, and they enjoyed access to Spanish silver and gold as well. But the Sugar Act of 1764 cut off the more profitable French and Spanish markets, limiting them to trade with the English islands, which could not pick up the slack, and added duties to indigo and other goods as well. New duties, restrictions on markets, time-consuming hoops to jump through—all this added up to a slowdown in trade. None of this made sense to the Philadelphia merchants—the colonies would be importing fewer goods, and they had lost some of the ways they used to make remittances. Why would the British impose such things?[48]

At roughly the same time, the Currency Act of 1764 ended Pennsylvania's practice of issuing paper money as legal tender. Old paper could circulate until it expired, but from that point on debts to English merchants could only be paid in specie or other kinds of commercial paper. According to Jensen, merchants argued that it would depress the sale of dry goods, make it harder to collect debts, and hurt produce exports. Pennsylvania had enjoyed a stable currency during the first half of the eighteenth century, and Philadelphia merchants felt like they were victims of an act prompted by the bad currency of neighboring colonies.[49]

Parliament passed the Stamp Act in the spring of 1765, and it was to go into effect on November 1. Rather than using paper money, colonists had to pay for the stamps with specie, which was not easy to come by. Parliament meant for the funds raised to pay for the army on the frontier. Merchants found it especially annoying because of all the different kinds of paper they used that would need to be stamped: ship clearances, bills of lading, bills of sale, newspaper advertisements, and more. When their neighbors responded to the Stamp Act with a more widespread resistance movement, the merchants decided to act. They met in October of 1765 and passed a resolution that began with the following set of facts: "This province is heavily in Debt to Great Britain for the Manufactures & other Importations from then, which the Produce of our lands have been found unequal to pay for." Until Parliament repealed the unconstitutional Stamp Act, Philadelphia merchants would cease shipping and importing goods. Most of the city's merchants signed, including Baynton, Wharton & Morgan.[50]

Benjamin Marshall wrote that feelings ran high that fall. He called the measure "the most cruel & oppressive Stamp Act" in one letter and referred to "Horrible Stamp Paper" in another. A lucky few had shipped goods before November 1, but afterward ships and cargo were stuck in port. Even if some had been willing to leave, most of the stamp offices had closed, and there were no papers to be found. In December those willing to risk it obtained papers from a reopened customs house and sent ships with flour and bread to Spain and Portugal. Marshall refused to take that risk, however. Defiant colonists began manufacturing their own cloth in Philadelphia, and Marshall and others called on British merchants to put pressure for repeal on Parliament back in England.[51]

Upon the Stamp Act's repeal, Baynton, Wharton & Morgan wrote to Benjamin Franklin to express their happiness over Parliament's decision, hoping that other "alterations in commercial laws" would follow. "These are events which will undoubtedly restore the Affections of Americans to the Mother Country," they continued, which has shown "an inclination to act justly and equally, with her children."[52] Despite such cheery sentiments, Baynton, Wharton & Morgan had already begun looking west for new markets, targeting the fur trade through Fort Pitt. The firm eventually gave up on their old networks as they forged new ones. The opening of the Ohio Valley seemed to represent a great opportunity to make their fortune.

John Baynton had first expressed interest in the Ohio Valley during Pontiac's Rebellion. In an undated letter to a trader named Robert Callender, situated among letters from October of 1763, he wrote that he believed that the "Indian war" would last for another half year or more. The firm was already planning to send goods to Illinois, and there were other "goods intended to be sent down the Mississippi." Since it was late in the year, Baynton wondered if they should send goods to Mobile and then up the Mississippi by bateau to Illinois. The firm told Callender that they were strapped for cash and asked if he could advance them £1,000. Baynton also wrote about land purchases, trying to find a way to make up for "Indian losses" during the war. Over the next few years, Baynton, Wharton & Morgan focused on Illinois. By the fall of 1766, Baynton's old business of trading with various European ports had almost ground to a halt. In 1767, they shipped nothing overseas and instead put all their resources into trying to capture the fur trade in Illinois, an endeavor aided and abetted by a man with decades of experience trading in the West named George Croghan. The amount of goods they sent to Illinois equaled half the value of goods all licensed traders sent to Canada to trade for furs. In addition, six weeks after sending the letter to Callender, Baynton's partner Samuel Wharton attended a meeting at a tavern with George Croghan and a few others, where they hatched a plan to obtain compensation for losses in the form of a land grant from the king.[53]

France and Spain sent the first explorers and built the first settlements along the Mississippi and Ohio Rivers during the first half of the eighteenth century. When the Seven Years' War began, Philadelphia would be the port that gave England their entry into the Ohio Valley, as Philadelphia merchants began supplying the British army west of the Appalachian Mountains. After the war,

George Morgan, the youngest member of Baynton, Wharton & Morgan, would go to Illinois in hopes of cornering western markets to lay the foundation for settlements to come, and Samuel Wharton would head in the opposite direction to seek a land grant from the king. Rivalries between their firm and others would follow, setting the stage for a showdown in the West.

Shifting Boundaries

A year after the war ended, George Morgan married his partner John Baynton's daughter and seemed quite content traveling and doing business along the East Coast. But when his firm decided to try to capture the fur trade in Illinois, his partners sent a large shipment of goods to Fort Chartres, with Morgan stationed there to look after their interests. His travel accounts and business records are filled with encounters with a wide variety of people along the Ohio and Mississippi Rivers, including Native Americans and those of European descent. Over the next five years, he developed a contentious relationship with French merchants and rivals from his own colony, as well as English officials. Despite the fact that the venture ended in failure and he returned to Philadelphia, Morgan would find himself entangled in the fate of the western waters of North America until the end of his days.

After the war, Philadelphia merchants sought connections to the Riverine West down the Ohio to Illinois and up the Mississippi through New Orleans, hoping to capture the fur trade for themselves. The territorial shuffle after the war left French inhabitants scrambling to secure their future all along the Mississippi. George Morgan encountered an international world in Illinois, and his travel diaries reveal much about encounters between settlers from various empires, as well as Native American tribes. In Illinois, Morgan bought and sold slaves and had to deal with French settlers, Spanish officials, and the British military as he strove to make a profit, but he failed to make meaningful connections with his neighbors in the end. Meanwhile, the agent of another Philadelphia firm, an ambitious trader named Oliver Pollock, began making inroads to the south through New Orleans, and he managed to move freely between empires in a way that Morgan never could. With both banks of the Ohio and Mississippi Rivers under the control of rivals, commercial people of both European and Native American descent did the best they could to keep imports and exports flowing.

Travel accounts from early commercial ventures on behalf of Baynton, Wharton & Morgan reveal their first impressions of what expanding Philadelphia's hinterland down the Ohio and Mississippi Rivers would entail. Urged on by George Croghan, Baynton, Wharton & Morgan's first forays into the West did not always run smoothly. Tensions ran high in western Pennsylvania for years after the Seven Years' War ended. As George Morgan, the firm's agents, and army officers traveled downstream from the Ohio's headwaters on their way to Illinois, though, their travails reveal an international world on the western waters. They paint an equally fascinating picture of life on the Mississippi.

The man who convinced the partners that they could make a fortune in Illinois was Irishmen George Croghan, who had come to the American colonies as a young man in 1742. With the help of an Indian trader named William Trent, he became a trader himself, acquired land, and kept a store in Lancaster County, Pennsylvania. Emulating the French rather than the British, Croghan traveled to Native American villages to set up trading posts and learned their languages. He made a name for himself by setting up a trading post with the Senecas on the shores of Lake Erie, where he learned to speak fluently with a number of tribes and married into a Mohawk family. In the process, he pushed farther into the region than English authority warranted. The Iroquois made him an honorary sachem in 1746. The French dominated the region, but Croghan's trade networks pushed back in the name of the British, and he would be asked to represent the empire in a number of treaty negotiations in the years to come. Sir William Johnson, newly appointed superintendent of Indian Affairs, chose Croghan as one of his deputies in 1756.[1]

The British halted trade with Ohio Valley Indians in 1763 during Pontiac's Rebellion but opened it up to licensed traders at British forts in 1764. Worried about the French sending goods up the Mississippi to Illinois, General Gage urged the governor of Pennsylvania to expand trading operations with the Indians in June of 1765. Colonists living in the region did not like traders selling weapons and ammunition to their former enemies in exchange for furs in the aftermath of the Seven Years' War, but Gage believed that the traders had to sell all manner of goods to the Indians or lose them to alliances with the French.[2] Johnson may have intended to use George Croghan's networks and influence to Great Britain's advantage, but Gage wasn't so sure.

Baynton, Wharton & Morgan sent a shipment of goods west in early 1765, but survivors of the Seven Years' War in the backcountry destroyed it en route, claiming that the Philadelphia merchants were sending scalping knives to their enemies. Croghan had been negotiating with Pontiac and returned to Philadelphia in the fall. The fact that Croghan's gifts for negotiating with Native American tribes had shipped with the Philadelphia merchants' goods aroused Gage's suspicions, and he declined to pay Croghan's draft at first. Samuel Wharton assured Gage and others that their goods had only been meant to be stored at Pittsburgh until trade opened. Croghan withdrew to show that there was nothing shady going on. The venture was meant to be split four ways between the Philadelphia firm and three western traders who had ties with Native Americans—Croghan, Robert Field, and Robert Callender. Field and Callender pulled out soon after Croghan, leaving the firm of Baynton, Wharton & Morgan on its own.[3]

The partners decided to try to engage in the Indian trade again the next year. The firm entered into a contract with Edward Morton to send twenty wagons full of goods to Fort Pitt three different times. Six hundred packhorses were added later. Baynton, Wharton & Morgan sent four carpenters from Philadelphia to build ships and hired sawyers and others to get the job done. The work did not go smoothly—the men ran out of supplies, and some of their tools went astray. But that fall the partners managed to send sixty-five boats to Illinois under a combined crew of over three hundred men.[4] Initially they had hoped to send boats back to Pittsburgh with furs and pelts, but they found that sending boats back up the Ohio was all but impossible. They shipped the furs south through New Orleans in the end.

A man named James Dobson took care of business for Baynton, Wharton & Morgan at Fort Pitt. In a series of letters from late 1765 through the spring of 1766, he gave a sense of what was going on there. In December, Dobson wrote that he felt like he was caught in the middle—a few men wanted to "break their engagements," but Major Murray insisted that they stay. He expected a high volume of skins to come in soon. Dobson identified one troublemaker as a trader named Alexander Lowry. In March, Dobson sent five bateaus to Illinois with their goods, and he had already sent a big load of pelts back east, but he had trouble finding enough labor to build their boats. He reports on the actions of another of the firm's agents, John Jennings. The newest load of the firm's goods arrived from Philadelphia in April, and Dobson wrote that between seven hundred and eight hundred shirts had gotten wet in the wagons. Some were being dried, a washerwoman had charge of more than half of them, but the others were spotted with mildew that would not come out. Shortly thereafter, George Morgan would be the man on the spot himself, and he would get their business back on track.[5]

The first travel accounts penned by George Morgan and his agents reveal the international riverine world of western rivers as Atlantic rivalries spread to the interior. As Dobson noted, John Jennings made the journey on the Ohio from Fort Pitt to Fort Chartres in the spring of 1766 with the first five boats loaded with the firm's goods. Jennings kept a daily log of distances traveled and the weather, as well as a description of what he and the other men saw on shore and the people they met. Other than one encounter that worried his party early on, they had a remarkably peaceful journey and met a wide variety of the region's inhabitants, especially Native Americans. The boat crews took precautions, watching carefully for signs of trouble, but their fears never materialized. A party of Shawnees in four canoes traded fresh meat with them in exchange for biscuit and tobacco near the Scioto River. The Jennings party traded for meat in a similar fashion with another group as they headed down the Ohio. Jennings mentioned small groups of what he characterized as "Indian cabins," "the cabins of warriors," "hunters' cabins," and "large Indian villages." Below Louisville, they heard gunfire, and he assumed that Indians were hunting nearby. Heading up the Mississippi at last, when Jennings encountered "a large French boat," his party put up their flag and rowed to shore to meet them. Along the way he made note of ruined forts, picturesque views, and inscriptions carved in a tree to mark the graves of two Frenchmen who died there the year before. Nearly a month later, Jennings neared his destination in Illinois, where he chauvinistically characterized the French he saw as "very bad" farmers.[6]

That summer George Morgan followed, and in letters to his wife he echoed many of Jennings's observations, tending to label everyone he encountered as either French, English, or Indian. He chose to ride in the boat commanded by an army officer named Hutchins rather than in the one with Indian agent George Croghan because he wanted to gain a better understanding of "the plan of the river." The party had to move slowly, apparently to show their peaceful intentions, and Croghan, as the Crown's representative, spoke with Native Americans they met along the way, including a party of two hundred at the Scioto

River. As they continued downstream, Morgan hired Native Americans to hunt buffalo for their larder, as well as turkey and deer. The youngest partner expected Wharton to follow, and then he himself would head home down the Mississippi, with a stop at Pensacola. Apparently Morgan's wife worried about his safety. Her father, John Baynton, tried to put her mind at ease by arguing that peaceful relationships with Native Americans relied on trade, which was, after all, the whole point of the venture.[7]

Accompanying Croghan and Morgan was Captain Harry Gordon, chief engineer in the Western Department in North America, and he took particular note of the French in Illinois. Upon arriving at Fort Massiac, he wrote that the French fort at this spot had been used to protect their trade from the Cherokees and recommended that the British do the same "to prevent illicit trade being carried on up the Wabash." Buffalo and salt for meat could be obtained easily by hunters in the area. The village of Kuskuskies on the Mississippi comprised eighty houses, most built of stone, and residents raised large numbers of cattle and hogs. As Gordon traveled inland, he ran into more French and Indian towns. Gordon encountered a man named Laclede at Point Court, aka St. Louis, who he said controlled all of the Indian trade to the north on the Missouri, Mississippi, and Illinois Rivers, as well as the shores of Lake Michigan. Gordon described the Frenchman as "sensible," "clever," and "active" and concluded that taking the trade from him would not be easy. But Gordon hoped that English possession of Illinois would finally show the Native American tribes that the British were superior to the French. Gordon suggested placing forts on the Illinois River and at La Baye to capture the region's trade and keep the French out.[8]

Gordon also described trade between Illinois and New Orleans. French boats were large, weighing 20 tons and requiring twenty oars. It took the crews between two and three months to come upriver. They made the trip twice a year, but they returned to New Orleans only half loaded because there wasn't much produce to ship from Illinois. They did send lead from a mine on the French side of the river. The trip down river only took about two weeks, but the window of opportunity depended on floods and high water that occurred in May and June.[9]

After concluding his first round of business in Illinois, George Morgan kept a journal of a trip from Kaskaskia to New Orleans down the Mississippi in November 1766 and left his own impressions of settlements on the Mississippi at that time. He wrote of a Spanish meadow and the English and French sides of the river. Many days were foggy. He often saw multiple "French hunting parties" out seeking buffalo and bear on both sides of the river. Morgan and his party ate buffalo meat on the trip, sometimes provided by others they met, other times procured by a member of their own party. Natchez had been named for a tribe of Indians destroyed by the French in 1730, he wrote, and was now home to a garrison of British troops from Scotland consisting of forty-four men and four officers. In his opinion, the site didn't look to be a very effective spot for an outpost because the river was so wide at that point that they couldn't easily stop anyone trying to slip past. Morgan stopped there for a day to dry out some pelts, before moving on.[10]

George Morgan encountered many more Frenchmen and Native Americans in the final stretch of his journey south. He stated that there were a couple of Native American settlements up the Red River and a "considerable French settlement with Fort & Garrison" on its banks. There were more settlements along the Mississippi, some with "new French huts," and Morgan saw fifty slaves from Pointe Coupée harvesting cypress trees to be floated to New Orleans the next spring. In his telling, Fort Coupée provided a focal point for two hundred families, eighty-five of them spread along the river. Several men had three dozen slaves, more owned twenty, and newcomers owned a handful each. They grew cotton, rice, indigo, and tobacco. Morgan noted a visit to the confluence of the Mississippi and Iberville Rivers where he stopped to see "the boundary between the French and English in America" (see fig. 2.1).[11]

John Jennings made the same journey for Morgan and his partners two years later. He began his journal with a description of a tense time at Fort Chartres in the spring of 1768. Various Native Americans seemed to be testing new alliances, and Jennings made distinctions between friendly and unfriendly tribes. In late June he headed south down the Mississippi for New Orleans. As with his trip down the Ohio two years before, he encountered French hunting parties and Native Americans in canoes on the river. He wrote that Natchez afforded a great view of the river and then noted the presence of a new Spanish fort and an Acadian settlement beyond. Acadians, who had first settled in Maryland after being expelled from Canada in 1755, came to Louisiana a decade later, where the Spanish governor welcomed them with open arms, and most of them settled near Natchez. The governor wanted them to be provided with food and supplies as they got settled, granting land to heads of household, though not to single men. The Spanish advised them against trying to plant corn, telling them that wheat and tobacco would be the most useful to them. Interestingly, the governor also wrote in his instructions that those in charge had to be careful not to let newcomers beg—they would whine and ask for more, he wrote, but the governor wanted them to become productive members of society.[12]

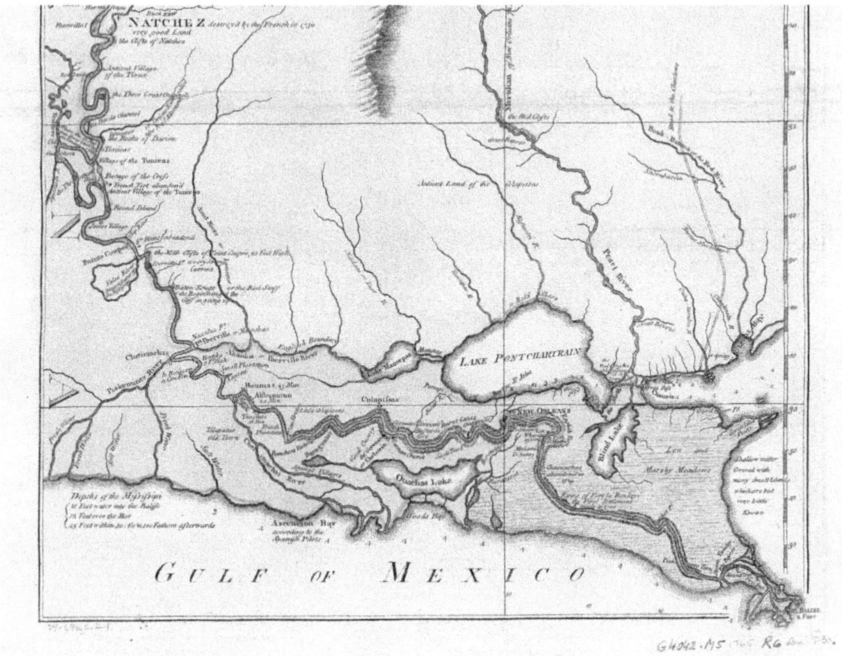

Figure 2.1. The Lower Mississippi from Natchez to Fort Balize. The Iberville River connected the Mississippi with Lake Pontchartrain. Lieut. Ross and Robert Sayer, *Course of the River Mississipi from Balise to Fort Chartres; Taken on an Expedition to the Illinois, in the Latter End of the Year 1765.* Courtesy of the Library of Congress

As Jennings continued down the Mississippi, he seemed to be impressed by France's Pointe Coupée, describing a settlement with a fort and church on the Spanish side of the river opposite. The local economy supported exports of indigo, rice, and Indian corn. Farther downriver, Fort Bute seemed to be in bad repair, and he noted that German settlements were producing the same crops grown upriver at Natchez, though they supported mills as well. All these groups were the legacy of French attempts to bolster their numbers on the Lower Mississippi.[13]

The popular conception of France's New World empire usually centers around the coureurs de bois—traders in canoes who traded for furs and left little mark on the territory. But when travelers like Jennings and Morgan mention seeing Frenchmen, they were usually doing other things. They encountered many French hunting parties and passed French forts on shore. Though at first Jennings belittled French farmers, both he and Morgan later described them producing wheat and utilizing slave labor to grow tobacco and other crops. Other words used in reference to the French include *villages*, *huts*, and *families*. They were rivals for the territory as much as for the fur trade. George Morgan would need to find a way to do business with them if his business were to prosper.

Though George Morgan seemed intent on learning as much as he could about the Riverine West and its people on his first journey down the Ohio, it did not pay off in the end. His business in Illinois did not go smoothly. Baynton, Wharton & Morgan had always managed to pay the firm's agents and their transport bills, but the firm couldn't generate enough income to pay their creditors, and it would not end well for them. In the beginning, Baynton, Wharton & Morgan intended to profit from their business venture to Illinois in three ways: supplying the British troops, selling goods to French settlers, and acquiring furs from Native Americans. That meant being on good terms with both General Gage back east and whoever commanded Fort Chartres in Illinois (see fig. 2.2). Gage gave them the contracts for supplying the army, and the military commanders in the West oversaw their relations with the French and various Native American tribes. Their relationship with Gage was generally good, but George Morgan would run into trouble dealing with the various officers in charge of the fort.

Baynton, Wharton & Morgan had a serious cash-flow problem by the fall of 1766. They had heavily invested in goods, but large-enough quantities of furs had yet not arrived from the West to pay their debts. They wrote to William Franklin, wanting to know if he would ask his father to secure a loan for them in London—they needed someone to advance enough money to Richard Neave to cover their drafts for a time. They had first asked William Johnson to expedite a land grant tied to their losses in 1763. By the fall of 1767, they threw up their hands and invited their creditors to look at their books, but the creditors found that the situation was not as bad as they feared. Baynton, Wharton & Morgan could claim £120,000 in assets against £80,000 in liabilities. Eight of their creditors came together as a board of trustees to supervise their business over the next three years. All expected great profits to come from the Illinois venture.[14]

When the British army took over in 1766, the French in Illinois felt hopeful about their future. They were allowed to continue worshipping as Catholics, and the British acknowledged their property titles and right to trade freely. The British commandant didn't interfere in local matters, allowing the French to keep the peace in their own settlements much as they had before. Before Baynton,

Figure 2.2. The Illinois Country in the eighteenth century. © Seth Rainey

Wharton & Morgan's goods arrived from Philadelphia, British officials purchased goods to gift to Native American tribes from local French merchants in Illinois. The British did require that the French pledge their loyalty to the Crown, but most of the French did not take that step, and some moved across the river to Spanish territory.[15]

John Jennings stored the first shipment of goods mostly at Kaskaskia in the spring of 1766, with a small portion sent on to Fort Chartres. When George Morgan arrived a few months later, he opened stores at Cahokia and Vincennes, before finally settling down to run the business at Kaskaskia. Trading with the French proved difficult. The French preferred to trade with New Orleans as they always had—the English didn't seem to have anything special to offer in the end. In New Orleans they could get cheaper goods and use their produce to pay for them. Morgan preferred that all customers pay in cash, which they did not have, though he did take their produce or livestock as payment when it could be sold to the army. If the army didn't need it, he couldn't sell it. It couldn't be shipped east over the mountains in any cost-effective manner, and the English couldn't sell in New Orleans, though Benjamin Franklin did smooth things over there on one or two occasions. In the end, Morgan sold over half of that first shipment to army personnel and the rest to French inhabitants.[16]

George Croghan believed that getting along with the French farmers would be crucial to Great Britain's success in securing the region, for they would be the key to provisioning the troops, and he proffered practical advice. Croghan reported to General Gage that they could not procure enough supplies from the Lower Mississippi River, rowing against the current. Supplies could come from Fort Pitt, of course, but building boats and hiring men to man them would be expensive, especially because once they arrived in Illinois they would be "an intire Loss to the Crown, as they cannot be brought up the Ohio again." But the French inhabitants began to cross the river at the war's end. In George Croghan's opinion the only "means of inducing many of those who have removed to the Spanish side, to return to our's with their Cattle &tc" was to offer them cash for their crops and meat. He wrote that the French farmers were very unhappy because British suppliers like Morgan paid them with notes on New York or London. Because they lived too far away to ever redeem the notes themselves, they had to sell them to merchants in New Orleans, who only paid them 40–60 percent of their face value. Croghan concluded that if we don't "break their connextions with the people of New Orleans," the few Frenchmen still living on the English side would "remove to the Spanish side" as well.[17]

The British Crown decided early on that holding Illinois cost too much and ordered General Gage in New York to find a way to bring costs down. In turn, Gage sent Lieutenant John Reed to take over in 1767, with orders to exert control over the French traders. He expected Reed to stop any dealings between the French on the Spanish and English banks. Reed didn't like the French—he thought they were dishonest and went behind the army's back to scheme with Native American tribes. Many of the French had married Native American women, and they spoke easily with their wives' families and others in their own tongue. Reed fined them for minor offenses, imposed taxes, and charged them fees to do business. George Morgan relayed to his partners that Reed treated his neighbors unfairly. Though Morgan didn't speak French, he and the French merchants united against the British army for a time. Morgan and his associates wanted a civil government to make it easier to buy land, and the French merchants wanted a civil government to facilitate trade—military rule didn't work for any of them. George Morgan's secretary James Rumsey helped the local inhabitants petition the British Crown for their rights under English law. "Trade cannot exist," they wrote, because we lack "a civil government."[18]

Despite such early signs of common purpose, tension grew when Morgan lost out to French and Spanish traders. British regulations stipulated that Morgan could not go to the Native American tribes in search of furs—they had to come to him. But the French and Spanish could go wherever they wanted, and the French offered goods from New Orleans at about 30 percent lower prices than Morgan could offer them from Philadelphia. Their networks were already well established, and they pretty much went on as before, even though their actions were now illegal. George Morgan complained to his partners that the French bribed the British officer in charge at Fort Chartres to go up the Illinois and Wabash Rivers with goods, but Morgan refused to stoop to such tactics. He did not give Native Americans their due, crediting French actions rather than Indian choices when he concluded that French influence with tribes along the Illinois River would keep Baynton, Wharton & Morgan out. Morgan did try to hire Native Americans to bring him furs and attempted to buy furs from French traders in St. Louis, but neither venture proved successful.[19]

While trying to reinforce the firm's backing by British officials back in New York during the summer of 1767, Samuel Wharton identified some of the problems Morgan would have trading for furs in Illinois. Wharton complained that British policies made it difficult to move pelts from one colony to another. He believed that the army allowed the French too much access to trade at Port Vincent and argued that the French should only be allowed to trade in British territories if they had a license from the commissary of Indian Affairs and bought their goods and sold their pelts at Fort Chartres or another British post. Wharton expected the army to stop "any Spanish or French Hunters (save those who are British Subjects)" from traveling to the Ohio from New Orleans. He blamed the loss of their contract to David Franks on the quick turnover of officials within the Board of Trade. According to Wharton, someone in England had asked Franks for a bid, he provided one that undercut Wharton and his partners, and they lost their contract.[20]

OK as edited?

Historian Jacob Lee concludes that the reasons for George Morgan's failure in Illinois went beyond British regulations. Accompanied by a Seneca Indian named Silver Heels with connections to George Croghan, Morgan found himself excluded from Native American kinship networks in Illinois. Pontiac and his followers along the Great Lakes hated the English for forcing their people to migrate west over several generations. He would recruit Illinois Indians during his rebellion, but mostly because they were open to a pan-Indian message for other reasons. Illinois Indians hadn't lost their lands yet, and they had been marrying both French traders and planters and each other across tribal lines for decades. They didn't like the English much, finding them arrogant, and there was no way Morgan could break into Illinois society with a wife and other ties back in Philadelphia. He just didn't fit in. Add to that his suspicions of French merchants and British officials, and you have a man mostly isolated from his fellows in Illinois no matter what their background.[21]

George Morgan carried on despite setbacks. In December of 1767 he told his partners that they could make a fivefold profit on tinware, especially if they packed it with coffee rather than shipping it to Illinois empty. The goods must arrive by June, he wrote, because that was when most of the Native Americans in the region came to trade. Morgan intended to keep trying to trade English goods to Native Americans for furs and to trade dry goods and groceries to his French neighbors in exchange for cattle and wheat. Selling provisions such as meat and flour to soldiers brought in reasonable profits, as did sales to the Royal Department of Indian Affairs.[22] Atlantic rivalries meant forts and soldiers, and Philadelphia merchants found them to be a ready market.

George Morgan also had to forge a relationship with another set of officials to engage in the Atlantic trade. Any merchant wishing to engage in commerce in the West knew that gaining permission from the Spanish governor to pass through and do business in New Orleans would be essential. In early 1766, Wharton indicated that Morgan had tasked him with asking Governor William Franklin of New Jersey for "a letter of recommendation to the Governor of New Orleans." Franklin declined, with the excuse that the partners resided in Pennsylvania rather than his own colony. In February of 1768 Samuel Young informed George Morgan that only ships with provisions were allowed to land in New Orleans; vessels with dry goods were required to have a permit from Spain. Before leaving Philadelphia for Illinois in the fall of 1769, George Morgan asked a colleague in New Orleans to obtain permission from the governor of Louisiana for Baynton, Wharton & Morgan to do business there. Morgan wanted to ship peltry to New Orleans before transferring the cargo to a ship heading for a British port. In 1770 he once again asked a partner (Baynton this time) to ask Franklin for a letter to the Spanish governor "as he did for Mr. Obrie in 1767," because he might need to repack their peltry or sell some of their flour. Morgan advised another colleague in 1773 that he should ship his pelts through New Orleans because merchants could usually find a ship there ready to take cargo to Philadelphia or New York, especially in the summer.[23]

As another offshoot of the Atlantic World, George Morgan sold slaves to the French in Illinois. An associate named James Rumsey purchased more than three dozen slaves for the firm in Jamaica and brought them down the Ohio River to Illinois in 1767. It's not clear why, but Samuel Wharton told his partners that he thought Rumsey should transport the slaves "as his property." Wharton also hoped that an associate named Irwin had laid in a good supply of Indian corn because it would "make cheap & strengthening food" for the slaves. By the end of the month, he worried that their cargo was late because the slaves might "have made a bold push for their liberty." A slow passage could be trouble in more ways than one, Wharton wrote—even if the captain and crew avoided a ship-wide revolt, the slaves might become too weak to be sent West for a time when they finally arrived.[24]

The cargo did arrive safely, but Morgan recounts that Rumsey lost seven of them, as well as two white men, on the journey from Pittsburgh to Illinois. In December Morgan wrote his partners that Rumsey had arrived just as a group of Frenchmen planned to leave for New Orleans in search of labor. Morgan offered them slaves in exchange for pelts, specie, bills of exchange, or produce to be paid in May, so they decided to stay and make deals with him. Morgan intended to sell slaves for at least 400 Spanish dollars and hoped that "we have it in our power to make a monopoly of all the flour in the country by purchasing it with negroes." In February, however, he wrote to his partners that sixty slaves were expected from New Orleans in the near future, apparently undercutting sales. Some of the firm's slaves remained unsold in April, and Morgan put them to work building a cabin and planting corn and tobacco on land he had taken in payment for a debt. In June of the following year he still had a few left, and he wrote that another merchant had sold slaves for less than Morgan charged and that other inhabitants had sent to New Orleans for slaves to be bought for 200 Spanish dollars apiece. Still, Baynton, Wharton & Morgan managed to sell forty-two men, seven women, twelve boys, and five girls in Illinois.[25]

In 1768, Gage recalled Reed and sent Colonel John Wilkins. Wilkins passed through Philadelphia and met with Baynton and Wharton, who offered him a commission and an annual payment in exchange for favoring their firm. This deal would cause Morgan no end of trouble. He couldn't make enough profit to pay off Wilkins, and their relationship deteriorated. In the meantime, Wilkins installed Morgan as the president of a new Court of Inquiry meant to settle trade disputes, which sided with an Englishmen against a Frenchman in the first case that came before it. The French complained to Gage about Wilkins's corruption, and they grew farther apart from Morgan.[26]

The border situation in Illinois continued to be very fluid, with Spanish territory on the opposite bank of the Mississippi and Morgan chafed under Wilkins's military rules and restrictions. At Kaskaskia in the summer of 1769 Morgan wrote to a colleague that "no person whatever officer merchant or inhabitant can cross the river from either side without a written passport," likening the residents to slaves. Morgan compared the situation in Illinois unfavorably to that on the Lower Mississippi—"the strict prohibition against foreign trade will I suppose prevent the free intercourse which the English had with the inhabitants of New Orleans."[27] But determining the nationality of those on the river was not always easy—Samuel Wharton had referred to French and Spanish hunters who were British subjects not long before. People might switch sides in the interior of North America, and those who lived in the West found ways to use the boundaries to their advantage. Morgan himself noted that after his Seneca ally, Silver Heels, was murdered outside his cabin one night, one of the assailants "escapd over the river." English soldiers and French inhabitants alike attended the funeral.[28]

Even after so many ventures had fallen through in Illinois, George Morgan came up with one last plan to make money: opening a distillery. Morgan needed permission to do so, and in a proposal to Colonel Wilkins he argued that such a business would make the best use of "old grain" residents hadn't been able to sell elsewhere. Buying spirits from the East and New Orleans had proved to be very expensive—producing their own in Illinois made sense because flour was in fact cheaper than it was in Philadelphia or New York, and he could buy "Indian corn." In retirement, Morgan would experiment with different crops on his farms in both New Jersey and Pennsylvania—perhaps the genesis of such activity started in his time in Illinois, when he proposed trying to grow rye, buckwheat, and barley, among other grains. Morgan flattered Wilkins and stated that his intent was to improve the area for all inhabitants and produce a benefit for his Majesty's service. He had already brought in millwrights to provide flour for the troops, proving his worth.[29]

All his work came to naught, however, and years later George Morgan seemed to blame the disaster on both Samuel Wharton and George Croghan. He characterized Wharton as a man of wild schemes who moved too fast and took too many risks. Wharton was to be the one to go West, but when Wharton invited Morgan to his home, his wife told the younger man she was pregnant, and then both husband and wife cried, begging Morgan to go in Wharton's stead—only for six months, they promised. Morgan portrayed Wharton as a man who didn't understand the fur trade in the West and had been led astray by George Croghan. Morgan portrayed himself as the holdout, only persuaded against his better judgment by his father-in-law John Baynton's trust in their partner. But Morgan's own correspondence at the time seems filled with schemes to grow rich. The first time he descended the Ohio, Morgan seemed taken with Croghan at times, describing him as "the most enterprising man," who appeared "pleased when he was not and indifferent when pleased."[30]

The year 1768 proved to be an important turning point in the West for Philadelphia merchants. As tensions on the Eastern Seaboard rose, the British moved their troops back east, abandoning military contracts, and merchants from Great Britain did deals with the French, cutting colonial merchants out of the loop and keeping the fur trade out of American hands. Colonel John Wilkins, the British commander in Illinois, assured Baynton, Wharton & Morgan in May of 1768 that he would favor the firm above all others. But that summer the contract for military supplies went to David Franks and a man named William Murray instead. In October, George Morgan didn't seem worried that Franks's business would undercut theirs, but General Gage back east sided with their rivals. Morgan returned to Philadelphia for good in 1771, and in the end Baynton, Wharton & Morgan did triumph over David Franks in the courtroom. Franks's business of supplying the army never recovered after the British decommissioned a number of forts and sold Fort Pitt to Alexander Ross in 1772.[31]

To succeed in Illinois, George Morgan needed to make meaningful connections with rivals on opposite banks of the river and opposite sides of the cultural divide. In his early days there, he and the French merchants united for a time against British military authority, but their amity did not last. Perhaps Morgan's efforts were doomed anyway because the British abandoned Illinois within a few years of occupying it. But the career of Oliver Pollock, another merchant who got his start in Philadelphia, proves that such connections between empires could flourish in the Riverine West.

New territory acquired at the end of the Seven Years' War awakened interest in the other end of the Mississippi River as well—the Gulf Coast. Baynton, Wharton & Morgan investigated the opening of East and West Florida, though Oliver Pollock, the agent of another Philadelphia firm, would have a much greater impact there. Initially working for the Willing family, Pollock settled in Havana and began a relationship with an official named General Alejandro O'Reilly. When the Spanish took over New Orleans, O'Reilly would be tasked with integrating New Orleans more seamlessly into the Atlantic World, and Pollock would soon join him.

Trade with the Gulf Coast tempted many Englishmen after the war. Baynton, Wharton & Morgan wrote to a trader in Mobile named Francis Poussett asking for his opinion about trading with the Spanish, as well as trading with the French and Native Americans at Mobile and up the Mississippi. Poussett's correspondence indicated that the Philadelphia firm had shipped goods to be traded to the Chickasaws for pelts and deerskins. Baynton, Wharton & Morgan also had a military contract of some kind to supply the garrison. Poussett urged them on more than one occasion to send any "Spanish assortment" of goods they had on hand, and perhaps even order more from London. Poussett sold flour and rum for the partners and had his own deal with a Pensacola merchant to sell flour in New Orleans.[32]

The French wanted to trade with the Spanish and keep the English out during the first half of the eighteenth century. After the Seven Years' War, the Spanish were slow to occupy what they'd gained by treaty, but once they did, they hemmed and hawed between suppressing the English and welcoming their business. Interest in both West Florida and Illinois came to a head in England and America in the 1760s, but the Spanish were unsure of what to do about it. New Orleans just couldn't support itself at that time, and trade back up the Mississippi never really overcame the river's current, though the French tried. Furs continued south through New Orleans from English, American, Spanish, and French traders upriver.

Scholars believe that the British were unsure of what to make of Louisiana after the war and preferred to concentrate on Florida. Historian John G. Clark argued that the English had to settle for the Gulf Coast ports rather than New Orleans, hoping to lure in Spanish ships with cheaper and better English goods. They believed that if they could corner the fur trade in the Southeast, the Spanish would come to them for goods. The British intended to use rivers, lakes, and canals in West Florida to connect the coast to Natchez, bypassing the delta and New Orleans (see fig. 2.1). But they couldn't overcome the strong ties Spanish merchants already had in New Orleans, where they could usually obtain English goods anyway. New Orleans would continue to be the link between the Atlantic World and the interior of North America west of the Appalachians.[33]

The Treaty of Paris gave Great Britain possession of the territory east of the Mississippi, and Spain took control of the territory to the west, including New Orleans. The British began shipping flour and other foodstuffs to New Orleans in 1763, and they moved to occupy Kaskaskia and Cahokia, trading with the French inhabitants in Illinois and trying to muscle their way into the fur trade. British merchants tried to make Natchez their main trading post by way of the Iberville River and Lake Maurepas, but they never successfully diverted trade from New Orleans, and they incurred the wrath of a number of Native American tribes along the way. Louisiana Creoles resisted turning over the territory to the Spanish in 1768, but the Spanish under General O'Reilly took control by force the next summer. The Spanish wanted the Lower Mississippi to be integrated into their commercial world, and at first O'Reilly aimed to cut the English out, kicking British merchants out of the port. A man trying to collect debts for Baynton, Wharton & Morgan, among others, found himself thrown in jail the following winter.[34]

Initially, the British had high hopes for the region. The spring after the war ended, Francis Poussett in Mobile wrote Baynton and Wharton that "we flatter ourselves here of the certainty of every agreeable piece of news that New Orleans is absolutely ceded to the Spaniards," and that summer he wrote that all the French in the region "have unanimously agreed to become English subjects in consequence of the Spaniards taking possession of New Orleans."[35] Three years later, a British captain in New Orleans reported something similar to the ministry—the French deeply disliked the Spanish and worried that the Spanish governor would create a monopoly, enforcing duties that would destroy their trade. According to him, French merchants spoke of moving out of New Orleans and setting up shop in British territory instead, if they could be assured of protection. Captain Marsh concluded that the merchants felt no loyalty to an empire that would give them over to another after they had worked so hard to hold Louisiana. He attributed some of that attitude to religion, citing tension between Catholics and Protestants.[36]

Englishman Jacob Blackwell provided another view of New Orleans trade in 1766. He wrote that the Spanish would buy linens and other goods, take them to Vera Cruz on their own ships, and return with other trade, including cash to pay the army. He denigrated the trade with the French that had gone on before, stating that much of it through Mobile had been rum passed on to Native Americans for furs, and all the while the French were telling the tribes not to trust the English. Samuel Wharton wrote something similar that same year, complaining that the French were "poisoning the minds of the Indians against us," denying any Native American agency just as his younger partner had. Blackwell thought that the French were enough of a problem that the English would need armed forts to watch them even after the Spanish took control of the region. He finished up by praising the area around New Orleans, noting that it would produce sugar cane.[37] A year later, Captain Marsh wrote to Brigadier General Haldimand that the English merchants trading at New Orleans sold flour and pork to the Spanish and the French. The Spanish governor wanted eight thousand barrels of flour a year and sent most of it to Havana. The English merchants also sold slaves. Marsh didn't find much trade in pelts, but other sources indicate that furs found their way out of the West through the port. Marsh also remarked on the rivalry between Europeans who competed for alliances with Native Americans along the Mississippi.[38]

Clearly New Orleans, located in the Mississippi Delta 100 miles from the coast, would play a key role in trade west of the Appalachian Mountains as interest in the interior of North America grew after the Seven Years' War. During the first half of the eighteenth century, Spanish and French colonies in the West Indies and South America hadn't been able to supply New Orleans with the flour they needed to keep the colony fed, and the French didn't want to trade with the English or their colonies, no matter how weak their own settlement on the Lower Mississippi became. The Spanish had no such scruples when they took over, and despite the fact that official policy often closed off trade on the river, officials in New Orleans allowed trade with Philadelphia to bloom and grow. The situation was ripe for a man like Oliver Pollock, who aimed to make himself indispensable to the Spanish and then, in turn, useful to Americans during and after the Revolution.[39]

As a young man, Oliver Pollock left Ireland and arrived in Philadelphia in 1760, and then he moved to Carlisle with his Scots-Irish father, brothers, and a nephew. His brothers became the owners of a grist mill and a tavern, but Pollock decided to move back to Philadelphia to try his hand at trade a couple years later. With a vessel, a crew, and the backing of some merchants, he took consignments of flour, rum, lumber, and indigo from Philadelphia and New York to the West Indies, shipping back molasses, tea, coffee, spices, and sugar.[40] Pollock settled in Havana and immediately began perfecting the art of crossing back and forth between empires whenever he pleased.

First claimed by Spain in the sixteenth century, Cuba changed hands during the colonial era. Spanish planters had imported slaves to provide labor, and then the French took control for a time. During the eighteenth century, England took control, but Spain claimed the island once again by the end of the century. The two did battle during the eighteenth century, with the British occupying Havana during the Seven Years' War, but Spain once again took possession after the Peace of Paris. Cuba would remain part of the Spanish Empire for over a century thereafter. The British Navigation Acts outlawed trade with Spanish ports, but since Pollock was a British citizen, officials allowed his ships to trade in Philadelphia, the West Indies, Europe, and New Orleans. Under normal conditions, Spanish policies would have cut him out as well, but

Pollock lived year-round in Havana for a time and made friends. Spanish officials signed off on his trade with Spanish and French ports. He later wrote that after "18 months of assiduous study" and "the constant practice of mercantile transactions in an eminent house to which I was attached," he could do all his business without an interpreter. Over the course of five years, he plowed his profits into more ships and more trade. Historian Kathleen DuVal concluded that Pollock managed to be English and Spanish simultaneously through the "Spanish trade privileges" he leveraged by way of personal relationships.[41]

One of the most important of those personal relationships was the friendship he struck up in Havana with another Irishman, Alejandro (Alexander) O'Reilly. Born in 1722, O'Reilly left home, as his father and others had before him, to join the Spanish army, choosing to serve a Catholic king. During the Seven Years' War, he also served in the armies of Austria and France. Charles III promoted him to major general after he led Spain's invasion of Portugal. After the war, he was sent to establish Spanish rule in Cuba and Puerto Rico. When the residents of New Orleans revolted against Spain's first governor in 1768, the king sent O'Reilly into action once again. He arrived with twenty ships and two thousand men in the summer of 1769, had the leaders of the rebellion arrested, and pardoned everyone else. Six of the arrested men went to jail in Havana, and O'Reilly had five executed by a firing squad.[42]

The leaders of that rebellion were some of the most wealthy and well-connected merchants and planters in the region. Unhappy that France had ceded the territory west of the Mississippi and New Orleans to the Spanish, many worried about Spain's restrictive trade laws and the impact they would have on their business. A truly international group—French, Acadians, and Germans—sent the Spanish governor, Antonio de Ulloa, packing and seized the port. During the short time in which they controlled the city, the men established a bank to provide loans and credit. New Orleans merchants feared that their tobacco couldn't compete with that of the Spanish colonies and that they would lose French markets for their furs and skins.[43] One scholar concludes that by targeting this group of economic elite, O'Reilly could "gain control of the colony swiftly and with decisive action."[44]

Ulloa's own account presents an interesting picture of the population of Louisiana at the time. The conspirators were merchants concerned that Spanish regulations were destroying trade. They convinced the hard-drinking inhabitants of New Orleans to go along by arguing that, thanks to the Spanish, they would have to give up their Bordeaux and drink much poorer wines from Catalonia. Retired officers and some of the larger plantation owners upriver seemed to have not listened and tried to ignore the affair. German settlers who had been in Louisiana for decades and the newly arrived Acadians were both persuaded that the Spanish Crown withheld money owed them or failed to give them a proper rate of exchange for paper money from Canada. The merchants told the Acadians that the Spanish would send their men to work in the mines and their women and children would live in poverty. The conspirators actually approached the English at Pensacola for help, though it was refused, and then tried to convince other merchants by using Pensacola's resurgence under English rule as proof that the Spanish would destroy them. Thus does Ulloa paint quite a picture of a wide variety of Europeans exchanging information and discussing the pros and cons of living under the rule of different empires.[45]

With magnificent timing, Pollock arrived with flour after O'Reilly had quelled the uprising but, looking ahead, feared he would not be able to feed his troops. At any rate, though the price of flour rose after the revolt, Pollock sold O'Reilly the flour at a much lower price. Much later, Pollock recalled that flour had been selling for 30 Spanish dollars a barrel in New Orleans. When he arrived and saw three thousand hungry troops, he asked O'Reilly to set his own price. O'Reilly would not, so Pollock himself set the price at 15 Spanish dollars a barrel. This represented the beginning of Pollock's fortune because O'Reilly told him that he would "have free trade there so long as [he] lived, complying with the regulations of the country as usual." Pollock could trade freely in Louisiana, and O'Reilly also gave him a contract to supply the troops in the future. Philadelphia's provisioning trade proved vital to the survival of New Orleans under Spanish rule.[46]

When O'Reilly arrived in New Orleans in 1769, he wrote that he had "found the English entirely in possession of the commerce of the colony." They traded with the German settlements and sold furs to France in exchange for goods. When it came to selling goods for specie, the English had the advantage because they sold their goods more cheaply than anyone else.[47] In September, O'Reilly issued a proclamation stating that "in order to remedy the great improprieties that result every day from the ease in which foreigners enter the city" without permission from Spain, inhabitants of Louisiana were forbidden to meet with or host any foreigners without passports. Inhabitants were also not allowed to provide any transport or guides for the same or buy merchandise from anyone on the Mississippi or any of the lakes without formal authorization from O'Reilly. Anyone violating that order would be fined, with one-third of the money going to anyone who informed on such persons.[48]

Despite O'Reilly's public proclamation, New Orleans needed flour, and

O'Reilly continued to rely on Pollock, who in turn brought in other merchants from Philadelphia. Thomas Willing and Robert Morris had been the backers of Pollock's trip to the Mississippi Valley in 1769, where he sold flour as their agent in New Orleans for half the current price. Born in England, Morris came to America with his father and apprenticed with the merchant Charles Willing in Philadelphia. While working in the West Indies, Morris struck up a friendship with Pollock. After Willing died, Morris partnered with his son to establish the firm of Willing & Morris in May of 1757. When the Spanish sought flour after a disastrous season of hurricanes in 1769, Willing & Morris stepped in and shipped flour to New Orleans. Pollock brought rice for them to sell in Philadelphia and sold Illinois corn and wheat in the West Indies. A few years later, some Spanish merchants questioned their dominance of the Spanish trade in the West Indies, but the government ignored their petition, apparently satisfied with what the Philadelphia merchants could provide. In 1772, Willing & Morris sent ships as far away as Quebec looking for enough flour to satisfy the Spanish colonies. But in New Orleans it was Pollock who negotiated the contract to supply New Orleans with flour, and other British traders would follow his lead. By the fall of 1770, ships were arriving from Philadelphia, New York, and Illinois.[49]

Governor O'Reilly next took steps to put an end to smuggling, sending an expedition down the Red River to Natchitoches and other places to assess the situation of the far reaches of the colony and have the people swear an oath of fidelity to the king. In his instructions, O'Reilly asked for the men to make note of troublemakers. He wanted them to be careful, though, to be sure those they accused were really on the wrong side of the river and not simply victims of jealous neighbors. The new governor wanted his men to make a census of people and cattle and take note of the road and soil conditions. O'Reilly instructed them to let the inhabitants know that he would treat them fairly and they would prosper under a kind king. He wanted reports about Indians and promised to send gifts to create alliances. O'Reilly told his men to warn Native Americans not to shelter deserters, and he hoped that Native Americans would inform the Spanish about any armed men in the area. He also expected them to try to discover the cause of any dissension along the river.[50] Back in New Orleans, O'Reilly invited representatives from over a dozen smaller tribes along the Mississippi to meet with him to discuss their place in the Spanish Empire. One leader asked the Spanish to "grant us the same favors and benefits as did the French." O'Reilly presented him and others with medals and spoke in favor of peaceful relations between Native nations, the English to the east of the Mississippi, and the Spanish on the western bank. All of these actions eased the transition from French to Spanish rule.[51]

O'Reilly's policies proved wise because the French continued to wield much influence along the Mississippi River. The firm Maxent, Laclede & Company from New Orleans proved themselves to be loyal to the new Spanish governor after establishing St. Louis as a fur trading outpost in 1764. The French had first given the firm a monopoly over trade on the Upper Mississippi in the year before the west bank officially became Spanish. Laclede scouted the area that fall, chose his site, and began constructing his settlement in February. The site represented the first suitable place to land boats below the Missouri and Illinois Rivers on the Mississippi. Well-drained high ground contained plenty of wooded areas, as well as rocks suitable for building. A Spanish official didn't arrive to take charge until 1770, but when he did, he seemed satisfied with what he found.[52]

The future didn't seem quite so hopeful to English settlers in West Florida. They took note of political turmoil to the north because it disrupted their commerce. A letter writer from Pensacola complained that General Gage had pulled troops from Natchez and other forts on the Mississippi in 1767, supposedly to save money. But he speculated that the troops were actually needed in Philadelphia and elsewhere to quell reaction to the Townshend Duties. The letter writer referenced Dickinson's "Letters from an American Farmer" and seemed to agree that the British treated the colonists like slaves rather than freemen.[53] But the settlers in Florida needn't have worried, for commerce would only continue to grow after the American Revolution—Philadelphia merchants would see to that.

Oliver Pollock succeeded in forging connections between Philadelphia and the Riverine West where George Morgan had failed. The Spanish wanted to integrate Louisiana into their commercial world and loosened trade restrictions in the years before the American Revolution, so the governor who replaced O'Reilly did not enforce the rules against trade with the English nearly so strictly. He allowed Spanish planters to buy goods from English boats on the river. In 1772 Pollock became the official supplier of flour for the garrison at New Orleans. Pollock and others expanded their businesses so much that in May of 1774 at least one report noted the presence of seventy boats north of New Orleans. By 1776, Pollock sold slaves, dry goods, coffee, tea, wine, and glassware as far north as the Wabash River, a tributary of the Ohio. Though the Spanish Crown may have disapproved, the English presence had grown greatly on the Mississippi in the years before the Revolutionary War, with the Spanish governors looking the other way when Pollock and others could supply provisions for their colony.[54]

Territories and boundaries had shifted between empires after the Seven Years' War, and Philadelphia merchants, Native Americans, and Spanish and French colonists had to make new alliances in the Riverine West. Baynton, Wharton & Morgan sold goods and slaves in the Illinois Country but failed spectacularly in the end. At the same time, they and other Philadelphia merchants were making inroads into trade along the Gulf Coast. With the Spanish now in charge of New Orleans, Pollock, a man with the skills to bridge the gap between two empires, gave Philadelphia merchants entry into trade on the Lower Mississippi. But their commercial connections only represent half of the story of Philadelphia merchants on western waters. Land speculation would go hand in hand with their business ventures.

Land Grants

The other half of Baynton, Wharton & Morgan's plans for the West would divide the firm into enemy camps. George Morgan had long complained that Samuel Wharton had been meant to act as the company's representative in Illinois but had always found an excuse not to come. Reports of Samuel Wharton's politicking indicate that he had happily shed his Quaker sensibilities for the finer things in London when he went abroad to make their case for a land grant in person, and he cut his partners out of the deal in the end. As the company went under in 1772, Morgan wrote Wharton that "it appears to be your intention to aim at justifying your attempt to exclude me from an equal share." When Baynton died at the age of forty-seven the next year, Morgan accused Wharton of worrying his father-in-law to death. However, it would not only be Baynton, Wharton & Morgan's plans that came to naught—the American Revolution would upend everyone's attempts to become the recipients of land grants from the king.[1]

Philadelphia merchants wanted to do much more than corner the market on western commerce, and they plunged into land speculation schemes with all the resources they could assemble. Great Britain had doubled its territory in North America at the end of the Seven Years' War, and Philadelphia merchants planned to help the empire consolidate its hold over the eastern half of the continent. Samuel Wharton took the tried-and-true path of trying to gain the favor of the king, driving a wedge between himself and his partners in the process.

Rivals from Pennsylvania and other colonies tried to thwart him at every turn. At the same time, Oliver Pollock speculated in land in Florida and Louisiana from both the Spanish and English Crowns. The colonization of North America offered what seemed like a limitless supply of land to those from England, and Philadelphia merchants were among the first in line to acquire it.

During the first century plus of the British colonization of North America, settlers could obtain title to land in a number of ways. They could obtain it from someone who had been granted territory by the Crown; they could purchase it directly from Native Americans, hoping that the colonial officials would ratify their claims; or they could purchase it from someone else who had had their purchase from Native Americans ratified by colonial authority. Many of the purchases were of dubious provenance. Colonists might buy territory from someone who they knew did not actually control it and then use the colonial courts to impose the deed on another group that had not sanctioned the purchase. Colonists might do all the paperwork for a purchase but never actually pay for it. Other kinds of trickery included the infamous Walking Purchase, in which, rather than adhering to the spirit of the agreement (the amount of territory a man might travel across on an average day), the colonists cleared straight paths and sent out runners to claim much more territory than the Lenape intended. Still, there existed the principle that, outside of direct grants from the Crown, colonists could purchase Native American lands—in other words, the British acknowledged that Native Americans might legally control territory.[2]

By the 1740s, though, some colonial elites began to push for vast swathes of territory in the colonial backcountry. British interest in western Pennsylvania began in earnest when men from Virginia, Maryland, New York, and Pennsylvania negotiated the Treaty of Lancaster with the Six Nations (the Iroquois) in 1744. Pennsylvanians entered the fur trade with a vengeance and outdid New Yorkers for the first time a few years later. Appointed in 1748 justice of the peace of the area that would be delineated Cumberland County the next year, George Croghan had the job of ousting squatters. Fifteen years later, he claimed that the grateful Onondagas had granted him a 200,000-acre tract of land for his troubles.[3] One of the earliest scholars to focus on colonial land schemes wrote that most prerevolutionary land projects followed the same four steps: "form an association, petition for a grant, secure an extinguishment of the Indian title, and proceed with sales to settlers."[4] In 1748, a group of Virginians including Robert Dinwiddie, Robert Carter, and George Washington's half brother Lawrence formed the Ohio Company with a group of London merchants. The Crown granted them land, hoping to counter moves by the French, but the French in turn extended their fortifications south and east beginning in 1752. Two years later, Virginia officials sent Lieutenant George Washington with an armed force to check out the situation, expel the French, and build a fort of their own. That encounter led to the Seven Years' War.[5]

In the meantime, unhappy Philadelphians who claimed that western Pennsylvania belonged to their colony began making plans of their own. Benjamin Franklin proposed two colonies between the Ohio River and Lake Erie at the time of the Albany Congress in 1754, and others became interested as well, including a mapmaker named Lewis Evans and a merchant named Samuel Hazard who had even greater ambitions, seeking a proprietary colony of his own. George Croghan had control over most of the trade with Native Americans at that time, and by 1750 the French went so far as to put a bounty on his head, with the British making serious inroads into the fur trade. Over the next few years, he participated in many a negotiation, sometimes acting against the Crown's interest. When the French destroyed the Native American town that had been Croghan's base of operations, he returned to Philadelphia, with war breaking out not long after.[6]

In 1756, Sir William Johnson, British superintendent of Indian Affairs for the Northern District, appointed George Croghan deputy Indian agent for the Ohio Country because of his contacts in the West. Over the next seven years Croghan used his position to start trading in western Pennsylvania once again, and he made various deals with Ohio tribes for land titles—all activities supposedly precluded by his official position. Just as Pontiac's Rebellion began when the war officially ended, Croghan left Pittsburgh, headed for London, and resigned his position when ordered back. Receiving Crown approval for the 200,000 acres of land he claimed in the Mohawk Valley had always been at the forefront of his mind. Upon his return from England, Croghan sought out men interested in land speculation to further his own plans. Various scholars have characterized Croghan as a supremely self-interested character with an insatiable appetite for land schemes, and men of his time noted the same, but historian William Campbell concludes that the Pennsylvania proprietors "found his aggressive spirit useful."[7]

It was through George Croghan that Baynton, Wharton & Morgan would be pulled into plans to seek compensation from the Crown by a group called "the Suffering Traders." In 1754, Croghan and other fur traders who had their goods destroyed during the opening salvos of the Seven Years' War petitioned the Crown for cash compensation. At war's end, the number seeking relief expanded to include the "Sufferers of 1763." A dozen of them, including Croghan, David Franks, and Samuel Wharton, met in a tavern in Philadelphia in early December of that year to talk about how to move forward with their claims. They decided to send Croghan to London as their agent to ask the Board of Trade for 200,000 acres of land instead. Croghan drew Baynton, Wharton & Morgan into the plans by promising them control over trade in the West.[8] Croghan and Wharton developed a deep friendship, and that spelled trouble for the other partners. Samuel Wharton was the main force behind the partners' interest in land speculation, and he had his agent William Trent buy up claims from other sufferers in order to gain a controlling interest in the effort to obtain a land grant from the king. Wharton and Trent's plans excluded some of the early claimants, and others refused to join the new plans, instead petitioning London for a fairer distribution of the land than Wharton had in mind. Thus, competing factions were trying to make their voices heard. As a sideline, in the spring of 1766 Croghan, Baynton, Wharton, Morgan, and others established the Illinois Company to buy French territory on the Mississippi River in Illinois; that plan never amounted to much, though shares in the company were listed as assets of the firm when Baynton, Wharton & Morgan later went bankrupt.[9]

Baynton, Wharton & Morgan also corresponded with the governor of New Jersey, Benjamin Franklin's son William, who wrote about colonizing Illinois. France would be on one side of the Mississippi, so, to protect British interests, the empire needed to establish a presence on the opposite bank. The forks of the Mississippi would be the key to the interior, William Franklin wrote, the "most important place in all the inland parts of N.A.," and declared that Native Americans would be their enemies. The Crown should purchase from the Indians all the land east of the Mississippi and between the Illinois and Ohio Rivers, as well as 50 miles back from the Mississippi, including the territory that had belonged to France. Wharton and Croghan met in September of 1767 and agreed that they needed to push for a boundary line so that they could open up lands to settlement. Like Franklin, the two argued that a war with Native Americans loomed on the horizon and that the Crown should acquire enough land to satisfy settlers while drawing a line that protected Indian hunting grounds to satisfy Native American tribes.[10]

Samuel Wharton joined George Croghan in shifting their focus from Illinois lands back to territory south and west of Fort Pitt. There were plans in the works to replace the Proclamation Line of 1763 with a new boundary at the Ohio River instead. Samuel Wharton represented the Suffering Traders at the negotiations that yielded the Treaty of Fort Stanwix in 1768. Among other land cessions, the treaty granted Wharton and his group 1.8 million acres in present-day West Virginia and Kentucky. But these lands had also been claimed by men from Virginia; in addition, some of the original Suffering Traders were angry that they were missing out. Croghan advised Trent and Wharton to go to London to confirm their grant.[11] The colonists had no seats in Parliament, of course, but they had always made their presence felt through agents—men from the colonies who went to London to try to influence trade policy. Going to court meant socializing with English nobility. Philadelphian Benjamin Franklin had been famous for charming the men in charge, but others would not be so lucky. With so much land now up for grabs, a new wave of colonists invaded London looking for favors.

Samuel Wharton sailed to London in January of 1769 to press for "imperial recognition" of the claims, asking for payment in land. What Wharton found, though, was disagreement among officials about how to handle the new treaty. Lord Hillsborough had taken over as secretary of state and said that private grants had no place in treaties. According to William Trent, Wharton began making social connections in London, parading around with a sword and wearing clothing that was decidedly un-Quaker. Making use of his connections to Franklin and Walpole, Wharton pulled British speculators, members of Parliament, various officials, and wealthy merchants and professionals into his scheme, and the resulting land requests ballooned to 20 million acres in present-day West Virginia and Kentucky by December. He kept living large, though, and by the end of the next year he feared being arrested for not paying his tailor, among others.[12]

When the Earl of Hillsborough became the secretary of state for the colonies, the situation changed, forcing Wharton to switch tactics, but then Hillsborough changed tactics in turn. Hillsborough urged Wharton and his cronies to seek a larger amount still, proposing a true colony. Scholars conclude that what Hillsborough really wanted was for the whole thing to collapse under its own weight in order to embarrass Benjamin Franklin. But the Treasury Department ended up approving it and sent it on to the Board of Trade in 1770. Hillsborough did all he could to delay it, though, and the Board of Trade did reject it in 1772, only to have that decision overturned by the Privy Council. Hillsborough resigned, and the fate of the West passed to other hands.[13]

Through all his machinations, Wharton kept his partners in the dark. In

April of 1770, Baynton wrote to Morgan that Thomas Wharton assured him that brother Samuel would get the job done. But Baynton wrote that his spirits were low, and he felt exhausted. With Morgan away, Baynton wrote, he had nobody to talk to. A week later Baynton wrote Morgan to say that Thomas and Samuel were citing different totals for the land grant—5 million versus 6 million acres. A couple weeks later Baynton suffered a bad attack of gout and had to stay home, "flat on my back, unable to move." By May, the tenor of the letters went further downhill—he wrote long letters to friends detailing lies Wharton had told him. He and his son-in-law, George Morgan, had acted with honor, Baynton wrote, but the Whartons had not.[14]

Samuel Wharton cut his partners out of his new scheme. When John Baynton wrote asking for news of their affairs, Wharton replied that since Baynton and Morgan had not put up any money toward the purchase, they were out. Baynton replied that he and Morgan had sunk all their money into the Indiana Company and efforts to save their business in Illinois. Morgan had long been unhappy with the way in which he had become the company's sole representative in the West and blamed their troubles on Samuel Wharton and George Croghan.[15]

George Morgan wrote to his partner in London in January of 1772. "Our unfortunate Illinois adventure originated solely with you," he argued. Wharton had never come to relieve him in Illinois, and he had tried to secure deals for Baynton and Wharton rather than the new firm that included Morgan, while at the same time taking money from their partner's children. Despite these harsh words, Morgan claimed that he had kept these opinions to himself and still hoped that some good would come of it all if the three partners remained united as they closed out their business in Illinois. An angrier letter followed in April, with Morgan declaring that corresponding with Wharton never accomplished anything so he would only write of business thereafter.[16]

George Morgan wrote to Samuel's brother Thomas that May, saying that people were asking him and Baynton about the Ohio lands Samuel was chasing. Since Wharton had told them nothing other than the fact that the lands lay along a river, Morgan suggested that one of them go out west to "make a proper survey." He volunteered, stating that it was a good time of year to visit, and a friend who could accompany him was heading that way. The trustees approved, Morgan wrote, and he hoped that Wharton's lawyer would as well.[17]

The way Morgan described Wharton is telling. In his affidavit, he stated that Wharton didn't send him a single polite letter after the Treaty of Fort Stanwix had left him in an envious position. He found Wharton vain and insolent. If

Wharton wrote from London at all, Morgan claimed, his brother Thomas never passed those letters on to his partners. Morgan doesn't spare himself in the affidavit, nor Wharton, nor Croghan—the only person Morgan truly had a good word for was his father-in-law, John Baynton. When Baynton died in 1773, Morgan blamed his death on Wharton's treatment of him.[18]

In 1772, the Privy Council sided with Wharton against Lord Hillsborough, and all seemed in order for the establishment of a colony Samuel Wharton intended to name Vandalia. Native Americans were to be notified of the new colony, Croghan met with various tribes that summer, and Wharton was to be appointed governor. He began plans for a mansion in Pittsburgh. Samuel Wharton meant for Vandalia to be a royal colony. Wharton and others had hit upon the idea of trying to convince the Crown that they could direct settlement across the Appalachians in an orderly way and extend British authority better than the authorities of the original colonies, who seemed unable to control their people. Wharton and his allies promised to facilitate trade and create alliances with Native Americans, and they wanted the right to distribute land for ten years as compensation for administering the venture. At the end of that time, the remaining property would be divided into seventy-two shares to be drawn by lot. But Vandalia ended up in legal limbo, despite Crown approval.[19]

In the meantime, rivals for the territory were making headway in western Pennsylvania. In November of 1773, Thomas Wharton wrote to Samuel about news of Fort Pitt and the vicinity. He informed his brother that George Morgan had recently returned and brought news of Croghan making deals with Native Americans thanks to groundwork laid by Samuel back in London. But James Dobson visited Philadelphia for funds and reported that "the country is thickly settled for 150 miles below fort Pitt" and that residents had established two grist mills. Thomas warned his brother that "some companies" have large tracts there, "the Principals" from Philadelphia. Thomas instructed Samuel to make sure they got clear titles to their land in London and wrote about the wisdom of establishing "a Loan Office"—be sure to "settle this point with our great partners" before coming home, get permission "for the Governor to pass such a law."[20] A rival from Virginia decided to make a move as well. Governor Dunmore sent troops to stir up the trouble that resulted in a conflict fittingly called Lord Dunmore's War. Thomas Wharton believed that his brother's plans for the region were in real jeopardy.[21]

In 1773, it seemed that Vandalia might actually become a reality. Samuel Wharton fell ill, however, and could not push for his plan vigorously thereafter. The Boston Tea Party in December created more delays, and the plan never recovered after that. Wharton held out hopes for the colony as long as he could and began to seek a smaller amount based on lands George Croghan had purchased a couple years earlier. He made plans for Croghan to purchase land from the tribes privately in the summer of 1774, going so far as to suggest to Croghan that they bribe members of Congress for approval by offering eight of them a partnership in their land schemes. Twice Wharton and Croghan used the tactic of playing on fears of war with Native Americans if their plans were not approved.[22]

Examining Thomas Wharton's letters and Clarence Alvord's account of Samuel Wharton's maneuverings makes it clear that these land plans were all about currying favor with the right people in England. Thomas mentions paperwork again and again, stressing proper planning. Samuel kept coming up with reasons why it was legal to purchase from Indians. They were actively asking, what's our place within the empire? They saw their path to success beginning with a land grant from the king. This story is different from old characterizations of the British Empire as a dock-to-dock administration or a narrative about isolated colonists.[23]

Croghan and Wharton's ambitions were not unique. Other Philadelphia merchants also speculated in western lands after the Seven Years' War. Like David Franks, Barnard and Michael Gratz were Jewish and used those ties to build their networks. The brothers came and served for a time as apprentices before striking out on their own through various business ventures, but they came around to speculating in land in the end. Land speculation became irresistible to many merchants during this time, with Great Britain doubling their claims to territory in North America following the Peace of Paris.

The Gratz brothers began their commercial careers working for their cousin Solomon in London. Barnard arrived in Philadelphia in 1754, and his younger brother joined him five years later. When Barnard came of age, his father's estate would set him up in business, and their uncle furnished connections in the Atlantic World. Michael Gratz's first adventures included trips to Halifax, Georgia, and the West Indies, and the brothers traded along the Gulf Coast to New Orleans in 1765. But marriage and new kinship networks in Lancaster, Pennsylvania, eventually turned their attention to the Ohio Valley. The children of both men married into Virginia and Maryland families with long histories of land speculation in the West.[24]

During the summer of 1770, Michael wrote to Barnard, who was at his

Comment on p. 74: Find this error that the author noted: “some caps on p. 74.”—Please advise.

uncle’s place in London, about business failures in Philadelphia and disappointments in Pittsburgh. He also reported that Philadelphians were very serious about nonimportation. It would be dangerous to cross them, Michael wrote, but perhaps they could continue to do business with Fort Pitt and the backcountry by way of Baltimore. The brothers seemed determined to press on with trade no matter what, and a little thing like a nonimportation movement wasn’t going to stop them. At least one scholar judges them to have been much more successful in Illinois than George Morgan, even if their share of the business there was small. They benefited from the advice of Morgan’s ex-secretary William Murray.[25]

David Franks, George Morgan’s nemesis in Illinois, would also prove to be one of Wharton’s chief rivals in land speculation schemes. In addition to the Gratz brothers in Illinois, William Murray represented Levy & Franks in Indiana. Franks invested in the Illinois Company and pulled in many family members, along with James Rumsey and the Gratz brothers. The company store at Kaskaskia bore his name: David Franks & Company. Franks wrote to James Rumsey asking for more news of ore that had been found in the area, hoping that they might find silver. In 1773, the venture became the Illinois & Ouabauche (Wabash) Company, pulling in more and more investors over the next two decades. It all came to nothing in the end, just like Wharton’s plans, but the paper trail they left behind stands as a testament to their ambitions.[26]

As the Seven Years’ War came to a close, the British found themselves faced with a dilemma: their territory in North America had doubled, and they had land-hungry colonists who wanted to move west. But the possibility of war with Native Americans remained a real threat. The Proclamation of 1763 gave the Crown more direct oversight of land purchases from Native Americans in the newly acquired territories. Private citizens could no longer directly purchase it and have officials ratify it afterward.[27]

These rivals nipping at Samuel Wharton’s heels took a different route in their quest for western lands. During the lull between the repeal of the Townshend Duties and the passage of the Tea Act, land speculators in America hit upon a new legal argument to justify land purchases directly from Native American tribes. In 1757, British officials had issued an opinion that pertained to the East India Company acquiring lands in India from independent princes. The company could arrange to buy land without any permission from the king if it came from regions within their charter, but conquered lands could only be granted directly by the king. The East India Company essentially acted in place of the king based on their charter in the first case. A copy of the Yorke-Camden Opinion circulating in America omitted references to the East India Company and stated that the opinion granted rights to anyone who wanted to purchase land directly from Native American tribes.[28]

There is some dispute among scholars about who first doctored the opinion and started it on its rounds in North America, but there's no doubt that William Murray, who went west representing the Gratz brothers, tried to use it to his advantage in 1773. He met up with George Croghan in Pittsburgh and claimed that Croghan gave him the go-ahead in May. In June at Fort Gage in Kaskaskia, Murray met the officer in charge of Illinois, Captain Hugh Lord, and asked about purchasing land, but Lord denied the legality of Murray's plans. Murray went ahead anyway and purchased lands from Illinois tribes in July. After he informed Lord of his actions, Lord wrote Gage, but Gage temporarily yielded to Sir Frederick Haldimand. A couple of French settlers got wind of what Murray did and tried to copy him. Murray attempted to get Lord Dunmore to back his purchase by promising that the new territories would be part of the colony of Virginia, and Dunmore passed the word to George Washington. Meanwhile, the Gratz brothers discussed their plans with James Hogg back home in Philadelphia, and he, in turn, informed Richard Henderson. Gage sent word from England in February of 1774 that all the purchases were illegal as far as the Crown was concerned, but the colonists ignored this. Patrick Henry told Thomas Wharton about the Yorke-Camden Opinion, who passed the news of Murray's actions on to his brother Samuel in September of 1774. All of this maneuvering just goes to show how widespread land speculation schemes were. It's also clear that William Murray, like Samuel Wharton before him, presented his plans to acquire territory as a way to keep western settlement orderly.[29]

That September, Morgan wrote to James and Joseph Thomlinson in the name of Baynton, Wharton & Morgan to warn them of people using fraud to claim western lands on the Ohio near Grave Creek. Apparently, some were felling trees or marking them with their names and claiming that they had made improvements when they'd done no such thing. Such would then try to "sell their rights," but Morgan wrote that claims would only be upheld if men actually settled there with their families. The settling of disputes would require witnesses to the facts, and Morgan warned that anyone who tried to intimidate actual settlers would not have their claims supported. The following month, Morgan wrote to Richard Winston, a lawyer who was trying to track down remittances from Illinois for Baynton, Wharton & Morgan. Morgan judged his affairs in Illinois to have been "unfortunate" and vowed to never go back except by "necessity." He still seemed to be hoping that Wharton would come through for his partners. Morgan stated that he "once thought Mr Rumsey a Man of Honor" but had decided that Rumsey had gone from bad to worse. Morgan's friend Thomas Hutchins had once characterized Rumsey's behavior as treacherous and rascally. Morgan won a judgment against Rumsey and Franks in the end.[30]

But Pennsylvania rivals were not the only obstacle to successfully claiming land in the West. Lord Dunmore's War illustrates the importance of rivalries between colonies. As one of his final acts before resigning, Lord Hillsborough abandoned Fort Pitt and pulled out the British troops. George Croghan, writing to Thomas Wharton, indicated that this was not necessarily a bad thing—it might lessen tension with Native Americans. The people who lived in Pittsburgh were less happy, though, and petitioned the Pennsylvania Assembly for protection. At first the assembly did not respond, but the actions of Virginia's royal governor would change their minds, and the assembly ended up approving the raising of troops in 1774.

Thomas Wharton wrote to Thomas Walpole about the way things heated up between Virginia and Pennsylvania over the lands at the forks of the Ohio in the winter and spring of 1774. Lord Dunmore had instructed a man named John Connolly to raise a militia at Fort Pitt for the express purpose of claiming the region. Connolly and others were advertising lots for sale in lands farther down the Ohio. Their grant needed to be settled as soon as possible. Pennsylvania officials had arrested and jailed Connolly, though they released him soon after. Wharton opined that the "anarchy & confusion that prevails on our frontiers" would only grow worse as more people headed west.[31]

Connolly returned to Fort Pitt and declared that it belonged to Virginia. In April of 1774, Governor Dunmore made the takeover official and renamed the fort after himself. Apparently those in the area submitted to Dunmore's actions, as Virginia established a court there soon thereafter. The following May settlers in the area met to officially approve of actions Virginia took in pursuit of independence. Dunmore tried to organize an Indian attack against them but failed, and a Pittsburgh militia under the command of John Neville took over when Dunmore's garrison retreated and restored the name Fort Pitt. Over the next two years, Virginia and Pennsylvania agreed that the Revolution should be their prime concern, and Virginia ceded the area back to Pennsylvania.[32]

Samuel Wharton's brother Thomas wrote pretty extensively about Lord Dunmore's War, linking it to both land surveys and trade. In May of 1774, he wrote to Samuel about George Morgan's actions with respect to land in Illinois.

Some lands had gone down so far in value that he wished they had sold earlier. Thomas reported that Baynton, Wharton & Morgan had settled accounts with David Franks and William Murray and that Morgan had sold some of the Illinois land to two other men. The mess in Illinois was certainly a Philadelphia affair.[33]

At that point, British policymakers threw another variable into the mix. Quebec became a British colony at the end of the Seven Years' War, but most of its inhabitants were still French more than a decade later, and because they were Roman Catholics, they had no representation in the government. Through the Quebec Act of 1774, Great Britain set up a government that allowed parts of the French system to continue, including land tenure and civil law, and allowed Catholics to become government officials if they took an oath of allegiance. What got some Americans in an uproar was Parliament's decision to extend Quebec's boundaries to the Ohio and Mississippi Rivers to deal with French settlers there and pursue Indian policy. British colonists with interests there were outraged, feeling that Parliament had in effect given control of the region back to the French. What is interesting here is that passage of the Quebec Act was partly in reaction to William Murray's attempt to purchase land directly from Native Americans.[34]

But land speculators like merchant Thomas Wharton did not immediately protest. They thought that putting the Ohio Valley under the jurisdiction of Quebec might halt Lord Dunmore's plans. Wharton didn't seem to think that Quebec would be as interested in spiking their plans for Vandalia as Virginia seemed to be. When Morgan, Croghan, and others tried to reorganize plans into the Indiana Company, it seemed pretty clear that land speculation had topped the fur trade as their primary goal. In the end, though, when it became clear that protecting the fur trade was in fact the intent of the Quebec Act, the land speculators decided to lobby the Continental Congress for land instead.[35]

Clarence Alvord argued that discouraging settlers from going west was exactly what Parliament had in mind when they allowed French law to extend to the Ohio Valley. During the debate over the Quebec Act, those who supported it in Parliament referred to the Proclamation Act of 1763 as a failure—it had neither stabilized the fur trade nor kept settlers out. According to Alvord, it was a continuation of the old argument about establishing a new colony versus extracting resources, and Alvord concluded that Parliament looked backward to extraction once again. But Americans wanted to settle west of the Appalachians, and there was no way Great Britain could stem the tide.[36]

As Americans set their sights on the interior of the continent, many recognized that knowledge of the course of western waters would be central to their plans. On his very first trip down the Ohio River, George Morgan made the acquaintance of Ensign Thomas Hutchins, who would eventually be named the first (and only) geographer of the United States in 1781 and go on to leave his mark on land surveys in the Northwest thereafter. In the early 1770s, Hutchins began working on a map. George Morgan wrote to a friend seeking information about the Upper Mississippi: "Engineer Hutchins a particular friend of mine is about publishing a map of the interior rivers and lakes in America." Morgan sent a proposal from Hutchins to his partner in London, hoping to find a publisher. Hutchins had been surveying all the Ohio's tributaries, with an eye toward settlement. Morgan wholeheartedly approved, writing to Hutchins that "great dependence is placed pointing out the best water communication between the west branch of the Susquehanna & the Allegheny River & the Potomack & the Yahagany or Cheat River." Morgan also told Hutchins that he had been promised a map from a Father Harding that was "a very exact draft of the River Mississippi from Fort Chartres to its sources," in addition to another of the Monongahela and Little Kanawha, and later asked him about adding other rivers, including the "little & big Giandot & the Great & Littel Totter Rivers."[37]

After failing to secure a land grant, Samuel Wharton sought shelter in France when the war broke out and returned to America in 1780. After taking an oath of allegiance to his home state, he represented Delaware in the Continental Congress from 1782 to 1783. The next year he served as a justice of the peace, and in the early 1790s he served as a judge for the Court of Common Pleas. He died in 1800, leaving George Morgan as the last survivor of the firm of Baynton, Wharton & Morgan. Barnard Gratz and William Murray united the Illinois and Wabash Companies in 1779, with "plans of settlement and government" and "locations for the first cities," which they proposed to the Virginia legislature based on purchases made before the war. They wrote of proprietors and a small number of chief settlers drawing lots and choosing lands before opening the territory for sale. But the Virginians had no intention of allowing any prerevolutionary claims to stand. The company turned to the Continental Congress next and, like others before them, tried to add politicians to the list of shareholders in a bid for their support. But nothing ever came of their plans.[38]

Philadelphia merchants also speculated in lands at the other end of the Mississippi River. Letters from someone identified only as "R," printed in three installments in the *New York Gazette* in 1773, showed interest in getting people to invest in Louisiana. Over dozens of pages, the author gave detailed descriptions of the Mississippi, many of its tributaries, the landscape, settlements, people, flora, and fauna drawn from a half century's worth of maps and travel accounts written by those men who had visited the Riverine West. Oliver Pollock needed no urging and bought land on his own while helping his friends acquire land grants in West Florida as well. Like Wharton, Pollock sought the favor of a king, but one from a rival empire.[39]

Beginning in 1769, Pollock successfully applied for four land grants from Great Britain, one near Manchac and three on the Mississippi River near Baton Rouge and Pointe Coupée. He helped his Philadelphia colleagues Thomas Willing and Robert Morris acquire land grants nearer Pensacola, where they cultivated rice. Like those of the French and Spanish before, Willing's and Morris's plantations relied on slave labor. A man named Alexander Henderson acted as overseer to nearly three dozen slaves between the two plantations, whose tasks included setting up levees and cultivating rice. Pollock oversaw the finances and marketed their rice in New Orleans. After clashing with Henderson, Pollock turned more of his attention to acquiring land with Thomas Willing's brother James. After war broke out, Pollock bought land more suitable for growing indigo on the Mississippi, and he ran a trading post for passing ships as well. With the English out of the way, the Spanish made no move to confiscate settlers' lands, and Governor Miró allowed Pollock and others to reconfirm their land titles between 1785 and 1787. Pollock had to declare bankruptcy after the war, but once he became solvent again, he was back in Louisiana buying lots in New Orleans.[40]

Englishmen and Americans were also looking to settle on the east bank farther upstream and went as far as probing areas across the river. The French had first established a trading post at the confluence of the Arkansas and White Rivers as early as 1686. Soldiers and traders occupied the spot sporadically thereafter, before the Spanish took possession by treaty at the end of the Seven Years' War, though they didn't physically occupy it until the early 1770s. General O'Reilly had sent instructions for setting up a command in 1769. The Spanish intended to use the spot in much the same way the French had—as a waypoint for boats traveling between Illinois and New Orleans, and as a trading post with local Native American and white hunters who brought in meat, skins, and furs from the surrounding rivers. O'Reilly specified that Indians were to leave their weapons at the door and would not be permitted to drink alcohol. Yearly gifts for the Native Americans would be provided, cementing alliances, and the post's commander was encouraged to have the Indians be on the lookout for and report wandering traders who didn't belong there. Not wanting to provoke any international incidents, O'Reilly wanted the commandant to "prevent any harm coming to the English who navigate the Mississippi River" and to make sure that any Native Americans "crossing this river" do not "cause injury to the English inhabitants." The job of commandant included keeping the peace between the English and local Native American tribes.[41]

The man who signed his letters with a simple "R" carefully noted the hunting territory of various Native American tribes. So many rivers in the West served as the Mississippi's tributaries, he wrote, that its drainage was vast. His focus on water routes was very reminiscent of George Morgan's correspondence with Thomas Hutchins. "R" described the various kinds of boats used by the French, as well as the waypoints they used on their journeys, and also made note of Spanish trade. Making light of French efforts on the Lower Mississippi, the Englishman wrote that industrious American settlers could make the place a paradise. The last letter described various Indian tribes in the area and gave a history of French settlement during the first half of the eighteenth century.[42]

When the British set up the colony of West Florida, they chose Pensacola as the capital instead of Mobile because it had a better harbor and healthier climate. French residents thought of moving to New Orleans until they learned that it would remain under Spanish control. Natchez seemed to offer the best prospects for crops and trade, but it was isolated, and the British grudgingly built a fort but ignored pleas for transportation improvements. Land business had to go through Pensacola, and only a few grants went to merchants, with one large grant given to an English lord, but actual settlers were few. The British did have good relations with the Choctaws at that time.[43]

The situation began to change in 1770. Settlers came from Virginia in groups, bringing slaves with them. A man named John McIntire came from Pennsylvania prepared to establish a sawmill and gristmill, and he let the powers that be know that others were prepared to come from the backcountry of his colony too, as well as points south. In 1771, the British decided to allow land business to be conducted at Natchez and agreed to help tide over newcomers with corn and salt. Settlers began arriving from New Jersey and New England as well. The British rescinded some of the easy land policies in 1774, but the population continued to expand and spread out in a scattered pattern utilizing slaves or paid white labor. The British settlement south of Baton Rouge was called New Manchac, and it functioned as more of a commercial hub than an agricultural one. A man named John Fitzpatrick imported goods from New Orleans, Pensacola, and Mobile, often having to pay his suppliers with tobacco, indigo, and other crops. Manchac linked British settlements from Baton Rouge to Illinois with Britain's Gulf Coast ports. A man named Richard Carpenter continued doing business on the "River Mississippi" in May of 1775. Robert Bagnall delivered to him rum, flour, molasses, and salt to be sold for John Collins of Newport. He also had commercial paper from Daniel Clark and Alexander McIntosh. Collins bought and sold slaves, and more flour changed hands.[44]

The last of the land speculators who sought to use the imperial system to gain favors from the king lost their bids for colonies of their own, and a new kind of land speculation would begin during the War for Independence. George Morgan and other Philadelphia merchants had successfully expanded Philadelphia's hinterland down the Ohio River and to the Illinois Country, even if Morgan's firm itself failed in the end, and Pollock and others had set their sights on the Gulf Coast. George Morgan and Oliver Pollock were both colonists who understood the imperial politics of expanding a king's interests, be that king English or Spanish. After the American Revolution, Philadelphia merchants would instead be citizens of a new republic, and a new generation would successfully integrate the western waters from Pittsburgh downstream to New Orleans into one commercial network, closing the loop.

PART TWO

NATIONAL PORT

During the American Revolution, a new generation of Philadelphia merchants set their sights on western markets and lands in a different way. Men like John Reed and Standish Forde used military contacts to get their start. George Morgan served the new nation at Fort Pitt, while Oliver Pollock did all he could to help the cause of independence in New Orleans—both men chose the new nation over old loyalties to Great Britain. There was a feeding frenzy when states like Pennsylvania and Virginia raised money to pay their war debts by selling land warrants, with Philadelphia merchants taking advantage of living in the new nation's capital, where many land schemes originated. The quest for furs would always be a part of the plans for some men heading to the interior of the continent, but the American Revolution unleashed a wave of a new kind of land speculation among citizens of a nation who were no longer the subjects of a king.

Philadelphia merchants found that speculating in western lands did not bring as many rewards as they had hoped, especially when legal questions about navigating western rivers raised doubts about the future of the region. Eastern policymakers disappointed westerners when it came to gaining access to the navigation of the Ohio and Mississippi Rivers. The Spanish were nervous enough to give George Morgan a shot at building a colony between present-day St. Louis and Memphis as a gateway to their territory on the Lower Mississippi, but his plans for New Madrid hearkened back to the past. John Reed and Standish Forde represented the future, building mills and commercial connections on rivers from Pittsburgh to New Orleans. Newly independent Americans had to find a way to utilize a river system not under the control of the new nation.

Rather than the double-pronged approach taken by Philadelphia merchants before the American Revolution, afterward Reed & Forde connected Philadelphia to Pittsburgh by wagon, Pittsburgh to New Orleans by river, and New Orleans back to Philadelphia by ocean-going vessels, completing the circuit and bounding the lands to the west of the Appalachians within their commercial network. Daniel W. Coxe of Philadelphia and Daniel Clark Jr. of New Orleans became partners and created the most direct link between the ports. After the signing of Pinckney's Treaty, more eastern merchants flooded into New Orleans than ever before. The Louisiana Purchase only reaffirmed the takeover of the mouth of the Mississippi that had been taking place for years. At last, one nation controlled both banks of the Ohio and Mississippi Rivers at the same time, fulfilling the Philadelphia merchants' long-standing goal of integrating the western waters into the Atlantic World, providing the foundation of a new empire.

A Revolutionary War

One evening in September of 1777, a young man named Richard Checkley wrote to his friend John Reed about strolling through the streets of Wilmington, Delaware, in the company of Jacob Garrigues and Peter Anspach. Along with a friend who had enlisted in the army named Standish Forde, the five of them had made one of their first forays into business with a store in the Delaware port. After the war, Anspach ended up in New York, Checkley in Savanah, and Reed and Forde would become partners and build a business that extended from Philadelphia to New Orleans down the Ohio and Mississippi Rivers.[1] Just as George Morgan had, Reed and Forde set their sights on the Riverine West and experienced the highs and lows of doing business there.

Like the Seven Years' War, the American Revolution brought changes to Philadelphia. A new cohort of merchants got their start during the war, and it provided them with a chance to establish themselves in the city that would be the new nation's capital for a time. Meanwhile, George Morgan and Oliver Pollock across the Appalachian Mountains had their own choices to make when the world turned upside down. After the war, the new state of Pennsylvania raised money to finance their debts by selling land warrants for western territory, and Reed & Forde participated in the feeding frenzy unleashed by the wave of a new kind of land speculation. Once again, Philadelphia merchants intended to do business on the western waters.

John Reed and Standish Forde used military contacts to get their start. Reed worked to supply the Continental Army, making contacts with merchants such as Richard Lamb that lasted long after the war ended. Forde served in the army far longer than Reed, but he also lent his talents to finding supplies. Their first trading ventures in the peace that followed involved the coastal trade. Reed and Forde were among that cadre of traders who tried to make a name for themselves during the postwar boom but then had to find ways to stay afloat during the inevitable bust that followed. Historian Arthur Whitaker first drew attention to them as "merchant adventurers" in the 1930s, theorizing that they took risks because they were so deeply in debt. A half century later, Thomas Doerflinger characterized them as "social climbers." Because so much of Reed & Forde's debt was made up of unsold lands, and the rest of it, unsold goods, Doerflinger concluded that the pair simply decided to send the goods to Kentucky to be exchanged for tobacco and furs. The Kentucky cargo would then be sold for gold and silver in New Orleans, which would make its way back to Philadelphia. Whitaker came right out and stated that his article detailed Reed and Forde's role in trade on the Lower Mississippi only; it was not meant to be a complete study of their business. Doerflinger mentioned a store on the Monongahela but failed to account for their mill at the same place, as well as a store in Natchez. Who were John Reed and Standish Forde really? How do the firm's commercial networks broaden our understanding of the role Philadelphia merchants played on western waters?[2]

Insight into John Reed's first years as a commercial agent can be gleaned from the account of Joseph Erwin, who came to America with his family in 1768. Erwin began a four-year apprenticeship with one of Reed's mentors, a merchant named James Budden, in 1772 at the age of fourteen. He continued working for Budden, and sometimes for a merchant named Thomas Lawrence, a year after the end of his term. While an apprentice Erwin was allowed by Budden to send "small adventures" to the West Indies on the company's ships, and he wrote that the profits from those "nearly paid all my expenses—in the year 76, 77," when he was on his own. In addition to the salary he earned from Budden, Erwin supplemented his income by buying any "liquors" he could get his hands on and selling them at a profit to the army. From there, he worked as a clerk for another merchant, went to France as an agent, and eventually became a partner of a merchant on the continent. Budden & Lawrence also figured prominently in John Reed's early career, especially in 1777 and 1778, perhaps on terms similar to those of Erwin. Reed also accepted long lists of goods from army officers and scrounged supplies for them. Clearly family ties such as Morgan had used weren't the only path to a mercantile career during the last decades of the eighteenth century.[3]

John Reed kept busy during the war, sometimes in the army, other times not, and he spent some time in the West Indies. The spring and summer of 1778 seemed particularly busy, with General Clinton and the British army moving from Pennsylvania to New York and with General Washington and the American army following. In April, Reed set out to New Windsor to buy sugar but found himself stopped by the enemy's advance. The next month, a merchant from Bethlehem wanted him to sell their flour but hold the indigo until ships traveling with the French convoy arrived—he hoped they would pay more than local buyers and that Reed, as a private citizen, could buy goods from the ships. Lawrence was looking for knives and saddles in particular. Lawrence seems to have given Reed a letter for another merchant named Barret telling him that he had given Reed a large sum to spend without restrictions, but Reed might come to Barret for advice. In May, another contact warned Reed to be cautious—silver and gold prices were unstable, so he advised against buying fine articles, but coarse linen and saddlery would sell. Reed was in Boston that summer, for a merchant named Anthony Butler had advised him to stay there, as it would be the "most advantageous port for speculation." Less than a year later, though, Richard Checkley told Reed that life in Boston was hard and "hundreds of families do not get a morsel of bread for two weeks together."[4]

John Reed's first correspondence also reveals the world of single young men engaging in pursuits that had nothing to do with their commercial ventures. One scholar published five of them—letters that he labeled "gossipy." For some reason, he didn't include the letter in which Reed's friend Checkley declared, "I heard you got a girl pregnant."[5] He also informed Reed that their friend Anspach wanted Reed to tell a girl they both knew to come and visit him in camp. As for Checkley himself, he chatted up a young lady, only to find that she was married with two children. Anspach also had ties to a friend of Standish Forde's named Jacob Garrigues. When Anspach wrote to Reed in April of 1778 about hanging out in Boston, he called their group "the old hands."[6]

One of that handful of young men, Reed's soon-to-be partner Standish Forde, had closer contact with the army. A letter from Forde to Anspach in September of 1780 extolled the life of a soldier. At an army camp, he wrote that if he didn't have to attend to business he would stay with the campaign: "I know of no place a person can spend their time so agreeably as with the army, they are free from the eternal duns of military fine gatherers and all others of their stamp." He expected a spy to be hanged the next day. Forde wished that Anspach and others would write more, saying that he always found time to write to them.[7]

Standish Forde's will gives some clues to his life. He invested about $2,800 in 1781 to establish Reed & Forde. He seems to have had three children with a first wife, who had since died, and more children with his second wife, Sarah. Forde stated that he mostly lived off income from an estate he inherited from his father, drawing little money from the firm. Because Reed had pulled more money out of the firm by way of expenses, Forde hoped that his own family would get a larger share of the firm when he passed away. He expected $20,000 off the top, with the assets divided equally between them thereafter. He didn't seem to be implying that Reed had been wasteful, just that the firm had been Reed's main source of income. Clearly he trusted Reed because his partner served as one of the three trustees of Forde's estate.[8]

One of Forde's earliest investments was in a store in Wilmington run by a man named Jacob Garrigues. Their correspondence makes it clear they were friends who knew each other's families. John Checkley and Peter Anspach had goods there too, and these two men would continue to factor in Reed and Forde's business over the next few years. Forde brought Reed into this endeavor, but a letter from Garrigues seems to indicate that the business went downhill fast—Garrigues regretted moving his family to Delaware.[9]

There is no record of how or why the Reed & Forde partnership came to be when the other three scattered. The first official account of a Reed & Forde venture came from Thomas Skinner, who consigned tobacco and snuff to them in November of 1780. The first "Adventures" in Reed & Forde's daybook were to Virginia and the island of St. Eustatius in the Dutch West Indies in 1785. Other adventures followed to Georgia, Kentucky, the Mississippi, and New Orleans.[10]

Reed, Forde, and their friends got their start during the American Revolution. War opened up opportunities, just as it had for George Morgan's generation. Getting started as a trader was not difficult, and there was a high turnover rate through death, retirement, and/or failure. Merchants were men who were willing to take risks, responded quickly to change, and were innovative and flexible.[11] The war had brought Reed and Forde together through mutual friends, and after the war they invested heavily in western land speculation, along with the rest of Philadelphia's mercantile community.

At the same time John Reed and his friends were living the rowdy life in ports along the Eastern Seaboard, George Morgan and Oliver Pollock had to adapt to a changing world west of the Appalachian Mountains during the Revolution. Morgan took command of Fort Pitt in western Pennsylvania and served as the new nation's representative to the Delawares, among others, in 1776. The next year, the Continental Congress gave Pollock the official position of representing the new nation in New Orleans. Pollock financed George Rogers Clark's campaign in Illinois and served with the Spanish forces that captured Fort Bute and Pensacola. The two men had choices to make, and both decided that their futures lay with the new nation rather than the British Empire or Spanish Empire.

Many Native Americans west of the Appalachians were more inclined to support the British than the Americans on the eve of the Revolution. During the summer of 1775, Morgan went to Fort Pitt, having not given up on obtaining lands for the Suffering Traders. In the meantime, the Continental Congress had sent commissioners west to negotiate with the Delawares. One of their leaders, Koquethagecton (whom the Americans called White Eyes), struck up a friendship with Morgan, who helped the Delawares resolve a dispute with his old rivals the Gratz brothers. The Delawares ended up siding with the new United States, and the commissioners chose Morgan to act as the Indian agent headquartered at Fort Pitt. Over the next few years, he took charge of supplying Native American allies and trying to persuade others to join them as well.[12] George Morgan always counseled taking the path of peace with Native Americans farther west, but tensions rose between the Mingos and white settlers along the Scioto River. After a particularly volatile summer and fall of 1777, Virginia militia officers accused Morgan of treason. He had in fact continued to pursue lands that Virginians wanted and maintained friendships with men who sided with the British in the end. After an investigation, however, officials cleared Morgan and credited him with convincing most western tribes to remain neutral in the Ohio Valley.[13]

While in charge of Fort Pitt, Morgan looked for opportunities to take advantage of hostilities to expand trade with Spain. He contacted the new governor of New Orleans, Bernardo de Gálvez, in April of 1777, asking about his plans and the possibility of using New Orleans as a base to attack British forts on the Gulf Coast. Gálvez didn't reply until months later and took the position that officially he could authorize nothing. Morgan actively promoted sending a force south to men he knew in the Continental Congress. General Benedict Arnold followed up, and Morgan advised sending fifteen hundred men south to

New Orleans, where they could buy provisions, capture Pensacola and its harbor, and hold them after the war rather than allowing Spain to take control there. Robert Morris, Oliver Pollock's partner from time to time, weighed in on the debate, backing Morgan's plans and echoing the conclusion that such actions would help expand trade between the new nation and Spain on the Ohio and Mississippi Rivers.[14]

Oliver Pollock had advanced plans quite similar to Morgan's a year earlier. Pollock was no fan of Great Britain and especially hated all the regulations that interfered with trade. Spain had strict trade regulations too, but Pollock had always been able to find an official to grant him an exception. Historian Kathleen DuVal argues that Pollock thought that the new United States "could create a more commercialized society" free of "imperial restrictions." Pollock had a plantation on the Mississippi, a mercantile business in New Orleans, and had traded throughout the Western Hemisphere—the future of his commercial endeavors seemed bright as a world of free trade appeared on the horizon. The world was changing, and Pollock intended to be at the forefront of that change.[15]

Pollock first aided the Americans during August of 1776. At the behest of the Virginia Committee of Safety, General Charles Lee sent a militia captain named George Gibson along with sixteen men to meet with Governor Unzaga and ask for a supply of powder. They came disguised as traders from Pennsylvania, and Pollock introduced them to the governor, acting as translator. With his knowledge of the city, Pollock helped the men hide and avoid British agents. Lee had sent a note arguing that if the United States became independent, it would weaken the British navy, making Spanish possessions in the Caribbean and Mexico that much safer. Unzaga wrote to the Crown asking for instructions, and the answer came that Spain would be happy if the Americans attacked Pensacola and would send supplies by way of traders through Havana. The governor provided Pollock with the powder, who in turn gave it to Gibson, and, according to Pollock, some of the supplies did make it upriver to Pittsburgh.[16]

The Spanish recalled Governor Unzaga soon thereafter, however, and Pollock would find a better patron in the new man in charge: Bernardo de Gálvez. Gálvez began his military career by participating in the invasion of Portugal and was later sent to New Spain, where he rose through the ranks. Returning to Europe in 1772, he served in France and learned the language, which came in handy later. Gálvez arrived in Louisiana in 1777 as the new governor and did much to aid the Americans before Spain officially declared war on Great Britain two years later. When that happened, Gálvez led military expeditions to capture British forts and strongholds on the Lower Mississippi. The governor also helped Americans evade the British navy, allowed American privateers to sell their prizes in New Orleans, and helped fund Pollock to further his plans on the Mississippi. Pollock told Gálvez that he could provide much information about the American army, and in return, Pollock later recalled, Gálvez promised him protection for as long as he lived in Louisiana. Pollock remembered being handed money in the dead of night outside the governor's residence by Gálvez's private secretary John Morales, describing it as "very secret service money" to be used in service to the United States but obtained "chiefly on my own credit." New Orleans and the Mississippi River gave Americans a backdoor into the contested arena, and Gálvez propped it open.[17]

The Spanish saw the American Revolution as their chance to recoup losses they had suffered after the Seven Years' War and finally expel the British from Louisiana and Florida. Spain began sending loans and materials as early as May of 1776. Their entry into the war made it a true world war, as they attacked British strongholds in Europe. The Spanish navy helped keep the British navy bottled up down south when the Americans laid siege on Cornwallis at Yorktown in 1781.

Gálvez arrived on the scene at a time when the situation on the Gulf Coast and the Lower Mississippi proved particularly tense. The British seized Spanish ships, and the Spanish returned the favor. The British demanded not only that the Spanish release their ships but that they hand over Pollock as well. The British also attacked a mail boat on the Mississippi. Two French commissioners in New Orleans asserted that the French, in fact, were the ones with the power to say who could and could not navigate the Mississippi. Chaos reigned.[18] The American Revolution also gave Natchez a population boost. Peter Chester, the governor of West Florida, declared his colony "a secure asylum" and granted land to those who could prove they were loyal to King George. The population doubled over the next four years, and the slave population grew faster than those of European descent, with many loyalist slave owners arriving from Georgia and South Carolina. A British trader named Alexander McIntosh bought and sold goods at Pointe Coupée and became a landowner in the region.[19]

Farther upriver, more trouble brewed. Native American allies of the British in Detroit attacked settlers in Kentucky in 1777. George Rogers Clark led a group of volunteers against Kaskaskia, capturing the fort easily in July of 1778, and other British forts followed. The British recaptured Vincennes in December, however, with Clark returning the favor in February. The British remained in Detroit, and attacks on Kentucky continued over the next few years. When the British took over Illinois in the 1760s, masters had complained that they needed help controlling slaves. By the time Clark took over, he outlawed nightly revels and the commercial transactions of slaves. A couple of slaves were well-known for poisoning people. They used the Mississippi as a boundary to escape, but Clark crossed that boundary and caught them, and they were tried and executed. The public execution was a warning to all slaves in the region that things had changed. A new slave code would be part of claiming the region for the new United States.[20]

Historian Jay Gitlin judges the situation north of the Ohio thusly: "there was no conquest." Changing allegiance had long been a requirement of making a life in the Riverine West, where territory had changed hands at the conclusion of various European conflicts. French farmers and traders who lived there didn't provide much resistance to Clark's advance and mostly went about their business as before. Some traders stayed and traded with the Americans, and others crossed the Mississippi to St. Louis to do business with the Spanish. Gitlin calls the Upper Mississippi a "Creole Corridor" where the French strove to maintain their kinship ties with Native Americans to enhance trading opportunities. That would change only when Americans poured west en masse after the war, intent on making the territory their own.[21]

Still, Clark's capture of the Illinois Country proved to be one factor in France's decision to ally with the new United States. In 1777 and 1778 Pollock sent supplies and specie up the Mississippi and Ohio Rivers to Pittsburgh, borrowing the equivalent of over $74,000 from Gálvez and others over the course of the war, and the boats flew the Spanish colors. Pollock's goods were officially consigned to the Committee of Congress. Some shipments contained guns, ammunition, and provisions, while others included dry goods, hardware, medicine, and shoes. Americans on the Upper Mississippi made use of some of these shipments, but most went on up to Pittsburgh.[22]

Back in New Orleans, Gálvez wanted to capture Pensacola to block English appeals to the Chickasaw and Choctaw Indians. The English told the Native Americans that they should stay out of the war, warning them that Americans wanted their lands. Gálvez hoped to make alliances with Indians who had formerly allied with the French. Both the English and the Spanish hoped for Native American support but would settle for their neutrality. Europeans saw Native American support as crucial to their war efforts. The Chickasaws agreed to watch for Americans along the Mississippi during the war for the English, but they ignored many expeditions (such as Willing's detailed below) and mostly attacked shipments upriver instead, keeping the spoils for themselves. The only time they took official action was when George Rogers Clark tried to establish a fort in their territory in western Kentucky in 1780; they harassed the Americans until they left a little over a year later.[23] One scholar characterized the Chickasaws as "defenders of Chickasaw territory" rather than allies of the British.[24]

But Gálvez heard rumors of other colonists planning an attack down the Mississippi. A British merchant in New Orleans warned officials at Pensacola about George Gibson, the captain who had visited Pollock and taken powder upriver. Gibson asked a lot of questions too, and he made a lot of people nervous. Spanish officials disagreed about how to proceed.[25] The British responded by sending a frigate. The captain argued with the Spanish governor and left only after five British merchants told him that he was jeopardizing their standing in New Orleans. When the captain returned to Pensacola, he reported that American rebels would be a problem on the Mississippi. The Spanish cut out the British thereafter, and trade with Americans thrived under the duo of Pollock and Gálvez by late 1777. The British didn't push further, hoping to prevent a wider war in Europe.[26]

Even as Gálvez and Pollock began working together, another Philadelphia player began to make his presence felt. Thomas Willing's younger brother James arrived in Natchez in 1772 but hadn't really made a go of it as a planter or a merchant, despite Pollock's help. He returned to Philadelphia in 1777 just as the Continental Congress considered action in the West. After telling delegates what they wanted to hear about the situation on the Mississippi River, he seemed like a logical choice to take command of a mission. Although Morgan believed an expedition down the Mississippi should have been launched the previous fall, James Willing and his crew left Pittsburgh in January of 1778. Willing harassed a few Europeans on his journey and somehow managed to recruit enough men to triple his forces before reaching New Orleans. Willing's trip down the Mississippi seemed rather like a bull in a china shop. They waylaid various Englishmen, some of whom got word off to Pensacola. Willing arrived at Natchez and proceeded to seize slaves from men he held grudges against, while loyalists basically stood down. One group went ahead to Manchac and managed to capture a British ship in the fog. Willing followed, looting the plantations of men he did not like. Though word had been sent to Pensacola, settlers on the Mississippi were caught by surprise. Pollock had no choice but to prepare for Willing's arrival in New Orleans. He sent a group from New Orleans to help capture the British ship and persuaded the governor to offer sanctuary to anyone fleeing the British so that Willing could enter New Orleans while preserving Spanish neutrality. Gálvez let Pollock auction off Willing's loot. More harassment followed, humiliating the British, while Governor Gálvez stood by. British settlers complained to officials in Pensacola, to no effect.[27]

Gálvez refused to give ground and ridiculed those who complained, using the rules of the high seas to excuse Willing's actions. Gálvez also argued that he had no control over what Americans did in English territory, while keeping lines of communication open on both sides. The British took a harder stand and took back their territory one small bit at a time. They tried to enlist Indian allies to boost their numbers, in addition to offering land grants to settlers in the area. The British began stopping and searching Spanish boats heading north, in addition to English ones, looking for contraband. They had control of Natchez again by late spring. Gálvez began to worry about a civil war brewing in the vicinity of New Orleans.[28]

The British began watching Pollock even more closely. When the Spanish decided to expel British citizens from New Orleans, a couple of merchants took an oath of allegiance to Spain to allow them time to close their businesses. They got wind of Pollock's shipment and provided a description of his boat, hoping it would be captured. Pollock's boat was forced to turn around at Pointe Coupée, but he planned to try again. He would have to find other means, however. Because of all these shenanigans, the British decided to strengthen their forts. They sent another ship to supply Manchac, but it hit a log and sank. They lost much of the cargo, and the fort's supplies dwindled. The British did better at Natchez but still had trouble with men fighting among themselves. All this seemed very petty among men personally known to each other.[29]

In the meantime, Gálvez worried about provoking a war with Great Britain. Willing hung around New Orleans much longer than Gálvez expected, but Willing knew that he was persona non grata with many inhabitants of the region. The two men maintained a subtle truce, but Willing and Pollock argued about dividing their loot. Willing and his men wanted their share, but Pollock was more concerned about financing an expedition north. There was a lot of tension in the air that winter. Pollock complained to Congress, a scouting party was held up at Arkansas Post, and Willing didn't make a move until nearly the end of the summer, before finally ceding to Captain George. Gálvez allowed George to take men north with safe passage through Spanish territory after George agreed to leave English settlers alone. Some men got sick, and others deserted, but more than three dozen made it to the Falls of the Ohio to rendezvous with George Rogers Clark, Captain George's uncle, in September 1779. All Willing had accomplished was making the loyalists more loyal to Great Britain and bringing Pollock to the brink of bankruptcy.[30]

Spain entered the war in June of 1779. Even though his military advisors were against it, Gálvez started getting boats and men ready to attack Manchac and Natchez, believing that this would be the best way to defend New Orleans. Unfortunately for him, a hurricane in early August destroyed most of what he had been stockpiling while sparing the British. But Gálvez rallied the people of New Orleans by giving a speech announcing that they were now at war with England and that he was now the official rather than the acting governor. By the end of the month, his troops, German and Acadian settlers, and eight Americans, including Pollock, were ready to go. They headed up the Mississippi River and captured Fort Bute at Manchac in September; the British couldn't do much to resist because they were concentrated on defending the Gulf Coast.[31]

Oliver Pollock had lobbied time and time again for the United States to do all it could to secure free navigation of the Mississippi during the war. In 1782, he wrote to George Washington telling him that the settlement of the West depended on being able to navigate the Mississippi River and trade through New Orleans. Gaining control of England's claims east of the river would be crucial. The new nation also needed to think about a post at the Mississippi's mouth or someplace nearby to provide pilots capable of bringing ships through the delta to New Orleans. Pollock referenced the mutual benefit of both the United States and Spain and, acknowledging Spain's place in the region, characterized "the inhabitants of this country" as "pattern[ing] their court strongly" to facilitate commerce. But Pollock also concluded that the lands to the north of New Orleans might "soon become one of the first states in America."[32]

Unlike Reed and Forde, George Morgan and Oliver Pollock had started their careers when Philadelphia was a colonial port on the periphery of the British Empire. Morgan seemed to actually care about the fate of Native Americans who had to choose whether they would ally with the British or the Americans. There is no indication that he hesitated at all about throwing in his lot with the revolutionaries. Pollock may have decided that a new nation would foster a world of trade without the imperial restrictions he had labored under all his life, be they English or Spanish. Both would continue speculating in land once the war was over, just as they had before it began.

As Philadelphia merchants chose to become citizens of a new nation rather than remain subjects of a king, they made the most of new opportunities. War had come to the region once again, but a much different one than the conflict that had first begun Philadelphia's transformation twenty years earlier. This time merchants had to choose sides. And instead of chasing their share of a flood of incoming British bills of exchange, merchants looked to invest in the land warrants and public securities that the new state issued to raise the funds needed to fight for independence. They were going it alone, without their old British suppliers. Rather than trying to strengthen their place at the periphery of an empire, the question now was how to make Philadelphia the headquarters of a new nation's economy.

Just as making one's living in trade and land speculation often went hand in hand for many before the Revolution, the trend continued after. New states were offering land warrants to build their treasuries, and Philadelphia merchants especially jumped in with both feet. Rather than appealing to a king, land speculators were now buying certificates. Plans took off in Virginia and Pennsylvania, and land speculation proved to be especially vigorous in Philadelphia. A new era of buying and selling land had begun. Between the appeal of Samuel Wharton and others to the king for land grants before the war and the story of the land-office business during the first half of the nineteenth century came a transitional period when speculators bought and sold land warrants as a liquid asset.[33]

It began with the Virginia Land Acts of 1779, which specified four kinds of warrants. First, preemption lands were made available to those who had settled in western Virginia before the Revolution but had no title. They could purchase 400 acres for a small fee if they had planted a crop, as well as another 600 acres if they had built a house. Second, the state issued treasury warrants—40 pounds Virginia currency for 100 acres of land. Third, the state provided bounty warrants to soldiers and those who had provided Virginia with credit during the war. The final, more general category covered lands not yet taken. Those seeking warrants had the land surveyed, and then the state waited six months to see whether others wished to challenge the claim, after which the governor granted title. Treasury warrants came out in two series: 1779–83 and 1787–1952.[34]

In Pennsylvania, the legislature confiscated the Penn family lands after independence, arguing that the king had granted it for the good of the people, not the Penns' personal domain. Figures such as Pennsylvania Supreme Court justice Thomas McKean suggested selling the land to raise money but keeping settlers out until the war ended so as not to deplete the army. He favored selling lands to Europeans, reasoning that this would give them a vested interest in an American victory. McKean and others planned to pay soldiers with lands, and

Robert Morris suggested using lands as collateral for European loans. Once the war was over, the legislature first started the process of clearing old Penn family land transactions and issuing land warrants to soldiers. But many veterans did not want lands in the western end of the state, fearing attack by Native Americans and living so far from eastern markets. Auctions didn't bring in many buyers either, and speculators ended up buying up many of the warrants in the end. Land speculators would use three strategies to make a profit: holding land until prices rose, selling quickly to other speculators or land companies for a quick return, or developing the lands and selling to settlers using credit transactions.[35]

As they looked beyond the original colonies, newly independent Americans believed that seizing land from Native Americans and selling it to settlers would kill two birds with one stone: first, it would provide funds to pay the new nation's debts and invest in the future, and second, it would provide land to help citizens of the new republic start off right in their quest to create a "kingless self-government" based on a landed citizenry.[36] The Land Ordinance of 1785 established the precedent of surveying land prior to sale and settlement and setting up townships with a lot reserved for supporting public education. The Northwest Ordinance of 1787 set up a system whereby territories would become states. Massachusetts, Connecticut, Virginia, and North and South Carolina all ceded lands to the Confederation that they had claimed to the west under old colonial charters. But officials recognized that the biggest obstacle to their plans to develop the West lay in the fact that all trade on the Mississippi and its tributaries would have to go south through the port of New Orleans. Unfortunately, that port was under the control of a foreign power—Spain.

The treaty that ended the American Revolution laid the groundwork for uncertainty in the West. Article 8 of the Treaty of Paris stated that the navigation of the Mississippi River would be free and open to all British and American citizens. In addition, the boundary along the Mississippi River would remain at the center of the river, just as it had in the 1763 Peace of Paris, which had separated Spanish Louisiana from British territory east of the river. But after the American Revolution, the Spanish claimed the lands on the eastern bank for their own because they had been part of the triumph over Great Britain. The Spanish now argued that the entire river was theirs—the Mississippi would be a boundary no longer. Spain had sided with the Americans during the war primarily to drive the British out; they wanted the Gulf of Mexico to be a "Spanish Lake," with the Lower Mississippi serving as a buffer between

Mexico and the new United States. They had allowed Americans to use the river during the Revolution, and they would discover that trying to keep Americans out thereafter would be no simple task.[37]

Some Americans continued to approach New Orleans by sea. A New York merchant named Nicholas Low sent a brig full of flour to New Orleans, arriving in November of 1783. He had apparently consigned it to a man named Michael Connor, who wrote that he had to sell it for only 10 Spanish dollars a barrel. He wanted to hold it for a few days for a better price, but the Spanish intendant insisted that he sell it within twenty-four hours and send the ship on its way. Connor complained that it was impossible to do business in a place "where there is neither money nor produce nor even liberty allow'd a man to dispose of his property as he pleases." Another merchant warned a colleague that the Spanish would only admit flour into the port in the fall. The following March, a ship from Rhode Island arrived at New Orleans, and the captain asserted his right to move on up the Mississippi based on the treaty between the United States and Great Britain. The last official orders to Governor Esteban Miró and Intendant Martin Navarro had come in 1781 and stated that American ships could sail on the river for "the duration of the war." The Spanish officials didn't like it, but they assigned soldiers to accompany the vessel to make sure the captain didn't trade with any Spanish plantations or settlements on its way to Illinois. The two would lobby for Spain to close the Mississippi to all but Spanish vessels, in hopes that it would stop the settlement of the Ohio Valley if Americans had no access to markets. Spain responded by issuing a royal order to close the river in December of 1784.[38]

In order to gain access to the Lower Mississippi River, the new nation would have to negotiate with a Spanish official named Diego de Gardoqui. Born in Bilbao in 1735, Gardoqui got his start in trade in London through family connections, before returning to Spain to run the family business over the course of two decades beginning in the late 1750s. He held various government positions, all the while importing cod from Boston, exporting iron to Cadiz, and then exporting salt from Cadiz back to Boston. In 1774 and the years following, he became Spain's "point man," supplying Americans with cannons, weapons, munitions, gunpowder, uniforms, and tents during the Revolutionary War. Gardoqui served as the Spanish consul in London in 1783 and 1784, before being appointed as Spain's envoy to the new United States, arriving in New York City in 1785. The Confederation sent John Jay to Madrid to open negotiations, but he returned shortly thereafter to meet with Gardoqui in New York. The Spanish official's goals included firming up the boundary in the West and encouraging trade between the two countries while keeping tight hold of the Lower Mississippi as a buffer to protect Spain's possessions in Mexico and South America.[39]

Gardoqui quickly recognized a rift developing between the southern states and those to the north. New Englanders, New Yorkers, and Pennsylvanians worried the most about trade to the Caribbean and Europe. Southern slave holders speculating in western lands thought that the most important goal should be gaining access to the western rivers. Those didn't seem like mutually exclusive goals in the beginning, but they did in the end. John Jay focused his attention on expanding trade in the Atlantic, and the Jay-Gardoqui Treaty of 1786 would be the unsatisfactory result. It affirmed Spain's control over the navigation of the Mississippi River but opened up Spanish ports in Europe and the Caribbean to American ships and left the boundary of Florida up in the air. Those living in the West greatly resented it, as did southerners interested in land speculation, and the Confederation Congress never ratified it. Under the Articles of Confederation, the ratification of treaties required nine states, making it easy for the five southern states to block. John Jay had a reputation as a firm and successful negotiator, but circumstances forced him to tell Congress that, after two years of talks, he couldn't get Spain to agree to allow the new United States free navigation of the Mississippi River. Instead, Spain offered access to European ports, helping their commerce expand in the Mediterranean. Let the river go for now, Jay seems to have counseled, we can come back in the future with more leverage and get what we want. Some scholars argue that Jay, Jefferson, and Washington chose to bide their time until the pressure of numbers in the West would determine the outcome rather than fighting a premature war.[40] But John Jay hadn't reckoned with how strong feelings ran in the West and the steps Spain would take to stoke sectional tensions.

Before and after the Constitutional Convention, Gardoqui met with James Madison and continued to try to negotiate a treaty with the new nation. According to Madison, Gardoqui stood firm in March of 1787 about retaining control of the Lower Mississippi River and joked that "the people of Kentucky would make good Spanish subjects." The Spanish envoy believed that westerners desired trade through New Orleans so badly that they would side with the Spanish in the end. Gardoqui kept tabs on the action in Philadelphia with interest, and the tension he saw between regions only raised his hopes that Spain would come out ahead in the end. The year 1788, sandwiched between Confederation and Constitution, proved to be the most dangerous in terms of the new nation's risk of losing the West to Spain. As soon as he took office, President

George Washington took the trouble to tie the Ohio and Mississippi Valleys more strongly to the East. He made Thomas Jefferson secretary of state and appointed various men from the Carolinas and other points south involved in land speculation schemes to various War Department and territorial posts. The Southwest Ordinance came on the heels of that for the Northwest, and Kentucky became a state. There would be schemes put forth by land speculators for taking Yazoo and Nootka, but Kentucky, at least, had been placated. There was also competition from Georgia and the Carolinas, as well as attempts to make use of Natchez.[41]

Free navigation of the Mississippi would not become official until Pinckney's Treaty in 1796, but, in fact, the Spanish began making exceptions to the rules by 1787 for the same reason they had been doing so before the Revolution: they didn't have the resources to supply New Orleans on their own, and so land speculation proceeded apace with scarcely a pause. Though the Pennsylvania delegation had sided with the North against Jay's Treaty, other Pennsylvanians proved to be just as interested in western lands as anyone in the South. States had begun settling land warrants before the end of the war, and though there was plenty of action in New York, Virginia, Connecticut, and South Carolina, Philadelphians did the highest volume because they resided in what was then the political and economic center of the new nation. Speculation reached a fever pitch in the mid-1790s. Men like Thomas Paine argued that it wasn't a risky business because land would never lose its value. With so many people moving west, speculators expected an excellent return on their investments for years to come. Historian Hanno Scheerer labels their actions "rational": a new treaty with Spain that allowed trade down the Mississippi and the low initial cost of land should mean a good payoff in the end.[42]

Historians don't agree on the context for all this land speculation by Philadelphia merchants after the Revolution. British goods flowed into Philadelphia at a fantastic rate, with merchants importing double the amount of the busiest year before independence. Unpaid goods filled warehouses, stores, and homes, and bankruptcies followed in 1785. Thomas Doerflinger labeled it the "dry goods bubble." The only trade that remained stable were shipments to the West Indies, as too many traders chased too few bills of exchange—not many were available because exports had plummeted. Prosperity didn't return until the 1790s.[43] But Norman Wilkinson characterized Philadelphia trade a bit differently. He argued that although merchants continued in the staples trade after the war and some invested in manufacturing, shipping had lost some of its appeal. Tension between England and France allowed the Barbary pirates to thrive, and the seizure of ships became a real problem. Wilkinson wrote that merchants, bankers, and investors believed that they could influence land laws to their benefit, and land offered a safe investment—rising prices were guaranteed as more people moved westward. The merchants didn't have cash, but 80 percent of the land bought in the 1780s was paid for by certificates that represented public debt from the war years. Land speculators applied for warrants in other peoples' names. More and more wealthy men began to buy up land warrants, and speculation hit its peak between 1792 and 1794.[44]

One such Philadelphia merchant who speculated in western lands was John Clifford. In the winter of 1790, his contact in Pittsburgh, John Wilkins Jr., warned him that the land he was trying to claim was "situated on the Indian side of the river & entirely unsettled." The surveyor's name was Cunningham, and he was a member of the Pennsylvania General Assembly—Wilkins advised Clifford to do a little name-dropping. Wilkins reported that land values depended entirely on perceptions in Philadelphia because the speculators controlled so much of it. Wilkins and his brother, who eventually settled in Natchez, would continue to do business with various members of the Clifford family into the next century.[45]

Like many others, including some of the wealthiest and most influential men on the Eastern Seaboard, Reed and Forde speculated in hundreds of thousands of acres of land in western Virginia, western Pennsylvania, and Kentucky. Public securities show up immediately in the earliest pages of Reed & Forde's combination daybook/ledger—page 2, January 1785. The partners sunk much of their fortunes into land warrants, mostly in western Virginia and Kentucky. A man named James Elliot wrote from Louisville in December of 1783, telling Reed and Forde that lands were worth nearly $1 an acre and going up in value quickly. It would be hard to claim good land, though, because six thousand people had arrived from Virginia since the spring, and "clouds of warrants" were at stake. Elliot claimed that he had located the best vacant land available for them but had run into some legal troubles related to a power of attorney. He said that he was losing money and couldn't support himself, so he might not be able to honor their agreement.[46]

Reed and Forde's land speculations began in 1784 in Virginia with the survey of 300,000 acres the next year. They also bought land in Centre, Northumberland, Philadelphia, and Mifflin Counties in Pennsylvania. There are many entries in the daybook for the advertising and surveying of land in 1785, 1786, and 1787. Reed and Forde expanded their purchases into Northampton, Roxborough, and Wayne Counties in 1786 and 1788. More Pennsylvania lands followed in the mid-1790s, and the partners bought land in New York in 1800.[47]

A letter from Standish Forde in Richmond to John Reed back home in Philadelphia in December of 1785 gives details of their business at that time. He wrote about providing goods to establish a store in Alexander, with a man named Roane in charge, and warned that they would have to pay the balance by June, but that it could be done with certificates from any state other than the Carolinas or Georgia. Forde sent Baltimore bills and told Reed to send surveys and patents on land to Cruger & Company for sales. The patents needed to be registered, and both their names should be on the power of attorney. A. G. Martin would handle other sales for them, and Forde wrote that river tracts should not sell for under half a dollar, but other tracts were worth a third of a dollar each. He hoped for "something considerable" over the winter from the Fredericksburg store.[48]

Whenever possible, the partners tried to unload their acres in sizable lots. Reed and Forde tried to entice Judge John Cleves Symmes of New Jersey to invest in their lands for his schemes, but he ended up purchasing over 300,000 acres in Ohio along the Miami River from the Continental Congress instead, including the future site of Cincinnati. Reed and Forde managed to sell 3,500 acres to a man named John Davis who headed a group of families eager to make a new start on the frontier. In the fall of 1789, Reed and Forde wrote to Major Samuel Hanway in Richmond and a Mr. Davidson in Morgantown, telling them that the settlers from Virginia were on the way. They hoped that their contacts would help the newcomers locate and choose lands to suit them, and they mentioned Jersey settlers in the area as well—the prospect of land sales looked good. Reed and Forde preferred that the newcomers choose lands for farms that ran along straight lines and adjoined one another but stated that if some had to be farther away that would be fine. A letter from John Davis a year later, however, indicated that all did not go as planned, as Davis complained that the land was not of high quality and did not provide easy access to Ten Mile Creek.[49]

They knew that their lands would increase in value once settlement got underway. Though they tried to convince men like Symmes to buy in bulk and hoped that their London supplier might find investors for them in England or France, they wrote of preferring to sell to actual settlers whose improvements would enhance the value of their warrants from the start. At one point they offered to take bonds and securities for three-fourths of the price, and they would allow buyers to take up to three years to pay if they would put a quarter of the price down to begin with.[50]

Reed and Forde contacted men in Connecticut and Virginia, offering them a 5 percent commission to find buyers in 1787. Initial surveys indicated that their lands off a branch of the Monongahela contained iron ore, and they sent out feelers trying to find an experienced man to establish an ironworks, hoping to supply "all the settlements on the western waters." Whenever Reed and Forde wrote of land, they emphasized easy access to markets. Once they boasted that farmers would be able to drive cattle to the headwaters of the Potomac, as well as shipping flax, hemp, and tobacco by the same route. Other lands lay closer to Philadelphia or Baltimore trade routes, and settlers passing through on their way to Kentucky were said to provide another ready market.[51]

Reed & Forde's 1787 letter book is a telling one. Most of the letters referred to land, but there were others about trying to obtain tobacco in Virginia and turpentine in the Carolinas to sell in London. They had initially thought of shipping corn but found the prices too high. As Forde endeavored to put a cargo together, he also tried to collect on their debts, with little luck. It seems to have been an altogether unproductive year, and thereafter they turned their attention to the Ohio and Mississippi Valleys. Land speculators had three choices: the first two involved either holding land until the prices rose or selling their warrants to other speculators for a higher price. In the 1790s, Robert Morris tried the latter, buying land on credit and then selling to others in hopes of raising enough money to pay off the original loan. Reed and Forde would end up taking the third way: they sold land to settlers and invested in mills in western Pennsylvania to make their lands attractive and facilitate trade. As with the Seven Years' War, Philadelphia merchants emerged at the other end of the conflict with their sights set firmly on the West.[52]

The American Revolution shook up the world of Philadelphia's merchants just as the Seven Years' War had done twenty years earlier. The merchants who would help open up trade between the new United States and Spain in New Orleans in the 1790s, John Reed and Standish Forde, got their start during the war. Meanwhile, on the Gulf Coast Oliver Pollock and many others chose to support the British colonies to the north, and they would engage in land speculation thereafter as well. George Morgan made the same decision at the Ohio's headwaters. After the war, interest in the fur trade receded as states sought to pay off war debts by selling land, and merchants made the most of new opportunities. This did not bode well for Native Americans who controlled wide swaths of territory west of the Appalachian Mountains. Merchants would continue in their efforts to make the Riverine West part of the new nation in the decades to come.

Maneuvering in the Riverine West

John Reed and Standish Forde's subscriptions provide a window into their world. The list includes not only magazines but also payments to common funds that supported debating societies, churches, and schools. Reed and Forde also subscribed to Matt Carey's *American Museum* and a manufacturing society in August of 1787. The next year, they paid for a subscription to the Rumseian Society established by James Rumsey to fund his inventions. Subscribers included Benjamin Franklin and William Bingham, as well as the London banker Robert Barclay. Rumsey never finished his designs in the United States, but others would go on to develop steamboats based on his early work. Reed and Forde were open to and explored all avenues to extend their business in the wider world. They were more than simple land speculators.[1]

After the war, Americans could at last flood over the Appalachian Mountains into the Riverine West. But eastern policymakers moved too slowly to secure the rights to navigate the Mississippi in the eyes of many westerners, and a period of unrest arose along the Ohio River that made the Spanish to the south nervous about the frontiersmen's intentions. George Morgan made one more play for a land grant, this time from the king of Spain, but his failure highlighted another path to the future. While Morgan looked to the past, John Reed and Standish Forde sold land, invested in mills and transportation to get goods to market, and negotiated with the Spanish as citizens of a new republic. But those who aimed to settle the West found that doing business in a region not yet firmly tied to the new United States could be tricky.

Possession of the Riverine West seemed to be up for grabs after the American Revolution. Americans came to the Ohio Valley during the war hungry for land. For the most part, they didn't have money to pay for it. Their intent was to use their labor to produce crops, send the crops to market, and use the profits to secure their title to the land after. Doing so required access to Atlantic markets through New Orleans. Spain had allowed trade on the river during the war in its effort to help the Americans defeat the British, and western farmers got a taste of what access to trade through New Orleans could mean. All of Reed and Forde's land speculation plans hinged on their promise to settlers that they could get their goods to market. Unfortunately, policymakers disappointed Philadelphia merchants and western settlers alike when it came to the right to freely navigate the Ohio and Mississippi Rivers. The new United States was a confederation. Squabbling over the borders of colonies gave way to squabbling over the boundaries of the new states. While eastern policymakers experimented with ways to distribute land in an orderly way, westerners wanted to immediately engage in trade. They were already there, on the ground, and they wanted action. Philadelphia merchants had been buying up state land warrants and were also ready to move ahead. Once the war ended, patience with the Confederation Congress ended.[2] At a meeting in Lexington in the spring of 1784 Kentuckians passed a resolution declaring that, among other things, they had a natural right to trade freely on the Mississippi River. The Confederation must demand it of Spain, they resolved, and the government better not take no for an answer.[3] The Spanish followed events closely and worried about how far Americans in the Riverine West might go to get what they wanted.

Before the American Revolution officially ended, Oliver Pollock wrote to George Washington about securing access to the Lower Mississippi River. He had been maneuvering in Spanish Louisiana for more than a decade and wrote that the navigation of the Mississippi should be open to all "for the mutuall benefit of both nations." If the new United States could take over English territory at Natchez and points to the east, the new nation should establish a customs house on the Mississippi and "a port for our vessels, a place to deposit our goods." Pollock argued that lands in the Ohio and Mississippi Valleys could only be settled if they had access to New Orleans, hoping that territory to the north of New Orleans would be part of the new nation.[4]

Naturally, the Spanish had other ideas, but they faced a number of problems when it came to holding on to the Lower Mississippi. The number of Spaniards paled in comparison to the size of the population of other peoples in the region, and their military style of leadership, designed to hold the line rather than expand their reach, endeared them to no one. Each settlement had a military officer in command who reported to the governor of Louisiana, who reported to the governor of Havana, who reported directly to the ministers in turn. Though some governors had proved successful in the New World, others not suited to it came to power simply because they were next in line for the first open slot. In terms of commerce, historian Arthur Whitaker posited that the French were really in charge, Spanish markets had little use for American goods, and westerners, those of European descent and Native Americans alike, preferred English and French goods to Spanish ones. Americans kept coming back for more trade principally because they desired specie—be they eastern merchants like Robert Morris looking to increase trade in the Caribbean or Kentucky farmers wanting to sell their tobacco in New Orleans. Holding on to Louisiana proved to be very costly; Spain didn't seem to gain much, and newly independent Americans seemed determined to make the Mississippi Valley their own.[5]

This doesn't mean that the Spanish didn't try, of course. The Cedula (Order in Council) of 1782 allowed for trade between New Orleans, Pensacola, and the French West Indies. Spain tried to bring in Catholic settlers to the Lower Mississippi and legalized the slave trade there. The Spanish promised British citizens in West Florida that they could be Spanish citizens despite their Protestant backgrounds. They aimed for all of this to grow the population on the Lower Mississippi, in order to strengthen it as a buffer zone protecting their colonies to the west and south.[6]

Conflicting negotiations during the final stages of the American Revolution between England and Spain and between England and her former colonies had set the stage for trouble to come. At the highest levels of the Spanish government, officials disagreed about the level of threat represented by the new nation, and some wanted Great Britain to retain the East Florida coast as a buffer zone. England's treaty with the new United States stated that both could navigate the Mississippi and set the southern boundary at the thirty-first parallel. England's treaty with Spain did not mention the river but acknowledged Spain's right to West Florida as conquered territory. In effect, this meant that both the United States and Spain could claim that England had ceded Natchez to them, as well as lands Native Americans claimed as their own, which represented important fur trade territory. Spain would take the position that England had no right to

Figure 5.1. One interpretation of the Treaty of Paris boundary lines.
William McMurray and Robert Scot, *The United States According to the Definitive Treaty of Peace Signed at Paris Sept. 3d. 1783.* Courtesy of the Library of Congress

grant navigation of the Mississippi to the United States. But Arthur Whitaker concluded that when Spain closed off the Mississippi River it tried to go against two decades of custom—Americans had first traded on the river as British subjects, and then as revolutionaries trying to win independence with Spain's backing (see fig. 5.1).[7]

Letters to Diego de Gardoqui show that the Spanish were quite afraid of what Americans would do after the American Revolution ended. There are letters from Natchez, New Orleans, and other places that spread rumors about plans for Americans to attack Louisiana in the decade before the Pinckney Treaty. Spanish officials wrote about the force of arms the new nation could bring to bear. They also wrote about maintaining their ties to Indian allies. Their mentality seemed like that of men under siege. The Spanish official in charge of Louisiana at the time was Esteban Miró, who served as governor from 1782 to

1791. During the American Revolution, he participated in the 1780 Mobile Campaign and helped suppress a rebellion in Natchez the next year. During his tenure, keeping American settlers out of Spanish territory was part of his job description. Miró oversaw the rebuilding of New Orleans after much of the city burned down in a 1788 fire, and in the end, much like the others who proceeded him, he reached out to Philadelphia for help.[8]

What were Americans seeing on the ground in the Riverine West? Elizabeth House Trist's trip down the Ohio in the spring of 1784 proved both similar to and different from that of George Morgan and others twenty years earlier. Most of the forts lay in ruins. She was impressed with the land around Wheeling but found that other travelers passed it by as they headed for Kentucky. There are "such a number of boats continually going down the river" that hunters couldn't find game to feed the traveling party. Trist commented on settlements laid out to attract settlers. Families had boats tied up, and they were camping at Bear Grass Creek near present-day Louisville. Trist's party spent a week trying to pass over the Falls of the Ohio, and several "gentlemen" spoke kindly to her, including a young man from Ireland who "lately open'd a store at this place." As they passed the Wabash, Trist wrote that she had heard that there were prosperous French settlements upstream and that it was "a place of considerable trade."[9]

Trist heard Native Americans on the move one night but did not actually lay eyes on any of them until they were downstream of Louisville. She feared they would attack her party and wrote that the lower portion of the Ohio was considered more dangerous; however, they encountered fewer Native Americans than she expected. After they passed the Wabash, Delaware Indians in two canoes approached them. Trist wrote that they seemed friendly, and she gave a woman bread to eat and a handkerchief to shield her infant from the sun in the interest of having "friends at court." But she characterized the man who seemed to be in charge as a person of bad character because he had a reputation for attacking boats on the river. A few days later, another canoe approached, and, as before, the crew had their weapons out just in case there was trouble. But this time the men were French and heading to Tennessee "to trade." Trist characterized them as savages who were nearly as naked and dark as Indians. As they approached the Mississippi, her party passed an Indian camp, as well as herds of buffalo and deer. Life had proven to be much livelier downriver from the falls.[10]

But Trist did not enjoy their trip down the Mississippi at all. Fast currents and high banks made the going perilous that June. Uprooted trees caught in the river created their own hazards—once Trist wrote that "we got in midst of them," and she feared that "our boat would be tore to pieces." They had to tie up every night. As on the Upper Ohio, game grew scarce. About 100 miles downstream from the Ohio they encountered a party that had been on the river for three months trying to reach Illinois from New Orleans. Farther down, she worried about Chickasaw Indians robbing their boats. Mosquitoes proved a problem on both rivers. Her party stopped at one of the Mississippi's tributaries so that a group of men could take flour upriver to sell at a Spanish fort. They stayed on an island overnight and met up with people from "a large boat from the Illinois" heading south. When the men returned, she found that they had sold a hundred barrels of flour for $17 a piece—a high price. They encountered more French, as well as a settlement owned by a man named Barber and run by "a Mullato woman nam'd Nelly," whom Trist found to be an interesting hostess. Trist had looked forward to reaching Natchez, where the party was to unload flour, but upon arrival she received the sad news of her husband's death.[11]

When Elizabeth House Trist tried to return home to Philadelphia after settling her husband's affairs in early 1785, she found it difficult. She attempted to book passage on a Spanish ship bound for Cuba as the first step of her journey and considered traveling "via the cape" as well.[12] Trist wrote to her friend Thomas Jefferson that "there being no trade between the United States and this country, it seems almost impossible to get from here."[13] In the end, she traveled first to Jamaica and then on home. As they had before the American Revolution, Europeans of English, French, and Spanish descent and Native Americans interacted and plied their trade on the Ohio and Mississippi Rivers. There were plenty of friendly encounters between busy inhabitants, and travelers could hunt for game, trade provisions, or find a suitable host at the river's bank. Rivers dictated the pace of life.

Commercial accounts reveal other details about the region. When Richard Carpenter wrote to John Collins in 1784, it was from Baton Rouge. He complained about a protested bill exchange that had sat for two years in New Orleans. Part of its paper trail had been through Illinois, while other paper had come from Pensacola and mentioned the custom of West Florida in redeeming it. Collins wrote him a year later about making no progress with a government official on the Mississippi. Later Carpenter wrote of problems with a man named Samuel Flowers. Another letter from Daniel Williams mentioned congressional certificates that had depreciated, as well as an iron works. A merchant named David Wood Meriwether wrote about shipments of flour sent from Red Stone to Spanish settlements on the Mississippi down the Ohio in 1785, even though officially the Spanish had closed the river.[14] The Mississippi remained the main thoroughfare of the West.

Meriwether settled near Bear Grass (Louisville) and wrote his father that he and his neighbors had high hopes for the region but they would not be able to succeed without trade—subsistence farming had no attraction for him. Westerners recognized that all trade from the region would have to go south with the current through the Spanish in New Orleans.[15] In June of 1786, a trader from Tennessee decided to take matters into his own hands and headed down the Mississippi River with a load of ironware, flour, and other goods. Spanish officials stopped him at Natchez and confiscated his cargo. Rather than allowing him to continue down the river to make his way home by ocean voyage through the Gulf, the Spanish sent him on his way overland back north and east.[16] Others tried as well, and they, too, had their tobacco and flour confiscated. A couple of months later, George Rogers Clark seized the stock of three Spanish merchants near Vincennes, and his actions received widespread support. If westerners couldn't send their goods south, they wouldn't allow the Spanish to send anything north. A Georgia official published a pamphlet that circulated widely in the West and kept people stirred up about the situation.[17]

The next year a man named James Wilkinson decided to make use of the controversy to his own advantage. A Maryland native, Wilkinson proved to be more wheeler-dealer than merchant, but he first went to Kentucky as the agent of the Philadelphia firm Barclay, Moyland & Company in 1783. He had married into the wealthy Biddle family and claimed connections with Oliver Pollock and Philadelphia merchant Joseph Ball. Wilkinson set up his own store in Lexington and participated in territory-wide debates over separating from Virginia. In March of 1787 he headed for New Orleans with a load of flour, tobacco, and other foodstuffs to supply the port. Scholars suspect that he bribed officials along the way, and he definitely arrived prepared to make friends with the governor, Esteban Miró. Wilkinson told Miró about the mood in Kentucky and played on Miró's fears of an attack from the north. He convinced Miró that opening up limited trade with Wilkinson, acting as Spain's agent in Kentucky, would forestall an invasion. Wilkinson swore allegiance to Spain in August, and he was back home the next spring. There was considerable debate in Kentucky about separating from the United States, especially after the Confederation Congress declined to grant them statehood in July, but by November leaders in Kentucky decided to petition for statehood once more. Perhaps tempers cooled because Spain did allow for shipping to Louisiana that summer. Wilkinson and his cronies were exempt from fees, but others were charged a 15 percent duty to ship their cargoes south, with an additional tax added if they then exported their goods from New Orleans to Atlantic markets.[18]

One of Wilkinson's Kentucky associates, Harry Innes, wrote a letter to an official named John Brown, congratulating him on his election to Congress. He told Brown that if the Jay-Gardoqui Treaty came to the floor, Brown should argue that John Jay had been wrong to imply that it would have no serious impact on the West. Innes declared that God had made the river their only access to the Atlantic, and thus it was intended for the people and no government should control it, a rather radical stand to take at the time.[19] A Frenchman lately of Kentucky named Pierre d'Arges gained an audience with the Spanish ambassador in Paris to propose a plan in 1787: open up the Mississippi but charge a 25 percent duty on trade. To gain access to free trade, westerners in America were angry enough to consider defecting to Spain, he told the ambassador. D'Arges proposed acting as a Spanish agent to recruit Americans to settle in Natchez. The secretary of state agreed with this plan and dispatched d'Arges to Kentucky, though officially his mission was to check out Spain's border. This plan elevated Natchez's status in New Spain, and the first governor appointed, Gayoso, would prove to be capable and important in the years to come.[20]

In 1787, Spain finally modified their demands, offering some concessions on boundaries (though not Natchez) and establishing a commission to look into American claims to the Mississippi. But by then it was too late—the Confederation was done, but the new Constitution was not yet in place; there was nobody for Gardoqui to negotiate with. Gardoqui and Miró both disliked d'Arges; Miró replaced him as Spain's agent in Kentucky with James Wilkinson, and so the Spanish Intrigue began. Historian Arthur Whitaker argued that it would be more aptly named "the frontier intrigue with Spain."[21] Older histories had also focused on anti-Jay feeling among the anti-Federalists and land speculators, arguing that too few commodities arrived at New Orleans to matter in terms of western trade. This ignored the fact that plenty of westerners were land speculators themselves, according to Whitaker, and that plenty of trade unloaded at Natchez instead. He also argued that it was future trade that mattered—westerners felt that their future depended on opening up the Mississippi River. Westerners complained about two things: access to the Mississippi and Indian policy. For Whitaker, commerce trumped everything in the West, and that's why men like Wilkinson approached the Spanish rather than the English when they considered separating from the United States.[22]

Arthur Whitaker argued that Wilkinson took a cue from Clark and approached the Spanish as if to help them. Wilkinson advised Spain to do one of two things: either start a revolt in the West or bring Kentuckians to Louisiana. But Wilkinson wanted a monopoly himself, rather than having the Spanish open the river to Americans. Spain waited for the d'Arges plot to play out and then took the middle road with Wilkinson's ideas. In the end, they did open up the river with a high duty, hoping to persuade people to become subjects instead through land grants and the promise of religious toleration and free trade. Whitaker argued that Spain decided to bring Americans to Louisiana instead of trying to placate them in Kentucky, reasoning that many Europeans in the West weren't English, and the Loyalists at Natchez had settled quietly into the Spanish system after 1781. Wilkinson's most ambitious plans would never come to fruition because Thomas Jefferson loved the Spanish plan, believing that the seeds of integrating the Mississippi into the new nation without firing a shot had been sown.[23]

It wasn't only men from Kentucky who were angry; letters from men to the south reveal an intrigue in 1788 involving Tennessee, North Carolina, and the Spanish. The Jay-Gardoqui Treaty cropped up again as a sore spot, and southwesterners also expected the Confederation to take their side against Native Americans. Some of them decided to negotiate with the Spanish. While Wilkinson stirred up trouble in Kentucky, Gardoqui did the same in Tennessee. The man on the ground there was James Sevier. But it was never going to work out—the Spanish wanted to trade with the southern Indians, while the Americans wanted to eradicate them, according to Whitaker. The Americans didn't really trust any Europeans who made alliances with Native American tribes. James Robertson, the founder of Nashville, led a force to attack French traders at a place called Coldwater in the summer of 1787 because the Americans thought they were conspiring with Indians. Robertson wrote about settlers killed by Indians in the summer of 1788. Negotiations between Robertson and the Spanish went on for the next few months. The Americans wanted protection and trade. The westerners wanted more—from the East, from Indians, and from Europeans.[24]

In January of 1789, James Robertson wrote to Governor Miró that rumors of a planned attack on New Orleans over the past summer were false. These were the rumors spread by a British spy named Conolly. In turn, Robertson wrote, the Americans had heard that the Spanish were supplying Native Americans with ammunition to attack them. Worries were subsiding, he wrote, with signs that some trade down the Mississippi might open up again. Robertson wrote that "every thinking person in this country is fully convinced" that friendly relations with the Spanish, who control the mouth of the Mississippi, are in everyone's best interest. He concluded, "Nature seems to have designed the whole western County to be one people."[25]

In 1790, a glut of poor-quality tobacco in Seville lay behind the Spanish decision to greatly reduce the amount the government would buy for a good price at New Orleans each year. Natchez planters protested most vociferously. They stated that they had cleared land and imported slaves, and now Spain had taken away their market. The trickle of settlers into Louisiana stopped partly for this reason and partly because Kentuckians had a new market—supplying the US Army doing battle with Native Americans in the Old Northwest.[26] At roughly the same time, Governor Miró did allow Wilkinson to ship Kentucky tobacco to New Orleans. Pollock had first become acquainted with Miró as Gálvez's second-in-command during campaigns against English forts in 1779, and "from that time on" the two were "intimately acquainted." Believing that he had exclusive rights to sell tobacco to Spain, Pollock complained to Miró about Wilkinson's shipment. Miró told him that he had allowed it to "pacify the Kentuckians and the people of the western country, to prevent rupture between Spain and America, and in order to give time for negotiations between the two powers, relative to the navigation of the Mississippi."[27]

In the meantime, the new governor, Francisco Luis Héctor de Carondelet, took the massing of an American army on the Ohio as the prelude to an attack on the Lower Mississippi, even though Manuel Gayoso de Lemos, then in charge of the Natchez District, tried to tell him that the Ohio Indians were the target. Various American officials, British and American merchants, and local leaders like Alexander McGillvray played on his fears to stir up trouble with the Indians in the Southeast. Carondelet wanted to create an alliance between Spain and the Creeks, Choctaws, and Chickasaws, among others. He truly thought that Spain was on the brink of war with the United States. What ended up happening was that he undermined Spanish agents in Philadelphia.[28]

With such tensions in the air, perhaps it is not surprising that the French Revolution had an impact on what went on in the West. The Spanish ended up at war with the French and failed to follow up on plans to supply their colonies with their own manufactured goods and to loosen immigration rules. Because they didn't want to rile up French settlers in their territory, they allowed them to trade all they wanted with Americans on the Mississippi. With French markets closed, Americans moved in, openly changing from American to Spanish colors when they entered the Mississippi from the Gulf. In terms of Indian alliances, they didn't have enough funds to hold them, and the alliances they did have created tensions with the United States. Spain allied with Great Britain in 1793, a traditional enemy, and that didn't end well.[29]

Whitaker concluded that frontiersmen took the French Revolution much more to heart than easterners did, and it lay behind their argument about their natural right to navigating the Mississippi River. Thomas Jefferson made the same argument as the secretary of state when he sent instructions to diplomats negotiating Pinckney's Treaty a short time later. Edmond-Charles Genet arrived in South Carolina from France in 1793 and tried to organize attacks on the British from American ports. He hired privateers and headed for Philadelphia, but George Washington let it be known that Genet was way out of bounds. Some officials in the West denounced him, but settlers on the southern frontier cheered him on. This all added to unrest in the West.[30]

Perhaps a man named Smith summed it up best in an eloquent statement meant to accompany a 1793 map. He wrote that "the western people consider the navigation of the Mississippi as the light of the sun, a birthright that cannot be alienated." They expected the new federal government to secure their claim to navigate freely on western waters. Smith believed that any agricultural and industrial goods produced in the East could be just as easily produced west of the Appalachian Mountains as long as they had access to the Gulf of Mexico. In addition, people would not be satisfied with just getting by, he argued; they would want to be able to buy foreign goods as well. If another nation controlled New Orleans, it would "blast the mercantile schemes" of everyone who lived in the West.[31]

During the American Revolution, Americans had gotten used to using the Mississippi River for both trade and provisioning military operations in the West. The Spanish had allowed it because they wished to weaken Britain's hold on North America. But once they signed a peace treaty, the Spanish began to worry that more Americans would cross the mountains and want lands the Spanish had claimed. They wanted to maintain control over the navigation of the Mississippi, and westerners grew angry with American diplomats who seemed more concerned with securing Atlantic ports than securing New Orleans. There were no guarantees that any of the territory west of the Appalachians would become part of the United States. Those living in Kentucky and Tennessee insisted on being allowed to trade by way of the Mississippi River, but they weren't sure who could make that happen.

Into the middle of all this intrigue strode George Morgan, who had a plan. He had started his life as the subject of a king, and after the Revolution, when given the choice of serving a king once more, he took it. George Morgan established the town of New Madrid to try to help Spain hold the Mississippi Valley while guaranteeing a trade route for Americans. Morgan had kept pushing for his Indiana Company lands after the Revolution but accepted an offer from Spain to found a colony instead. Morgan envisioned New Madrid as the gateway for trade between Americans and the Spanish in New Orleans, but various intrigues scuttled those plans, and he abandoned them the next year. Morgan's efforts represented the last gasp of counting on a king for a land grant instead of speculating through land warrants and, eventually, the General Land Office.

After Morgan returned to Philadelphia in 1771, he dabbled in other land deals and looked into setting up lead and salt mines in eastern Pennsylvania over the next few years, but nothing came of any of those plans. Morgan continued his friendship with geographer Thomas Hutchins and provided him with many notes that detailed the land, waters, and plants of the Ohio Valley and Illinois. Known and respected by the Delaware Indians, Morgan found himself appointed as Indian agent for the Indian Affairs post at Fort Pitt in 1776, where he served until 1779. He returned to New Jersey thereafter to try his hand at applying scientific principles to farming, an interest sparked by his years in Illinois.[32] In 1788 he wrote a letter to George Washington about his experiments growing wheat that would be resistant to damage done by Hessian flies. Washington replied that he received the wheat samples and would distribute seeds to others to further the experiment.[33]

Morgan remained convinced that he could make a fortune in the West. The same year in which he wrote to Washington about his wheat he got together a group of investors to petition Congress to sell them 2 million acres of land in the Illinois County, basically the region the French had controlled along the Mississippi River for so long. The New Jersey Land Society offered one-third of a dollar per acre, and Congress actually accepted the offer at double the price. But Morgan hesitated because Congress held back some of the land along the river. Spain had charged the Spanish envoy to the United States, Diego de Gardoqui, and the governor of Louisiana, Esteban Miró, with the task of protecting the empire's interests on the Mississippi a year earlier. They closed the river to American navigation on the east bank but let it be known a few years later that American settlers would be welcome on the west bank. To one James White and his neighbors in the district of Franklin (present-day Tennessee), Miró promised land grants, free trade, and the freedom to worship as they saw fit without joining the Catholic Church, as long as they did so privately. All the Americans needed to do was separate from the United States, take an oath to the Spanish Crown, and agree to defend Spanish territory. During the summer of 1788,

Gardoqui found someone, perhaps their mutual friend Thomas Hutchins, to tell Morgan to apply to the king on similar terms to establish a colony on the banks of the Mississippi. Morgan did so, backing out of his deal with Congress.[34]

According to his biographer, one reason Morgan had not fared well in his various schemes throughout his life was that he had never been supported by a proper civil government. The king of Spain seemed to be offering the kind of stable backing that he needed. Morgan promised to bring many families with him and take an oath of allegiance to the king if his demands were met. Morgan wanted to be in control of the colony—appointing officials, distributing land, heading up militia units. He wanted a rank in the Spanish Army equivalent to his rank in the United States, 1,000 acres of land for his wife and each of his children, a salary, and word of the king's protection over his family. Morgan's land grant was to be opposite the mouth of the Ohio, and the king must promise free trade, support for schools, and the freedom to worship as they wished. The colony would provide a port of entry for Americans who wanted to trade with the Spanish in New Orleans. Give him all that, he proposed to the king, and Spain would control trade west of the Allegheny Mountains. This scheme was the last gasp of a man who lived much of his life as the subject of one king but looked to another king to make his dreams come true.[35]

Morgan moved fast, ahead of confirmation from Spain. For the initial expedition to survey the situation and the land, he published a handbill on October 3, 1788, hoping to recruit farmers and tradesmen of good character to accompany him. He told them to bring a firearm, ammunition, and a blanket. If anyone wanted a tent, they also needed to provide that for themselves. The first group of volunteers would receive 320 acres of land at one-eighth of a dollar per acre, with the choice of land based on the order in which they signed up for the expedition. All he asked was that their plots be four-sided. Many applied, and Morgan choose about seventy men from all walks of life, many of them Pennsylvanians of German descent. They set out from Pittsburgh with four boats on January 3, 1789.[36]

Before leaving, Morgan sent a report to Gardoqui, warning that the western population was on the rise, and the people resented taxes from the East when the government couldn't guarantee them access to markets. Spain needed to act fast, Morgan insisted, for the Ohio Valley had all the raw materials needed to manufacture their own goods if they failed to gain access to New Orleans. On the journey downriver, Morgan noted that Kentuckians were on the fence about allying with Spain and were interested in a British spy's propaganda currently making the rounds about the legality of seizing New Orleans. Morgan held freedom of religion and free trade to be the most important factors that would dictate the West's loyalty to Spain in the end.[37]

Morgan's handbill also laid out the kind of settlement he hoped to create. He wanted to recruit farmers and tradesmen, and he would establish a town that would welcome merchants. Teachers "will be engaged immediately," he wrote, and he also welcomed religious leaders. Morgan even stated that whole congregations could apply for land. In terms of economic incentives, he promised free navigation of the Mississippi and duty-free trade in New Orleans, where buyers would pay for their flour and tobacco with Mexican dollars. Morgan planned to set aside a plot for corn that would provide food at cheap prices during the settlers' first year in the West, as well as low-priced buffalo meat provided by hunters. Free shipping would be provided for a family's tools, as well as clothing, as long as the bundles weren't too bulky. Morgan intended to provide credit to help settlers set up their homes, bring in livestock, and plant their first crops.[38]

All looked ready to succeed when James Wilkinson upset the apple cart. Wilkinson had put his own plans in motion the year before when he approached Miró with plans to annex Kentucky. Kentuckians were ready to either negotiate with the Spanish for navigation of the Mississippi or take New Orleans by force. Wilkinson told the Spanish that rather than giving up control of the river, they should employ him as an agent to bring Kentucky under their control. All he asked in return was free trade in New Orleans for himself and his friends. Upon hearing about Morgan's plans the next year, Wilkinson told Miró that his rival was a land speculator who was twice bankrupt, and ties would remain strong between Morgan's colony and Kentucky—neither would ever be truly friendly to Spain. When Morgan arrived in New Orleans in May of 1789, he carried a letter of introduction from a man well-known to Miró—Thomas Hutchins—assuring the governor that Morgan would only recruit the best farmers, tradesmen, and artisans to settle on the west bank of the Mississippi. But Morgan found that Miró had already decided to rein in his plans. The governor offered Morgan the post of second-in-command at New Madrid, along with a small grant of land, and told him that although Americans could worship as they pleased in private, only Catholic churches would be allowed.[39]

Morgan spent a month in New Orleans making plans, returned to Philadelphia that summer, and took out advertisements for the colony, but he decided not to return to New Madrid in the end. George Morgan's biographer, Max

Savelle, speculated that Morgan's brother's death and his subsequent inheritance of lands in western Pennsylvania swayed him. The new federal Constitution was in force, and Morgan once again tried to win approval of the old Indiana Company grant. Though Morgan had aspired to be a merchant as a young man, once he began speculating in land, that remained his principal object for the rest of his career. Morgan retired to a farm outside of Pittsburgh, and when Aaron Burr came calling in 1806, Morgan wrote Thomas Jefferson to warn him of the former vice president's schemes.

A letter from New Madrid dated April 14, 1789, aimed at bringing in more people with its descriptions of fine land and clear lakes, also contained some interesting clues of what was to come. It seemed that the settlers Morgan recruited decided to ignore the advice of where to establish the town from people who knew the area. A group of French families that lived on the American bank suggested a site north of the mouth of the Ohio, and Americans from St. Louis thought they should build their town opposite of the mouth of the Ohio inland more than a mile. But they chose their own spot to the south and below another of the Ohio's tributaries. Perhaps it's not surprising that they complained of flooding over the summer and ended up moving their fort away from the river's banks. When Morgan failed to return, most of the Pennsylvanians went back east.[40]

Over the next few years, those in the West referred to the outpost there as L'Anse a la Graisse—the name New Madrid did not take hold immediately. John Halley, a Kentuckian traveling on a flatboat bound for New Orleans, described meeting Native Americans from various tribes, twenty Americans, and a few French traders when he stopped there just a month later. When Halley stopped there again two years later, he wrote of presenting the official in charge of the garrison there with a gift of two bacon hams when he received a pass to use at the next garrison downriver. Halley stopped a few more times, including at Natchez, and received a new pass for the next place south at each, before arriving in New Orleans.[41]

As for the French, they reacted to Morgan's land company grant with dismay. "The French inhabitants of Illinois" sent a memorial to Congress bemoaning the fact that Congress only intended to give them 400 acres per head of household instead of the 500 acres they had asked for. Congress decreased their reward, they wrote, because some thought that the French hadn't really suffered from Virginia's actions during the Revolution. The map Congress used for Morgan's grant was an old one, and the French were being cheated out of old Kaskaskia land, as well as grants from Americans in 1783. The French also worried about the ban on slavery in the Northwest Ordinance, stating that slave owners would be forced to move to the Spanish side of the river.[42]

After the Revolution, Morgan believed he would at last be able to make his claim to land in the Riverine West. Just as he had at last persuaded Congress to sell land to him, the Spanish king made him a tempting offer that would set him up as the leader of a colony of his own. Morgan went into it with all the enthusiasm he could muster, but James Wilkinson convinced Governor Miró in New Orleans to claw back most of the provisions that had attracted Morgan to the project, and he pulled out in the end. Perhaps it was just as well, because Morgan looked backward to a colonial past rather than forward to a republican future.

John Reed and Standish Forde intended to firmly tie the Riverine West to the United States by taking steps different from those George Morgan proposed. They would promote the growth of the new nation by supporting mills to attract settlers and sell their lots on tempting terms, ensuring that farms could get their flour to market. Reed and Forde's longest-lasting venture proved to be a store and flour mill on Ten Mile Creek, a branch of the Monongahela River, near Redstone, nearly 40 miles south of the Ohio River's headwaters at Pittsburgh. Morgantown in western Virginia lay 60 miles farther upstream. The French initially took control of the region at the beginning of the Seven Years' War, but the British pushed them out a few years later and established Fort Pitt. Colonel John Campbell laid out the city's first blocks in 1764, but Pittsburgh grew slowly during the American Revolution. Afterward, it would blossom thanks to men of commerce who outfitted settlers coming from the South and the East, heading for new homes in the Ohio Valley.[43] As for eastern goods destined for western markets, warehouses were needed to store goods when the Ohio ran low in the summer and winter, awaiting the river's rise in the spring and fall.

Standish Forde purchased the flour mill in August of 1788, hoping to export six hundred barrels of flour a year, in addition to beef, pork, and whisky. A young man named Caleb Copeland managed the business for them in western Pennsylvania. Reed and Forde regularly shipped goods to him, and he in turn collected flour to be sent to market in New Orleans. A letter from the spring of 1789 reveals some of the ins and outs of doing business in the West. Copeland had sent nearly two hundred barrels of flour on to Redstone. But, he wrote,

"Mr. Crow of Morgantown met us there and had the boat attached for a debt Mr. Forde owed him for examining some lands." Copeland averted disaster by giving Crow an IOU payable in three months and securing it with a debt from a third party owed to Reed and Forde signed over to Crow. Forde later took exception to Crow's high-handed ways. When Reed went west that fall, Forde told him to demand an apology and return of the bond Copeland had signed over. Reed was to threaten a lawsuit and ask for a more complete report of their lands, implying that the surveyor had not done his job.[44]

In addition to handling the goods for his own market, Copeland took charge of and arranged storage for goods heading farther downriver to Kentucky. At home, he often reported that business was dull and sales were slow, and at times farmers would only accept cash for their flour, refusing to be paid with goods. When their miller quit his post, Copeland recommended that his replacement be a millwright rather than a simple miller, indicating that men who could also take care of the machinery of the business were in demand. And though business may have been dull at times, other matters were heating up. Copeland wrote of sporadic violence between settlers and Native Americans, reporting that the Indians were "troublesome"—whole families of settlers had been killed within 15 miles of Ten Mile Creek, and more had been killed on the Ohio near Limestone, on the southern bank in Kentucky. By 1792, as he wrote to Reed and Forde, hiring hands to work on the boats had been getting more and more expensive—men were enlisting at garrisons in Kentucky for high wages.[45]

Caleb Copeland didn't always have an easy time of it, and sometimes farmers got the better of him. Overseeing a mill didn't quite work out. Still, it seems that Reed and Forde were doing more than just buying and selling land. Scholarly opinions about land speculation moved from labeling speculators as villains to arguing that many of them helped develop the regions, and Reed and Forde fall into the second category.

John Reed and Standish Forde would succeed where George Morgan failed by concentrating on commercial connections in the aftermath of the Revolution. The two men demonstrated how a partnership really worked in the late eighteenth century, as they alternated taking trips west. One would be home in Philadelphia while the other would be descending the Ohio and Mississippi, checking in on their lands and looking for business opportunities. One sent news east, and the other sent news west, trying to send it one city ahead of his partner. Two men, lots of trust—that was the only way to be in two places at once back in those days.

When it came to their plans to expand their network to New Orleans, linking the headwaters of the Ohio to the Gulf of Mexico and beyond, Reed and Forde used their partnership to take a very hands-on approach to business. In the fall, one or the other made their way across the mountains to tend to business in Pittsburgh and its hinterland, as well as Morgantown, and then moved on to Kentucky and, finally, Natchez and New Orleans. Forde made the journey in late 1788 / early 1789, Reed went west in the fall of 1789, then Forde a year later, and so on, usually taking turns. The partner who stayed behind sent letters with updates about prices in Philadelphia, Natchez, New Orleans, and Europe with any acquaintance who happened to be heading across the mountains, hoping to advise the traveler on the best way to invest their cash, goods, or flour, or perhaps the best way to collect their debts with news of notes that had been protested. During Reed's trip over the winter of 1789–90, it appears that intelligence did not flow back east quickly because Forde sent letter after letter asking for news so that he could arrange insurance for the trip.[46]

John Reed's meeting with the unfortunate Mr. Crow proved to be only one of many in the fall of 1789. Forde instructed Reed to visit Lancaster, Hagerstown, Clarksburg, and Morgantown, to collect debts and seek out goods, and then to take charge of the flour at their own mill and visit others along the Monongahela so that they could send as large a cargo as possible south. He mentioned a "clever fellow" he'd met the year before who could give his partner advice on which mills were the most trustworthy. Reed was to purchase oil at Redstone, to go with the kegs of paint the partners intended to send downriver, and to purchase butter and whiskey, as well as skins and furs. Forde wrote with news of a tinman heading Reed's way and asked him to find tin in Pittsburgh for the artisan and take payment in cups that would sell well in Natchez.[47]

Reed could obtain boats at Redstone, Forde wrote. He also advised that Reed should "take care to take down with you some spare tow to cork with in case of leaking—you can get pumps made near the mill at 1 doll. cash you should have one for each boat." Each 50-foot boat carried three hundred barrels of flour. Hands could be hired at Lancaster, and Forde told Reed to take care that they signed a contract to work all the way to New Orleans. Waiting at Pittsburgh for the river to rise with the fall rains proved common in the years to come. Dry weather might waylay travelers for weeks. Planning for one trip included asking a friend if he knew of anyone who wanted to transport slaves from Pittsburgh to Louisiana. If so, Reed and Forde would hire them from their owner to work on their boats heading west and south.[48]

Forde advised his partner to a use a lookout for sawyers—trees stuck in the riverbed with barely visible branches that could ensnare boats, as Elizabeth House Trist had encountered a few years before—on the Ohio. Despite such hazards, Forde advised traveling through the night rather than stopping on shore. Copeland had warned them that tensions ran high that year between Americans and the Indians of Kentucky. Once on the Mississippi, sandy beaches or low banks with willows were the safest places to land, if need be. High trees might look like good shelter, but they tended to come down in high winds because of the loose soil along the river. Reed was to be sure to have the passports ready at New Orleans.

A year later when Forde went west, he left a journal that revealed a similar process. During most of November, he traveled from town to town, conducting business along the various rivers and streams of the Upper Ohio Valley. He spent a couple of days waiting for wagons with goods to arrive from the East in Redstone, and then he loaded the goods and flour onto boats and headed for the Falls of the Ohio. Forde and his men accidently grounded the boats in the low river between the Ohio's headwaters and Wheeling, necessitating the unloading and reloading of flour on occasion, as they tried to move the boats downstream. The river's course proved to be deeper thereafter, and they made good time to Louisville at the falls.[49]

The Falls of the Ohio consist of a 2-mile stretch of rapids nearly 600 miles below Pittsburgh and represent the one major navigational hazard on the river's journey to the Mississippi (see fig. 5.2). George Rogers Clark settled there on the southern bank with others during the Revolution and attacked Native Americans to the north. Just as the growth of a commercial center was inevitable at the Ohio's headwaters, so too was the growth of such a town at the point where goods would have to be either moved by portage around the falls from one set of boats above to another below or stored, waiting for the river to rise enough for boats to make it over the rocky narrows.[50]

Once over the falls, Forde purchased flatboats and a Kentucky boat at Shippingport below. Bad weather forced them to stop on shore as they floated toward the Mississippi, and they rescued a man who had escaped from a group of Native Americans who had held him captive. They broke through ice on the lower reaches of the Ohio and then had to contend with low water and sandbars on the Mississippi. They arrived at New Madrid about seven weeks after leaving Pittsburgh. The town had been settled only the year before by George Morgan, who intended to reap the benefits of sending cotton and livestock south to Spanish markets.[51]

On one of Reed's trips, he sought to reassure Forde back in Philadelphia that

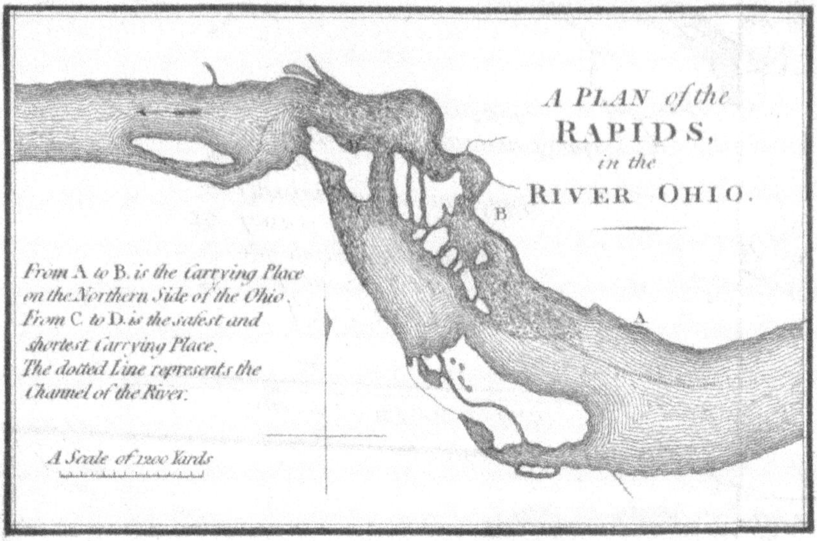

Figure 5.2. The Falls of the Ohio. John Filson, *A Map of Kentucky.* Courtesy of the Library of Congress

he would be safe. He said that he would travel in "a good boat of 40 feet the most manageable size," and for company, he had men who were good with rifles looking for a ride to the Mississippi. Reed stated that he didn't expect any problems heading south from there. According to him, attacks by Native Americans had been confined to the Ohio, with "a great many boats taken this winter." On the other hand, he told Forde, even though he didn't find any letters from his partner in Pittsburgh, Forde should make sure that any were forwarded because "boats are always coming." He painted the picture of a fairly busy river scene. His cargo on that trip included flour, lard, and goods from Philadelphia.

The partners didn't intend for all of the flour shipped from the Ohio's headwaters to reach the mouth of the Mississippi. From Natchez in January of 1792, John Reed directed William Shannon, one of their agents following behind him with the cargo, to sell a barrel here and there when he could, if there was a profit to be found. Reed told him to be on the lookout for any chance to trade flour for indigo too, which was bringing in good prices in Europe. A man couldn't be too long en route, however, for the flour that arrived down south first brought the best prices.[52]

An agreement between Reed & Forde and James Wilkinson from February 1790 lays out the situation precisely. Sending goods down the Mississippi to

Spanish territory was illegal, and their goods might be seized, so Wilkinson should use "the weight of his influence" to give them advice and secure credentials for them. In exchange for Wilkinson's letter to Gayoso, the Spanish official at Natchez, Wilkinson would receive one-fourth of the net proceeds of the goods they were sending. In addition, if any new business comes of it in Spanish territory after, Wilkinson would get one-third, but he would also share the costs and risks. The plan, Reed in Louisville wrote to Forde back home, was to "establish a profitable and permanent business down the Mississippi." Reed hoped to purchase a warehouse in Natchez to start them off. But the letter also revealed how difficult it was to get Wilkinson to pay his debts.[53]

Once Reed and Forde's goods reached the Lower Mississippi, a new array of commercial tasks awaited the partners, and they set up a store in Natchez. The British had taken possession of West Florida and Natchez, Mississippi, to the north in 1763. The settlement grew during the Revolution as a refuge for Loyalists. Settlers from the region "provided a lasting larder for New Orleans." Flour was in high demand throughout Louisiana and in Cuba as well. By the early 1780s, it was the largest town in the region north of New Orleans, with a population of one thousand free men and three hundred slaves. Residents sent regular shipments of indigo and cotton, as well as corn and tobacco, south to the Gulf of Mexico. Newcomers from the United States brought large herds of cattle in the 1780s. The Spanish encouraged further growth for a couple of years by guaranteeing a market for American tobacco in 1788. After the turn of the century, the Natchez District became best known for cotton production.[54]

American merchants in Natchez would continue to do business with Spanish settlements on the Red River through the end of the century. The Spanish brought in tallow, leather, horses, mules, and other goods from Mexico to trade with merchants from Natchez. A Frenchman named Louis Tarascon, who descended the Ohio and Mississippi Rivers in 1799, wrote that men could travel by land from New Orleans to Natchez in just under a week, buy cotton and other goods, and then take the cargo back to New Orleans down the river in five or six days, thus completing a profitable commercial circuit between the cities in two to three weeks. Tarascon reported that Natchez was full of well-stocked and well-managed stores. Trade through Natchez connected whole regions of the Mississippi Valley and the Southwest.[55]

Reed and Forde's original plans called for a man well-known to them from Fredericksburg, Virginia, John Lewis, to establish a store in Spanish territory. Lewis sent a letter to the Spanish minister to the United States, Diego de Gardoqui, expressing his interest in the Lower Mississippi. He wanted to make a new start, he said, and had heard that the Spanish wanted Americans to settle there. Lewis boasted of bringing fifty slaves (men, women, and children) with him, many of them skilled in a trade—smiths, carpenters, bricklayers, and rope makers. Reed and Forde, among others, vouched for Lewis, helping him gain permission to trade in New Orleans. Gardoqui not only answered in the affirmative but also wanted Lewis to send him two copies of the debates at the Virginia Convention. Arthur Whitaker speculated that it was Lewis who introduced Reed and Forde to James Wilkinson, knowing of their common interest in the West.[56]

After receiving official permission from Gardoqui, Lewis made a trip to New Orleans with goods provided by Reed and Forde—goods that hadn't sold at their store in Lewis's hometown. Some of the dry goods "may not do so well at Kentucky," Reed and Forde wrote, "but they will suit the Natchez."[57] Instructions for dealing with sherry, tea, sugar, powder, and chocolate followed. The partners quoted letters from contacts in New Orleans as follows: "that the Spanish government pay the planters for all the Tobacco they can raise @ 10 Dollars pr Hundred which they send to Old Spain and Mexico[—]they now allow them to bring this article from the American settlements above and a number of settlers from Kentucky and there abouts have got leave to come and settle in the Natchez District."[58] During the 1780s, the Spanish had not allowed Americans to trade in New Orleans, but they lifted that ban in 1788, partly because James Wilkinson convinced them that they might woo Kentucky and points west away from the United States. But Lewis had also been busy speculating in Kentucky lands and decided to settle there with his family in the end.[59]

Instead, a man named David Ferguson would run their store in Natchez. In the summer of 1790, he wrote that the hot weather might lead to spoiled flour. Flour prices were high, but there was little cash to be had, and most sales had to be done by credit. Ferguson also bartered flour for furs. Prospects were gloomy, however, and he advised against another shipment of goods. Planters had had their tobacco refused the past spring, and Ferguson used caution when extending credit. The next year, Ferguson proved much more optimistic—cash sales had been brisk, he wrote, and he expected to sell a big tobacco crop. A Mr. Cochran seemed to be their main competition, and Ferguson told the partners that their rival's selection of goods was "much better calculated for this place." He expected to have $700 or $800 on hand in cash for Reed when he arrived, and there would be a big crop coming in from contracts he'd made. That fall Ferguson reported that plenty of men from Kentucky were content to sell their tobacco for goods in Natchez rather than making the trip all the way to New

Orleans. Presumably, they then made their way home along the Natchez Trace. The tobacco crop was so good that year that many used it in order to settle their debts with the firm. In 1792, Ferguson wrote to Reed downriver that "the sales have been much better this spring than they have been since your commencement of business here." Unfortunately, Reed's reply from New Orleans the next week contained the bad news that the tobacco inspections had not gone well, which would curtail payments. Such was the lot of men trying to make profits on the Lower Mississippi.[60]

Reed and Forde strove to link the East and West together by helping those who wished to buy their lands get their goods to market. They didn't seek a leadership role or strive to found a town as George Morgan had done. Instead, they simply got to work personally escorting goods to market. Though the Spanish had officially closed the river, they found ways to make deals with Spanish officials to get the job done.

Newly independent Americans had to find a way to utilize a river system not under the control of one nation. After the Revolution, Philadelphia merchants exploited a new way of speculating in western lands but found that their investments did not bring as many rewards as they had hoped, especially when legal questions about navigating western rivers raised doubts about the future of the region. Eastern policymakers disappointed easterners and westerners alike when it came to gaining access to navigation on western waters. When the new nation moved slowly to stake a claim, George Morgan decided to throw his lot in with Spain, but others did not. John Reed and Standish Forde strove to build mills to attract settlers and sell their lots with tempting terms, and they successfully established commercial connections all the way to New Orleans by descending the rivers personally. The next step involved truly linking the commerce of the Riverine West to Philadelphia by way of the Gulf of Mexico, though even that left Philadelphia merchants and western settlers at the mercy of a foreign power. Clearly what was needed was bringing both banks of the rivers under the control of one nation from the Ohio's headwaters to the mouth of the Mississippi.

CHAPTER SIX

Completing the Circuit

In March of 1793, Daniel W. Coxe of Philadelphia and Daniel Clark Jr. of New Orleans wrote to inform John Reed and Standish Forde that they had formed a new firm in the southern port, hoping that together they would be able to facilitate more business for "our Friends." Clark wrote personally to the Philadelphia partners a couple weeks later to explain that competition between Coxe and himself had been harming both of their businesses and that he expected to have even more trade for them now that Coxe had become his partner. The voluminous correspondence between Reed & Forde and Coxe & Clark, among others, led historian Arthur P. Whitaker to dub Reed & Forde "merchant adventurers" and credit them with being among the first to open up trade between the new United States and Spain in New Orleans during the last decade of the eighteenth century.[1]

Before the American Revolution, Baynton, Wharton & Morgan had taken a double-pronged approach to expanding west, aiming at Illinois down the Ohio River and Pensacola by way of the Gulf of Mexico. But after the war Philadelphia merchants aimed to complete the circuit from Philadelphia down the Ohio and Mississippi Rivers and then back east by way of the Atlantic Ocean, which would bind the Riverine West firmly to the new United States once and for all. Reed and Forde opened up trade between the new United States and Spain by sending ocean-going ships to New Orleans. War broke out on the high seas in the 1790s, but imperial rivalries provided opportunities for merchants like Daniel W. Coxe and Daniel Clark Jr. to take advantage of.[2] Unfortunately, Reed & Forde began to run into real problems in 1794 just as new treaties made trade in New Orleans official and firms from New York and Baltimore rushed in to challenge the Philadelphians. The efforts of eastern merchants to fully integrate the trans-Appalachian West into the new United States would come to fruition with the Louisiana Purchase, when one nation at last controlled both banks of the Ohio and Mississippi Rivers, taking the first step toward creating a continental nation in North America.

In addition to sending flour and other goods downriver from Pittsburgh, Reed and Forde added a new dimension to their commercial plans by sending ocean-going brigs directly to the gulf-coast port loaded with flour, dry goods, and other items. The cargo shipped by brig could be sold in New Orleans or sent upriver to Natchez. Reed and Forde also profited from shipping cargo for others for the cost of freight, or by taking on passengers. One partner or the other took the trip from Philadelphia to Pittsburgh to New Orleans and back round to Philadelphia between late fall and early summer each year. Meanwhile, their brigs went back and forth between the West Indies and the Gulf Coast, as well as to Europe, on a regular basis (see fig. 6.1).

The first mention of New Orleans in a Reed & Forde daybook comes in March of 1787. It involved a man named Laidley paying another man named Vaughn for the passage of Archibald Menzies. The first adventure to New Orleans came in September of 1789 and included cigars, tea, and sugar. A handful of other names appeared in conjunction with the first adventure, as well as the store at the Monongahela. The second adventure followed the same fall and yielded profits from the sale of beaver skins. Reed & Forde launched a third adventure in the fall of 1790, with cash mentioned for the first time. New Orleans remittances started showing up regularly thereafter, and in June of 1791 came a line that read "public securities dr [debit] to New Orleans remittances." That same summer remittances from New Orleans included bear, deer, and otter skins, as well as sarsaparilla. New names popped up a few months later, and that fall, their fourth adventure included the shipment of sugar to another trio of gulf-coast businesses. There were follow-up entries for earlier trips in December of 1791, and they mention insurance premiums as well. Clearly, the overseas trade expanded their contacts greatly.[3]

Arthur Whitaker speculated that it was John Lewis of Virginia who introduced Reed and Forde to James Wilkinson. The partners backed Wilkinson's

Figure 6.1. The Lower Mississippi in the eighteenth century. © Seth Rainey

gambits down the Mississippi in 1788 and 1789 but were left with nothing but IOUs from Wilkinson totaling £2,300 that he never paid back. Reed and Forde had managed to procure a passport from Diego de Gardoqui, and Forde joined the expedition to New Orleans in 1789, but they still lacked an official Spanish permit to trade in the port. They next turned to Philadelphia merchant Joseph Ball, who obtained a permit for them from Oliver Pollock. Whitaker writes that although there are no official agreements to be found between Reed, Forde, and Ball in their papers, Ball clearly provided them with capital to begin trade.[4] Other records indicate that Reed was deeply in debt to Ball after Forde's death ended their partnership in 1806, so Whitaker's conclusion is most likely the correct one. In 1791, five of the nine ships that arrived in Philadelphia from New Orleans came with "cargoes that were consigned wholly or in large part to Reed and Forde." One of the ships was their own *Gayoso*, probably named for the governor of Natchez, Manuel Gayoso de Lemos.[5]

Much of Reed & Forde's initial correspondence with men in the port of New Orleans revolved around news of protested bills and lawsuits, shipping news, and orders for goods. A man named Daniel Hodge wrote most often, and in addition to his usual report on the legal front he stated that men were coming from Kentucky during the spring of 1789 and making good sales on both tobacco and provisions. During Reed's trip to the Riverine West from the fall of 1791 through the spring of 1792, Forde wrote letters hoping to catch his partner at various stages in his journey, advising him to buy as much indigo as possible because it was selling well in the East. He told Reed to invest in goods to send to Europe too—shipping rates had recently fallen, but tobacco was in high demand.[6] For a few years, they had been squabbling with their London suppliers over debts, but that fall Forde had high hopes for sales in France. "Hold the proceeds to our order," he wrote, "as it may possibly suit us better to sell Bills on France than direct the proceeds remitted to London."[7]

The range of business conducted between Reed & Forde and their contacts can be seen in entries related to a man named Jonathan Arnold who often accompanied their shipments involving tobacco. Arnold first showed up in Reed & Forde's daybook in conjunction with a partner in May of 1791—"sundries dr to sales a/Arnold & Holmes." Other entries followed: "to sales a/Jonathan Arnold for 3 HH [hogsheads] tobacco," and later that month, "to sales a/Arnold & Holmes, beaver and fox skins." A couple weeks later the amount of tobacco was much larger—seventy hogsheads split into two entries. And then in June: "Andrew Holmes dr to slaves Arnold & Holmes." A later entry reads "Jonathan Arnold for one half balance of Capt Petisclowe outfits." Sometimes Arnold sold the tobacco on his own and simply paid for freight, but in July Reed and Forde shipped tobacco on their ship *Gayoso* "in co[mpany]" with Arnold, and that same month, Arnold's entries included totals for porterage and sales. More tobacco followed, and then "to sales a/Arnold & Holmes for 2 bundles of beaver," as well as otter and deer skins, and in August, New Orleans remittances shipped on *Prospero*, again selling "in co with" Arnold. In December, a Reed & Forde entry makes reference to "his half profits" and "expenses at New Orleans," as well as to "commission on said sales [candles] with Jona Arnold."[8]

Lines in a daybook are not meant to reveal much about a business association, but Jonathan Arnold wrote a letter to his brother in Providence from New Orleans in 1792 that tells us more about what he experienced. After riding out a storm along the coast, it took twelve days to sail from Cape France to New Orleans. When he arrived in the port, he said that he was "kindly received by the officers" and had no problems with his cargo. Arnold wrote about a French baker who was supposed to buy flour and butter but tried to cheat them. The baker was still in the garrison, Arnold reported, perhaps because the Spanish governor had sided with the American merchant. Arnold wrote that markets were dull, butter sales were down, and they would take a loss. He relayed that "Andrew Holms is not yet arrived I hope he will not be ketched by the Indians," adding that men on other boats who had made the journey down the Mississippi said that Holms was still in Kentucky. Other news included the fact that Samuel Brenton, a New Yorker who now resided in the West Indies, also languished in jail; for what offense Arnold does not say.[9]

Daniel W. Coxe appeared as another regular associate in Reed & Forde's daybook. The first Coxe brother to show up there was actually William, partner for a time of John Donaldson. They bought cloth from him and were sometimes paid by others with drafts drawn on Donaldson & Coxe in 1785. Daniel W. Coxe's first entry comes in July 1791 and concerned an "Adventure *Gayoso* in Co DW Coxe." The outfitting of and loading of the brig took up a couple of pages of entries—it was a large and varied shipment. At one point, the partners noted that they paid Coxe £850.0.0 for his half of the cost. A few days later Coxe paid Reed and Forde £695.15.8. Thereafter, Coxe served as a regular fixture in the daybook in relation to various payments to and from third parties, notes and drafts, and other entries such as wagon fees to Pittsburgh. That fall, the three of them launched another venture with the ship *Prospero*.[10]

The planning that went into Reed and Forde's western ventures in the summer of 1791 and the business decisions that came during and after reveal much about the lengths Philadelphia merchants went to in order to extend their networks to the Ohio and Mississippi Valleys. In August, Forde visited their mill on the Monongahela to assemble a cargo of flour and other goods and arrange for the building of a boat to ship it downriver. Knowing that a fellow merchant wished to travel to Natchez, Reed wrote him and offered to help him go by river rather than by sea, arguing that it would be a faster and easier journey. If the man took him up on it, he would soon find out that Reed probably downplayed the toll various delays would take. In the meantime, Forde returned home, and Reed headed west. Forde wrote to Captain Thomas Porteu, the commandant at L'Anse a la Graisse, just below the Ohio on the Mississippi, that Reed would pass through with goods that could be paid for with either skins or a note on New Orleans. Forde and Porteu had met the previous year in New Orleans, and Forde reminded him that they had discussed the difficulties in shipping goods up the Mississippi River, in terms of both prices and lost cargo. Another of the tasks Reed meant to accomplish on the trip involved evaluating the situation of their store in Natchez. The Spanish governor in New Orleans had recently granted a three-year moratorium on the collection of debts from hard-pressed planters, and the Philadelphia partners despaired of ever collecting what was owed them there.[11]

A slave revolt in the French colony of St. Domingue in August of 1791 meant that Forde had to revise some of their plans. Ships bound for New Orleans had been detained, and Forde decided that sending a new shipment of flour by sea could allow the firm to take advantage of rising prices there. Forde referenced the slave revolt often over the next year, indicating that it disrupted trade for a time. Daniel Coxe had set out for New Orleans by sea on one of their brigs in July to sell goods in combination with Reed and Forde, so he would be there to take charge of the latest shipment. The new cargo included wine that couldn't be shipped to New York because they hadn't had the proper containers to unload it when the brig arrived in Philadelphia. Early the next year, Forde met with further setbacks because a cold winter had closed access to Philadelphia itself. Ships couldn't sail, meaning that the firm would be stuck with out-of-season items. A similar situation a few years later led to selling indigo for a smaller profit in New York because the ship couldn't reach Philadelphia when the prices rose.[12]

In the meantime, Reed sent a letter from Pittsburgh reporting that he had to wait there longer than expected because the river hadn't risen enough to begin his journey. That was the last letter from Reed for some months, and when news came from other sources that warfare had broken out on the Ohio River, Forde worried that the army might have demanded some of their flour to provision troops. Back in contact once again in March, Forde passed along the news that the slave revolt in the West Indies had resulted in high prices for molasses and sugar from Cuba—if Reed could obtain some at low prices in the Riverine West, it would sell well to Atlantic markets. Otter pelts were in high demand, and in fact pelts of all sorts would sell, except for bear skins. Furs and skins had to be packed carefully, though, because when shipments arrived with damage from worms their value dropped. Forde passed along similar news and instructions to Daniel Coxe in New Orleans, and in fact Forde instructed Coxe to open the accompanying letter to Reed if his partner hadn't arrived yet in order to complete the tasks himself.[13]

Reed and Forde dispatched ships regularly to New Orleans, and Reed would take one of them home in the late spring of 1792 after completing his business along the journey from the Ohio's headwaters to the Gulf Coast. The voyage from New Orleans to Philadelphia took about three weeks. Forde wrote to friends and associates in Fredericksburg, Virginia, that he hoped to visit them soon, but he could not leave until Reed arrived. One partner or the other always stayed in Philadelphia—Forde had written of riding hard to return from Ten Mile Creek the fall before so that Reed could set out on his fall trip. While he waited for Reed's return in May of 1792, Forde tinkered with their plans to invest in various kinds of state certificates and corresponded with old friend Peter Anspach in New York about US bank stocks. Congress had adjourned, he wrote a friend, without settling the issue of assuming state debts, but they might be able to arrange loans using leftover continental debts. Reed arrived home on June 7 and oversaw the firm's plans that summer.[14]

Reed sent a letter informing another merchant that friends in Natchez were well and that they had a brig departing soon if he wanted to send along any articles or letters to Louisiana. He instructed Captain Graisbury to stop at Cape Francois to obtain permission to trade in New Orleans from the Spanish consul with the help of a local firm and gifts that included candles and a small mahogany desk. When Graisbury arrived at Fort Balize at the mouth of the Mississippi (see fig. 2.1), a barrel of port and a piece of the most fashionable muslin for the commandant's wife would speed their way up the river, and Daniel Clark would take Graisbury to the Customs House to commence their business upon his arrival. Reed had seen for himself the great demand for Kentucky tobacco in New Orleans earlier that year, and he thought that their shipment from upriver might sell there, rather than needing to send it on to France. He wrote to Clark that he wished him to load up the brig with logwood for ballast, topping it off with furs and skins. Reed indicated that if others would ship goods with them at a high freight price, he could go that route instead of investing in a cargo of their own, or Clark could procure passengers. Taking on passengers sometimes yielded a higher profit than trading in goods. With the stops for Spanish paperwork added to loading and unloading cargo, a brig could make the round trip from Philadelphia to New Orleans and back in four months.[15]

Tensions on the Ohio River alluded to the fall before seemed to have grown by October of 1792. Fearing raids by Native Americans, Reed informed Captain Thomas Porteu that they would be sending a smaller parcel of goods than intended and would not be making the trip themselves. Robert Cochran would be their agent as he made his way home to Louisiana by way of Pittsburgh. Reed provided Cochran with an English translation of the letter written in French to Porteu. Perhaps Reed and Forde curtailed their usual trip because of a glut of flour from western Pennsylvania in New Orleans that led to lowered prices. In November, Reed told Clark that if he could buy damaged flour cheap it would sell in Philadelphia to bakers for making biscuits. Reed and Forde sought to expand the range of goods they shipped to New Orleans by sea, asking Clark about the market for dry goods, lime, marble, millstones, and mahogany furniture. They also intended to ship flour, cider, and bar iron to Savannah. Something must have changed by winter, however, because later correspondence indicated that Reed did make a trip west in early 1793.[16]

The following summer, other opportunities beckoned. A man named Charles Ewing contacted Reed and Forde, offering them some kind of ore that he intended to procure from the Chickasaw Indians in June. Forde sent a letter telling Ewing to "go among them" to obtain the minerals, contact Ferguson in Natchez for boatmen, and then ship it to Philadelphia through Daniel Clark's hands in New Orleans. Reed and Forde could not offer any dry goods but would send other sorts for barter. They did not intend to send any goods before Ewing had actually secured the ore, however. Apparently, they viewed this as a risky venture.[17]

According to Reed and Forde, by the fall of 1792 people in Philadelphia expected Spain to declare war on France any day. Reed and Forde hoped that Daniel Clark Jr. would still be able to obtain permission for them to trade in the Spanish port. They wrote to Captain Graisbury and warned him to be ready with both Spanish and American papers when he left the Mississippi River and entered the Gulf as he headed home. If the ship were to be boarded, Graisbury should convince those in charge that he was an American and try to return to New Orleans to ask for Clark's advice. A month later Reed and Forde instructed Captain Jonas Keen to hoist the Spanish colors at Balize, stop by and give the Spanish commandant a barrel of cider, and act as though the ship belonged to Daniel Clark Jr. When Keen visited Spanish ports in the region, they advised him to be respectful and avoid talking about politics or religion—if he did so, officials would be helpful.[18]

Rumors became reality when war broke out between Great Britain and France during the winter of 1793, with Spain joining in soon thereafter. Daniel W. Coxe and Daniel Clark Jr. established their partnership, and much trade followed. In June of 1793, Forde wrote to his partner that he had no news from the Mississippi since Reed had left on the firm's annual trip west, but he expected provisions to be in high demand in New Orleans, so Reed should buy as much flour as he could to send south. A little less than two weeks later, though, Forde reported that Captain Webb had arrived from New Orleans with $1,060, and Daniel W. Coxe had followed with an additional $2,000 in payments. Forde told his partner that all ships were now permitted to leave New Orleans for any United States port and to return there as well. He warned of reports of privateers along the coast. Forde wanted Reed to gather up all the flour, beef, pork, whiskey, butter, and lard he could in Kentucky to send to New Orleans. Later that summer, Reed and Forde, along with Captain John Wheeler, purchased the sloop *Ulalia* from another trio for unspecified Kentucky merchandise and $550. They spent the next two weeks repairing and outfitting the ship—buying all manner of timber, hardware, tools, and the like. On September 6, Wheeler sailed for New Orleans with a cargo of flour and cheese to be delivered to Clark in New Orleans. Along the way, Wheeler seems to have delivered a quantity of salt. At New Orleans the captain picked up indigo, cigars, and a group of passengers, including women and children, and headed back to Philadelphia on April 13, 1794. In June, the *Ulalia* made a voyage to a port in Haiti. The cargo included flour, pork, crackers, beef, and corn meal. The expenses included duties, passports, various fees at port, bags and twine, commissions on sales and purchasing, and perhaps the short-term use of a slave. It is likely that they would return with a cargo of coffee. The run to this port seemed to be the *Ulalia*'s regular route over the next few years, with wines, dry goods, oil, and spices added into the mix.[19]

Reed and Forde initially prospered during the opening years of the war. Americans flew Spanish colors on the Mississippi River and American colors once they reached New Orleans, where they could trade as neutrals. During the spring of 1794, Reed received news that a body of armed men were stopping boats heading for Spanish territory at the mouth of the Cumberland River—a number of adventures had been turned back. Reed and Forde had an easier time of it, thanks to their passports. Privateers captured the *Gayoso* as a prize at one point, but officials in New Orleans released it when it reached port. Reed and Forde also expanded their business in 1794 to Bordeaux, where they hoped to exchange both western lands and a cargo from New Orleans for brandy and wine, among other goods. Unfortunately, their French cargo fared poorly in Philadelphia, and other ships fell to privateers without the lucky escape afforded the *Gayoso* the year before. They closed their store in Natchez and managed to sell over $2,000 worth of their leftover inventory to government agents when the United States took over Natchez in 1797 as per Pinckney's Treaty two years before. Reed and Forde continued to consign cargoes to other Philadelphia merchants heading for New Orleans in the years that followed, but their most active years of trading on the Lower Mississippi were over.[20]

The Philadelphia merchant who forged the most direct link with the port of New Orleans was Reed and Forde's sometime associate Daniel W. Coxe, who entered into a partnership with Daniel Clark Jr. The first Daniel, brother of Tench Coxe, who began his political career as a delegate to the Annapolis Convention and moved on to become assistant treasury secretary under Alexander Hamilton, had been born into a well-respected Philadelphia family. Daniel Clark Jr. had been born in Ireland and emigrated for a time to Pennsylvania, before moving to New Orleans in the 1780s to work for his uncle Daniel Clark Sr., who had established his mercantile establishment in New Orleans the decade before. Quickly becoming fluent in both French and Spanish, Clark established ties to both fellow merchants and government officials in his new home. There were new opportunities in New Orleans after the war. Coxe brought his good Philadelphia name to the endeavor, and Clark brought his facility for languages and working the angles. When Coxe and Clark became partners, they provided one of the most visible connections between the two ports during the last decade of the eighteenth century.[21]

After the Revolution, trade between Philadelphia and New Orleans increased as American merchants sought access to specie. Merchants from other cities began to take an interest too, however. In 1782, a New Orleans merchant named Juan Baptiste McCarty made deals to buy flour from a New York merchant named Nicholas Low, a Baltimore merchant named William Smith, and his son Robert in Havana.[22] As previous chapters have shown, it all started with Oliver Pollock and others who made inroads into Cuba during the later stages of the Seven Years' War. Historian Linda K. Salvucci writes about the expansion of those ties during the American Revolution. Robert Morris wanted silver to pay the troops; Cuba wanted flour. After the war, when the British blocked trade with their colonies in the West Indies, Philadelphia merchants made up for that lack and then some with more Cuban trade. In the 1790s, if merchants brought slaves to sell, they were allowed to sell more flour in Cuba. Francisco Rendon was a Spanish agent in Philadelphia from 1779 to 1786 and came to know Morris well; he went on to be the Spanish intendant in New Orleans from 1793 to 1796.[23]

In February of 1792, Oliver Pollock wrote a memo characterizing the Lower Mississippi that allows us to visualize the port that sits 100 miles from the coast. He stated that the land west of New Orleans was "not entirely sunken" and that he thought it could be "reclaimed." Fort St. Marie lay between river and lake, and he thought that it would be a good center for trade, mentioning a nearby

Spanish settlement. Pollock believed that it was actually a more accessible spot for boats, but that New Orleans had an advantage when it came to communication with the lake. The Mississippi ran a very crooked course that required careful maneuvering—finding deep waters along one bank or the other involved following eddies. Because of this, Pollock came to the conclusion that boundary lines along banks of the river would not be very effective: "the river would be useless to both Americans & the Spanish were it not free to both in its whole breadth."[24]

Letters from a man named Don Estevan Pontalba provide insight into how residents were feeling at the time. Pontalba wrote to Miró in spring of 1792 about rum and sugar, Havana and Cadiz. One of his ships had a French name, and the others went by the names *Louisiana* and *Mississippi*. Pontalba wrote about the citizenship of ship owners and captains, which seemed to indicate that Coxe and Clark's dance was to make sure things were legal. The maneuverings of Spain and France, the Haiti revolt, and trade between the Caribbean and the Gulf Coast were all part of this story. Pontalba wrote that the state of mind on the Lower Mississippi was one of worrying about Americans—residents believed that the Americans were coming. Rice prices were high, and only those of European descent could afford it. He reported that "negroes can hardly get any." Plantation owners fed bread to their servants instead. Pontalba attributed some of the price fluctuations to the uncertainty over people he labeled in another letter as "the enemy." Pontalba painted a picture of a plantation economy well established in 1792. His news was full of crops grown by slaves—tobacco, rice, sugar. He wrote of trying to decide what to feed his slaves and about fears that the slaves would follow the lead of those at St. Domingue. People helped their neighbors—when one planter had trouble with water levels in the middle of the night, others pitched in to help.[25]

Into this evolving international place, Daniel W. Coxe and Daniel Clark Jr. decided to combine one's Philadelphia connections with the other's knowledge of the Gulf Coast. In March of 1793, Coxe and Clark wrote to Reed and Forde that they had formed a new firm, hoping that together they would be able to facilitate more business for "our Friends." They believed that trade in New Orleans would grow, especially if war broke out between England and France and Spain joined the conflict. They mentioned trade with the Spanish Empire specifically, stating that the government "will doubtless continue" to wink at "the mode in which the business is carried out." It would be Clark's connections that got the job done.[26] The relationship between Coxe from Philadelphia and Clark from New Orleans seemed to be a very warm and friendly one. At the end of one letter, Clark wrote about being "confined" in New Orleans for the past five years, complaining that he had never been in one place for so long. He seemed to be anticipating that Coxe would join him in the southern port, but if he did, Clark wrote that Coxe would need to learn to be patient. It's all business in Coxe's letters to Reed and Forde, but with Clark real friendship seemed to be involved.[27]

The governor at this time was Luis Héctor de Carondelet, having replaced Miró in 1791. Philadelphia merchants worried that he would try to shut down trade on the Mississippi during the summer of 1792. Philadelphia merchants had enjoyed good relations with Miró for the most part, but Reed and Forde expected Carondelet to be harder to get around and speculated that they would have to pay duties to trade on the river going forward. His time in office was plagued by unrest inspired by the French Revolution, then threats of French attacks in 1793 and 1794, and finally attacks by the British in 1796 and 1797. He had participated in the American Revolution in the Caribbean and at Pensacola. Carondelet tried to create alliances with Native Americans in the region and open up the port to free trade. Under his watch, the Spanish started building a canal to link Lake Pontchartrain to the Mississippi, but all his work came to naught thanks to Pinckney's Treaty. Still, this was the man in power during most of Coxe and Clarke's initial schemes.[28]

Daniel Clark Jr. wanted to expand their networks and connections. That same spring, Coxe and Clark told Reed and Forde that they had had trouble disposing of goods shipped on the *Betsy* and the *Molly*. Two ships from England had arrived the previous fall and glutted the market with dry goods, especially woolens and linen. They had a schooner there registered under Coxe's name, and it needed to stay that way. Transferring it to one of the captains would trigger a tax of 6 percent and a foreign duty of 21 percent if the ship didn't return. Clark complained about the quality of the flour, stating that he could only sell it to the baker who fed the troops. The Natchez contingent had just arrived in March with crops to sell, and Clark had yet to press them for remittances owed to Reed & Forde. Clark complained about the dry goods too, mostly stating that what arrived wasn't best suited for the market. Coxe & Clark sold at two to four months credit, writing that other merchants offered longer credit. Clark was hopeful about trade with the Chickasaw Indians, however, and wanted Reed and Forde to send more flour. In April, Clark wrote that "the probability of war between France & Spain has had a great effect on the price of certain articles," including wine, soap, and oil. A "handsome profit" could be made on any bargains, but he advised against sending any more dry goods in the near future. Later that month, Clark wrote that the government had forbidden all trade with French ports, but Clark had permission to trade directly with the United States, England, and Holland. As usual, Clark portrayed such goings-on as an opportunity to expand their trade. That summer, Clark's maneuvering between empires continued, but the situation worsened that fall.[29]

Trade between the United States and Bordeaux took off in 1793 for various reasons. In January of 1794, Daniel Coxe embarked on a trip to France on a venture he made in partnership with Reed and Forde. He arrived in Bordeaux in March and reported that "two thirds of their vessels came here in ballast in search of freights from England & Spain etc which I am persuaded is almost the sole cause of the general embargo." Coxe worked with a French merchant to sell their goods. France had laws about prices at that time that brought down the value of other goods, though hides, bear skins, and indigo would sell. Coxe intended to buy large quantities of wine on this trip, some of which Reed and Forde would then forward to Clark in New Orleans. At one point he bought 300 tons of "old wine" in casks in Paris using half of the "Virginia lands" as security. The bill would be due in eight months. Another Philadelphia speculator named Major Jackson was also in town trying to sell nearly 1 million acres of land, without success. When Coxe tried to leave in May, he ran afoul of government regulations and had trouble obtaining a passport. He sent the wine on, instructing Reed and Forde to add flour and dry goods to the cargo before sending it on to Louisiana. He managed to sell their cargo of cotton, pelts, deerskins, pimento, logwood, tobacco, and indigo.[30] The French were seizing ships at that time. Two set out for the United States in August and split up along the way. Unfortunately for Daniel Coxe, the one he took was captured by a French privateer, and he ended up being taken to Bermuda, where he had to fight to keep possession of his cargo.[31]

In March of 1794, Clark wrote to Reed and Forde that there were too many ships in New Orleans, recommending that they cut back. He deemed one ship too small to bring in a large-enough cargo of salt. Highlighting the differences between doing business with Spanish and British ports, Clark told Reed and Forde that he didn't have anything to send on the *Molly* that would sell at Spanish ports. Clark planned to send the ship to London instead and stop at New York on the way to pick up anything else that would fit in the hold. Indigo sold well in London, but some of the indigo he had on hand in New Orleans wasn't high enough in quality to sell there.[32]

Things were heating up between empires in the summer and fall of 1795. Coxe and Clark advised one of their contacts that if they bought a vessel to send to the port, they needed to be sure that the captain and first mate were either Spanish or residents of New Orleans for their first trip. Once in New Orleans, they could switch to an American crew. By October, there was a new Circular of Commerce that put a duty in place of 15 percent. Not being allowed to trade with any ports in the Spanish West Indies "considerably deranged us and will be most hurtful in the future," the partners wrote in October. They told their eastern contacts to ship finer goods in smaller shipments to lessen the affect. Clark advised Reed and Forde to sell or exchange the *Molly*, for she was too "well known to bring back under another name." Clark wrote Coxe that he alone had found a way to circumvent the duty and hoped that it would keep others away.

Reed and Forde pulled back from their efforts to corner the trade on the Lower Mississippi at roughly this time. They had ships seized by both the British and privateers in 1794, while rumors of French schemes halted the deployment of others. Reed & Forde wrote Daniel Clark Jr. that they could not fulfill a contract for shoes thanks to the Whiskey Rebellion in western Pennsylvania: "The shoemakers with whom we have contracted have all been on campaign against Western Insurgents."[33] They also closed their store in Natchez. Relations had not always been smooth between Reed & Forde and Coxe & Clark, and in 1796 they sank further. The Philadelphia partners complained that remittances were not forthcoming from New Orleans, but Daniel Clark Jr. blamed problems on Reed & Forde's choice of goods and shipping practices. A shipment of broken glass, the wrong color of nankeen, spoiled raisins—the list went on. Clark blamed some of the problems on deals between the Philadelphians, including his partner Coxe, that excluded him. Clark's connections with the powers that be in New Orleans gave him the upper hand in many ways, though. The domino effect, such as when companies like Conkling & Lloyd in New York suspended payments, also wreaked havoc.[34] The final years of their business continued on with trade in Europe, as well as investing in bank stock and trying to get rid of unsold lands. As with George Morgan, the fortune Reed and Forde expected to find in the West never materialized.[35]

When it came to linking trade on the Lower Mississippi and New Orleans to the port of Philadelphia, Daniel W. Coxe and Daniel Clark Jr. completed the circuit, integrating the commerce of the Riverine West with that of the Atlantic World. Reed & Forde set up commercial connections from Philadelphia down the Ohio and Mississippi Rivers, and Coxe & Clark provided a direct link between the ports. Coxe was a man of good stock with ties to the new government in Philadelphia, and Clark spoke fluent Spanish and knew how to work the system in New Orleans. The two men made the most of trading opportunities opened up by war in Europe and on the high seas.

Though Reed and Forde failed in the end, other merchants who followed in their footsteps succeeded. Pinckney's Treaty would bring a flood of merchants from New York and Baltimore who would compete with Philadelphia's contingent for control of trade on the Lower Mississippi River. Spain had rebuilt New Orleans after citywide fires in 1788 and 1794, and the city stood ready to become a major commercial port. France would enter the picture once again at the turn of the century, and in the end the United States would purchase Louisiana. At last, the Philadelphia merchants who had labored for a half century to integrate the western waters into the Atlantic World would see their goals come to fruition when one nation controlled both banks of the Ohio and Mississippi Rivers from Pittsburgh to New Orleans at last, and the United States would be well on its way to establishing a continental empire.

Jay's Treaty of 1794 had worried the Spanish because they didn't like to see the Americans cozy up to the English, and so they sought a remedy. The two nations signed the Treaty of Friendship, Limits, and Navigation Between Spain and the United States, more commonly known as Pinckney's Treaty or the Treaty of San Lorenzo, in October of 1795, and it went into effect the next August. The treaty settled the boundary between the United States and West Florida and opened navigation on the Mississippi River to both American and Spanish boats. Secretary of State Thomas Jefferson instructed the negotiators to argue that Americans had a natural right to trade on the Mississippi because trade on rivers and oceans should be open to all. "Spain does not grant us navigation of the river," he wrote; "we have an inherent right to it."[36] Americans no longer had to pay duties to ship cargo through New Orleans—that had been the biggest sticking point in the treaty negotiations and the provision that the Spanish held out on the longest before conceding. Americans flooded into New Orleans in 1796 and 1797. Spain tried to stem the flow by refusing to grant them land in 1798, but by then the Americans had become firmly entrenched.[37]

The Chickasaws would suffer the most under the treaty, which was signed without their consent. After the American Revolution, some Chickasaws wanted to expand their trade with the Americans, while others thought that Spain would be a better ally. Both nations wanted to build a fort in their territory at Chickasaw Bluffs (modern-day Memphis, Tennessee), but the Chickasaws refused them, wanting to keep their options open, though in the end they allowed the Spanish to build a fort at the Yazoo River instead. In 1794, land speculators from Georgia tried to lay claim to land along the Mississippi River and passed the Yazoo Act in early 1795, which ignored both Spanish and Chickasaw claims to the territory. The Chickasaws decided to allow the Spanish to build a fort at Chickasaw Bluffs after all, but the passage of Pinckney's Treaty later that year would render that moot.[38]

The United States established the Mississippi Territory in 1798, with a southern boundary drawn east from Natchez to Florida, leaving the Gulf Coast to the Spanish. But the Spanish did not abruptly disappear north of the new line. An account book of merchant Abijah Hunt from 1797–98 provides a snapshot of trade on the rivers between Louisville and Natchez. Hunt sold whiskey, ribbon, brandy, bacon, thread, linen, and tea to many men who held the rank of "Captain" in early June. Two weeks later, the pages were filled with mention of linen, silk, calico, brandy, cider, sugar, ribbons, and nails. The merchant arrived at Fort Massac on the Ohio in July.[39] Frenchman Louis Tarascon, who came to the United States during the French Revolution, seemed especially impressed when he arrived in 1799. Native Americans provided furs, Illinois merchants would welcome supplies, and French and Spanish settlements were within striking distance.[40] The Spanish figured prominently in Tarascon's journal as he described settlements in Illinois and along the Mississippi River near St. Louis.[41]

Hunt did most of his business that summer at Chickasaw Bluffs in Tennessee, staying through November of 1797. The Spanish were there that summer, seemingly intent on reoccupying it despite Pinckney's Treaty. The merchant sold lots of whiskey, nails, thread, and brandy. Entries at Natchez include women for the first time—both single and married. Many of the customers were soldiers, and the merchant listed a number of drafts on Philadelphia.[42] Louis Tarascon also wrote of Natchez, noting that merchants took certificates from the owners of cotton mills as payment, or cash from tobacco warehouses. They could trade at New Orleans or with Spanish settlements on the Red River that funneled to and from Mexico trade in tallow, leather, horses, mules, and flour, among other things. Pointe Coupée supported two sugar refineries. The sugar trade was going strong in New Orleans, and plantation owners made good profits from the labor of slaves.[43]

In 1798, Hunt moved on to Natchez. After the Revolution, Spain used the lure of land to attract Americans to settle at Natchez, allowing them to trade freely if they swore an oath of allegiance to the Crown. Many found it easier to acquire land there than in Kentucky, and the Spanish welcomed planters with slaves. After the passage of Pinckney's Treaty, it wasn't immediately clear whether the area would become a territory of its own or would become an extension of Georgia. Two years before Gayoso, as the Spanish official in charge of the Natchez District, had told the Chickasaws that Spain would never give up the region, and after the empire let it go, he feared that they might attack Spanish settlements. In addition, Gayoso hoped that unhappy whiskey rebels might come and bolster those who were loyal to Spain. When he became the governor of Louisiana, he only reluctantly gave way to the Americans in 1797. Over the next few years, more Americans came with slaves, and they brought with them a new technology—the cotton gin. Cotton quickly superseded tobacco as the region's most important export, and Susan Gaunt Stearns writes that Natchez cotton planters would be among those pushing the hardest for the acquisition of Louisiana when Spain ceded New Orleans to France shortly thereafter.[44]

Farther south, Abijah Hunt did business at Loftus Heights, Mississippi, about 40 miles south of Natchez and 6 miles north of the boundary line established by Pinckney's Treaty. The American army began moving in to occupy the Mississippi Valley in 1797, and they built Fort Adams there in 1799. A traveler named Fortescue Cuming wrote that the Mississippi was not particularly wide at this point, and the fort sat on a bluff 100 feet above the river, making it an excellent lookout post—"the fort completely commands it" with cannons in place. One could see "the meanders of the river for several miles." If the Spanish tried to make any military maneuvers, the Americans would see and stop them. The fort's personnel also collected cargo duties from ships coming north into American territory on the river.[45] Tarascon characterized Loftus Heights as the last outpost of the United States on the Mississippi, 6 miles from the border between the new nation and Spanish territory. Spanish settlements on the Red River brought in trade from Mexico to the Mississippi Valley. He credited the success of refineries in New Orleans to Spanish methods of cultivating sugar. Spanish control created trouble in New Orleans, though—goods had to be consumed in the city rather than being sent on to other Spanish settlements, though they could be traded to other nations.[46]

During the last decade of the eighteenth century, the Spanish transformed New Orleans. The French port had consisted of low, wooden buildings, susceptible to both fire and floods. In March of 1788 a fire broke out that destroyed over three-quarters of the city, including most of the public buildings. Governor Miró saw to it that the homeless had tents and that the merchants did not raise the prices of necessary goods. Ignoring Spanish commercial policies at that time, he sent ships to Philadelphia and New York for flour, rice, medicine, and other provisions and petitioned the king to pardon men who had been sent to prison for trading with the United States. Miró and other officials had been allowing illegal trade for years because the city needed supplies, but the fire pushed the colonial government to make such trade official. Oliver Pollock sold the city a pump fire engine. The Spanish intended to rebuild with brick walls, tile roofs, and wrought iron balconies when another fire in 1794 encouraged strict enforcement of the new building policies. Historian Cindy Ermus concludes that the 1788 fire was a "major, transformative event" that only strengthened ties between New Orleans and the United States.[47]

Related by marriage to Philadelphia's Pile family, a member of the Morgan family described some lean years in the mid-1790s even as New Orleans grew. Philadelphia merchant Thomas Morgan had a daughter named Rebecca who married an ocean-going captain named Samuel Pile. Her brother George W. Morgan, using both his father's and his brother-in-law's connections to establish himself as a merchant, moved to New Orleans in 1793. He seems to have gotten off to a slow start. In the spring of 1794, he asked his sister to send him two dozen pairs of shoes and 50 pounds of chocolate for the New Orleans market, and he offered to sell any cravats she made. In the fall, he sent her $35 to invest in hair powder. George characterized himself as poor and new to trade, a beginner, who needed to add to his "small capital." The next year, he wrote to his father that sales were "trifling," but he was always looking for a chance to speculate with a small sum.[48]

George's older brother, Thomas Morgan Jr., showed up in New Orleans from time to time, but he seems to have emulated their brother-in-law Samuel, becoming a ship's captain in the end. Though George had already resided in New Orleans for nearly two years, Thomas advised him to learn French and give Wykoff & Garland no reason to doubt him. George W. Morgan's relationship with that firm is not clear, but when they dissolved their business in 1798, Morgan hoped to partner with Wykoff himself. In 1799, Morgan wrote his sister that he had been in New Orleans for six years with no salary and thanked her for her help over the years.[49]

In New Orleans, the agents of Philadelphia merchants held their own, but others from New York and Baltimore made their presence felt. William Taylor of Baltimore sent a young man named John McDonogh to act as his agent in New Orleans in 1800, and another man, Shepherd Brown, the next year. McDonogh took a cargo to London in the summer of 1801 and returned with a shipload of goods to sell. In the meantime, Brown went upriver to Natchez to invest in cotton on Taylor's behalf. Taylor sent a cargo as far upriver as Loftus Heights in 1801. By 1802, Taylor was commissioning a large variety of goods to McDonogh in New Orleans, including dry goods, wines, and tools.[50]

A New York merchant named John Pintard visited New Orleans in 1801. Amid descriptions of the fort and the troops who manned it, Pintard chronicled the actions of officials determined to put an end to smuggling. Ships on the Mississippi hugged the shores, and not far from the city he took note of sugar plantations with slave huts and orange trees. The streets of New Orleans did not impress him; he described them as unpaved and filthy. Recent fires had twice destroyed much of the city, and current builders were reinforcing their work with brick. Pintard remarked unfavorably on the French influence on houses, furnishings, horses, and carriages. But of the inhabitants he wrote, "These people are full impressed with the growing importance of this city, which must very shortly become a vast commercial emporium." He complained that Customs House officials actually slowed things down, especially when more than one ship arrived at a time—written like a true merchant. In Pintard's opinion, New Orleans merchants didn't haggle much among themselves, and he complained about the lack of coffeehouses. He also described slaves and American Indians who lived in town. The people are healthy, Pintard wrote, and "laugh at our exaggerated accounts of its being sickly." Men from Kentucky gambled, and many of the unlucky ones returned home with nothing to show for their tobacco sales. Another merchant who commented on the continuing influence of the French on New Orleans asked his New York supplier to stop sending wine glasses, "as people live after the French fashion & drink only out of tumblers" except for a few Americans.[51]

Oliver Pollock had recorded his own observations about New Orleans and its vicinity in a memorandum. The island on which it stood was 60 leagues long, with the port in the middle of it, he wrote. He thought that the land to the west stood high enough to be made part of the city. Pollock's most interesting observation had to do with the Lower Mississippi River: he wrote that the river ran so crooked through New Orleans south that ships had to navigate from eddy to eddy looking for deeper water along the curves. Using the banks of such a river for a boundary would not work for either the Americans or the Spanish. The river needed to be free for all along its entire length.[52] But less than a decade later the new nation would solve the problem not by making navigation free for all nations; rather, the new United States would claim both banks of the Mississippi River for its own and set its sights on a continental empire that stretched all the way to the Pacific.

As it happened, the French were not quite done with the Lower Mississippi. A second wave of Acadians arrived in Louisiana in 1785. The French presence was also strong in Philadelphia in the 1790s—men who had been leaders of the French Revolution in the beginning but fled when it took a wrong turn. Philadelphia attracted them as the capital, and they made up as much as 20 percent of the city's residents for a time. They speculated in land and made plans to reclaim the Mississippi Valley.[53]

As slaves arrived in Louisiana from Caribbean islands in revolt in the early 1790s, fissures opened up between the French and Spanish over how to treat them. In 1792, Governor Carondelet issued regulations about the proper treatment of slaves in terms of how they would be fed, clothed, and sheltered, as well as calling for fair working conditions. A royal decree from 1798 stated that "those settlers ought to realize the Negroes are men and are under the protection of the laws, that their masters can correct them in a paternal fashion." Under Spanish law, slaves could testify in their own defense if accused of a crime. The French objected to Carondelet's stance and argued that treating slaves "leniently" only led to revolt, and there were even rumors that the governor intended for slaves to revolt in order to bring French settlers in line. But when they uncovered plans for insurrection in 1795, Spanish officials did act by hanging more than twenty men convicted of being ringleaders at Pointe Coupée and then displaying their heads at various crossroads as a warning to others.[54]

In 1796, Spain became entangled in the war between Great Britain and France and did not fare well. Spain had real economic problems and decided to cede Louisiana back to France in 1800 through the Treaty of San Ildefonso. Some regions changed hands back in Europe too. The terms of the treaty specified that France could take possession six months later, though the French didn't take over until 1803, just before the finalization of the Louisiana Purchase.

In economic terms, New Orleans had thrived under Spanish rule. The various governors had always worked around official imperial policies to keep the port open and the colony fed. Spain did block access to New Orleans from time to time, but local rulers usually made one exception or another as time went on until navigation opened once again. The wars of the last half of the eighteenth century had provided opportunities for many merchants, traders, and privateers to use back channels between empires to turn a profit while Europe fielded armies and engaged in naval combat. One scholar concluded that "what was legitimate trade one day became smuggling the next."[55] Tobacco, cotton, and flour from Illinois, Kentucky, and the Natchez area; sugar and slaves from the Caribbean; silver from Mexico and South America; and goods from London and Philadelphia (and later Baltimore and New York) all combined in a heady mix that fueled commercial growth. Before the United States took over, most men of business in New Orleans dealt in mixed cargoes, investing in whatever paid a high price from season to season. They poured almost all their profits into land and slaves, and the plantation economy grew on the Lower Mississippi. Nobody worked to establish banking or insurance industries until after New Orleans became an official American port. The value of exports from New Orleans nearly quadrupled during the 1790s, and by 1803 the export trade had become strong and stable.[56]

The United States agreed to pay France $15 million for over 820,000 square miles west of the Mississippi River in the spring of 1803. The Louisiana Purchase nearly doubled the size of the new United States. It included the port of New Orleans but did not include Florida or overlap much of present-day Texas, spreading north and west from present-day Arkansas and Oklahoma instead. Considering the significance of rivers like the Ohio and Mississippi to expansion since the middle of the eighteenth century, it is not surprising that the Lewis and Clark Expedition started its quest to explore the new territory on the Missouri River. They would find no handy water route to the Pacific Ocean, however. During the nineteenth century, the new United States would settle the Great Plains by overland routes, culminating in the building of railroads. There would be conflict aplenty, of course, among the new United States, Spain, and various Indian Nations west of the Mississippi, just as there had been to the east, but it would play out on a very different stage than that of the western waters that George Morgan, John Reed, and Standish Forde had come to know.

It was pioneering diplomatic historian Arthur Preston Whitaker who first used the careers of John Reed and Standish Forde to credit eastern merchants with laying the groundwork for the Louisiana Purchase. Other scholars had focused most of their attention on Thomas Jefferson's goal of acquiring land for farmers, and the size of the purchase itself would lend itself to emphasizing that as the main accomplishment of his efforts. But Whitaker asserted that "Jefferson's main purpose in the negotiation . . . [was] to protect and foster American commerce on the Mississippi." Other scholars had also focused on the actions of westerners themselves without giving proper credit to easterners, Whitaker concluded. But Reed and Forde had risked much to open trade with the Spanish port, and though they had to withdraw in the end, they had blazed the trail in "the development of the Mississippi trade, and consequently for our acquisition of Louisiana."[57]

After resisting opening up the Mississippi for trade to Americans for over a decade, Spain invested in New Orleans after Pinckney's Treaty, and commerce expanded accordingly. A new wave of merchants arrived from the East Coast to set up shop. And though Philadelphia lost its advantage in the port itself, it would be Philadelphia merchants who continued to supply residents of the Ohio and Mississippi Valleys with eastern goods by shipping them downriver from Pittsburgh before steamboats arrived to take goods upriver from New Orleans after the War of 1812. Rivalries remained between those of French descent who had remained under Spanish rule and everyone else. With the production of cotton exploding in Natchez thanks to the arrival of the cotton gin, Americans pushed harder than ever before for control over New Orleans, leading Jefferson to pursue the purchase of Louisiana. After over a half century of maneuvering for control of the Riverine West, one nation at last controlled both banks of the Ohio and Mississippi Rivers.

Reed and Forde had begun their partnership speculating in western lands, and they took turns descending the Ohio and Mississippi Rivers every year to build the commercial connections needed to get western crops to market through New Orleans. The next stage of their business involved sending ocean-going vessels to New Orleans, and they cultivated a relationship with Coxe & Clark—a partnership with one foot in the east and the other in the west. But after the signing of Pinckney's Treaty, Philadelphia merchants faced stiff competition from merchants pouring into New Orleans from other eastern ports, and Americans soon set their sights on total control over the Mississippi watershed. Rivals from Baltimore and New York provided new competition to Reed & Forde and Coxe & Clark. Reed & Forde's western business failed, though they pressed on elsewhere. With the Louisiana Purchase, the new United States added control over both banks of the Mississippi River to their control of both banks of the Ohio River. This represented the end of an era—rivals no longer controlled opposite banks of the Riverine West, and the new United States took its first step toward establishing a continental empire in North America. Europeans had created empires by crossing oceans; Americans created an empire by following rivers. Philadelphia merchants had been at the forefront of that effort, and they helped make it possible.

Epilogue

After giving up on establishing a new colony on the Mississippi River, George Morgan retired to a farm near Pittsburgh. His business correspondence had ended just as John Reed and Standish Forde began their careers in the mid-1770s. Morgan made no mention of the pair in his letter books, and he appeared only once in their records. In November of 1789, a bear skin "for Col Morgan" changed hands by way of Miles & Morgan in Reed & Forde's daybook for the price of £0.15.0.[1] Though they seem to have rarely crossed paths, the year 1806 proved to be pivotal for all three men. The partnership of Reed & Forde ended with Forde's death in April, and in August Aaron Burr paid a visit to George Morgan on his way west to foment rebellion. The year 1806 also proved pivotal for the new nation. The Lewis and Clark Expedition returned home in September, and with their failure to find a northwest passage to the Pacific, the United States would take up expansion by overland routes in the century that followed.

❋

Though the Louisiana Purchase gave control over both banks of the Mississippi River to one nation at last, the transition to American rule in New Orleans and its hinterland did not always go smoothly. A man named Mayberry wrote in February from Havana that he had had difficulties selling a ship and cargo, citing molasses, the northern states, and Spanish paperwork as the roots of his trouble.[2] Correspondence between merchants John Leslie and John Forbes sheds light on the short period during which the French took control of Louisiana for the last time. A Mr. Morgan from New Orleans had told John Leslie that a couple of Frenchmen claimed to have the authority for "the Indian Trade in Louisiana" and planned to set up shop at Mobile. They had presented a letter of introduction to Morgan, and it seemed like Leslie & Forbes intended do business with them. Leslie mentioned meeting Mr. Morgan in the coffeehouse (in London) and reported that the French had sent troops to St. Domingo. Leslie seemed to expect the troops to try to take New Orleans as Spanish officials headed to Pensacola. Leslie wrote that the French expected to open shipping on the river to Americans because they wanted their produce, but they would have to buy their merchandise from French merchants. "One of these French men I believe he who now goes out to N Orleans resided for years at Philadelphia in business there." Leslie commented more on the Indian trade. Florida would not change hands, he wrote, and he hoped that meant they could collect their debts from Native American tribes. Leslie expected the French government to be more powerful in the region than the Spanish in Florida and to corner the Chickasaw and Choctaw trade at Mobile. As for the future, Leslie thought that they would have to move their business to US territory, but restricted navigation on the Mississippi would be a problem.[3]

Following news of the Louisiana Purchase the next spring, Leslie told his partner that business had been dull for months, and many were trying to sell their ships to any interested parties. Americans were offering ships for charter and charging between £2,500 and £2,700, 5 percent pumage, two-thirds pilotage, and charges to stay in port. Charters allowed "60 running days." £500 had to be paid upfront, with the rest paid when the ship returned with new cargo. Leslie thought that those were "hard terms," and he was determined to come up with other plans. He referred to New Orleans and Mobile as "new American ports."[4]

Americans in New Orleans anticipated good things, however. In 1802, Benjamin Morgan wrote John A. Collins with news for his friends in Philadelphia about shipping on the Lower Mississippi. If they returned from Europe or the West Indies without cargo, they should consider coming to New Orleans first between February and July to buy flour and cotton at the best prices.[5] In June, George W. Morgan wrote to his brother-in-law, Samuel Pile, that large quantities of flour had been shipped down the Mississippi. Apparently, much of it went on to the West Indies, where it sold for $4 a barrel. Morgan wished that he could have gotten word to Pile sooner but wrote that he might still be able to make something of the opportunity if he arrived within the next four weeks. Like Benjamin Morgan, George W. Morgan recommended late winter through late spring as the best months to come to New Orleans and put together a cargo.[6] The next August, George W. Morgan wrote the following to his sister: "We are informed that this place is ceded to the U.S. if it be true there will opportunity for our brother at this place and for all industrious young men." At first, John McDonogh worried that New Orleans would lose Cuba as a market for flour when France took over and that his business would suffer. But by the fall of 1803 more and more merchants from such places as Boston, the West Indies, and Europe began to contact him about selling their goods on commission, and demands for cotton grew. McDonogh's business continued to expand.[7]

To the north in Kentucky, Congressman John Fowler sent a letter to constituents about the Louisiana Purchase in March of 1804. Fowler believed that the mood in Kentucky was one of "no price would be too high" to make the Mississippi Valley and New Orleans part of the United States. Congress had ended up paying half the total many feared, he reported, and it would be paid slowly over time, funded by the national debt. Fowler wrote that New Orleans and its hinterland would be as valuable as a market for industry as it had already proved to be as an outlet for western produce. Congress had taken on Georgia's Yazoo scheme and had plans in place to "extinguish" Indian control over lands in the West. The Lower Mississippi would be part of the United States at last, and Fowler tried to assure his constituents that common folk would benefit.[8]

A pair of lawyers seemed equally pragmatic. David Bradford left Washington, Pennsylvania, after the Whiskey Rebellion to settle in Bayou Sara, a Spanish settlement on the Mississippi south of Natchez. In March of 1803 he wrote to a friend back home that he feared that the French would "come to take possession of the country" at some point in the future. Cotton prices had dropped by half, and with them the price of slaves. He expected a peaceful takeover, though, writing that he did "not see that the change of nations" would create "a change in markets."[9] More than a year later, in September 1804, he wrote that he thought of moving south to New Orleans once the United States took control of the region. He betrayed his worry, however, when he noted that the Spanish could cut them off from New Orleans if the United States didn't take control of East Florida.[10] Robert McShane wrote to Abijah Hunt in May of 1804 that business in New Orleans was just like business in Philadelphia: "monopolized by a few, of well known & established character." He was having a tough time making a go of it as a lawyer in the port, writing that Livingston & Douglas and a couple others had taken all the business. McShane had been praised for his knowledge of French, though, and hoped to represent Frenchmen in the Governor's Court, where cases were conducted in both English and French.[11]

New Orleans' growth spurt received a check from a yellow fever outbreak in 1804, however. Two decades before, Elizabeth Trist had written often of the plague of mosquitoes during her first journey down the Mississippi, and mosquitoes would be the culprit for spreading the disease. Long-time residents who stayed out of the city in the summer were mostly unaffected, but she wrote that people in port succumbed whether they were accustomed to the climate of the Lower Mississippi or not. Charity flowed to help the victims, though, Trist wrote. A handful of years before this latest outbreak, George W. Morgan wrote to his sister about people dying in the city while others fled. "About three weeks past," he wrote, "we had the misfortune to lose our worthy Governor Gayoso which loss is much felt by our countrymen in general."[12]

A hopeful report of the region came the next year. Philander Chase wrote home to family and friends in Poughkeepsie, New York, about his impressions upon arrival in New Orleans in late 1805. Plantations fronted the river with a few acres each and then ran back inland. The soil was so fertile that they didn't use any manure to fertilize it. Planters grew corn, rice, sugar cane, oranges, and grapes. Chase thought that New Orleans was about one-third larger than Albany, with a large-enough harbor to shelter a vessel of any size. The city offered two banks, a courthouse, a convent, a Roman Catholic church, a government house, and military buildings to hold one thousand troops. Chase noted that during yellow fever outbreaks in the past the wealthier sorts retreated to the countryside for the three warmest months of the year, and most of the time a cool sea breeze blew through town. Most of the inhabitants spoke French, Chase wrote, but Americans were fast increasing.[13]

A German circular from 1805 referred to the Louisiana Purchase as the turning point in commerce on the Mississippi for others around the world. German settlers had come to the Lower Mississippi from time to time in the eighteenth century as one governor or another recruited them to suit their purposes. The early nineteenth-century circular still referred to "colonies" and "colonial products." The circular touted companies in Spain, Italy, France, the Netherlands, England, Havana, and New Orleans. Having the United States take possession would lead to "free commerce with the entire world"—an interesting phrase for that time. From the German point of view, the dry goods trade seemed to be most important.[14]

But at the same time that some in the West were planning for a future as

American citizens, others had different plans. After the duel that led to the death of both Alexander Hamilton and his political career in July of 1804, Aaron Burr looked to the West to find the power and acclaim he craved. He knew James Wilkinson well and had recommended that Thomas Jefferson appoint him as governor of Louisiana. Burr contacted Wilkinson and floated the idea of separating the West from the East and establishing a new nation, with themselves in charge. Both men knew of the unrest that had risen in the West during the 1780s and 1790s, and Burr thought he could capitalize on it. Burr traveled down the Ohio the next year looking for other allies, and he found a few, including an Irish immigrant named Harman Blennerhassett who had invested in boat building near Marietta, Ohio. In August of 1806, Burr visited once again and asked Blennerhassett to ready a military expedition down the Ohio to put his plan in motion. But, forewarned, the Ohio militia put an end to those plans in December, and federal authorities took Burr into custody in February of 1807, though the Supreme Court acquitted Burr in the end.[15]

Rumors swirled in New Orleans over the next summer and fall. Elizabeth House Trist, who had returned to New Orleans for a time, wrote a friend in June that she didn't think Burr would be convicted of any crime because of the partisan nature of politics. Another sign of tension involved the feud between Daniel Clark Jr. and Orleans governor William C. C. Claiborne. Trist's account of the resulting duel noted that the two men traveled to Spanish territory, where Clark shot Claiborne in the thigh.[16] Trist wrote Thomas Jefferson in October that she did not trust former Louisiana governor James Wilkinson. A gentleman she trusted was showing a letter to others purportedly from Wilkinson that led them to doubt not only his intentions but also those of Daniel Clark Jr. and Daniel W. Coxe. Transplanted Philadelphian merchant Richard Relf claimed to know nothing about it, though he engaged in business with Clark often. According to Trist, Wilkinson was known to have very direct ties with the Spanish, as well as permission to trade with them. Trist worried about a "mob" government, but it's not clear whether she meant in New Orleans or the United States as a whole. It seemed like some in New Orleans would have preferred Bonaparte, according to her. Some things remained unchanged, however: Trist mentioned five ships loaded with black slaves at the levee and worried about their health, fearing they would spread illness to town.[17]

And indeed slavery on the Lower Mississippi would only continue to expand. A man named Nathaniel Cox came down the Mississippi from Kentucky in 1806 to try his luck. Writing to a friend back home, he reported that sugar was the most important crop being produced in New Orleans. There was money to be made, less only the price of clothing and feeding slaves. "Sugar is a crop that never fails," Cox wrote, so long as people are drinking coffee and tea. But Cox urged his friend to bring his slaves to Mississippi instead to grow cotton, believing that his friend didn't have enough capital to establish a sugar plantation.[18] Cox established a ropewalk and ran a commission business. The commission business had paid more than $3,000, even though he got a late start, and he expected the ropewalk to make him $5,000 or more a year. That summer, though, his letters came from West Florida—sickness in New Orleans had sent him scurrying to Spanish territory.[19]

Letters from Nathaniel Cox also reveal some of the impact of the Burr conspiracy in Louisiana. Cox wrote that rumors that he was in league with the vice president left him feeling embarrassed and under scrutiny. Being from Kentucky seemed to have been enough to raise suspicions, and he received accusatory letters of this sort from the firm of Hart & Bartlet: "the former being enough for suspicion and the latter according proof of guilt." Cox went to Governor Claiborne, showed him the papers, and cleared his name—in the governor's eyes, at least.[20] In February of 1807, Cox reported that a Mississippi grand jury had failed to find any proof of Burr's guilt, but some had considered having him arrested by the military. Burr absconded, and the governor posted a reward for anyone who could capture him. Cox stated that he was glad to have it all over—the Burr scandal had made all other business in the area dull, and he was ready for things to get back to normal. A couple weeks later he wrote about "making rope to hang the rascally Spanioirds" and unsuccessful trials against Burr's conspirators. At the end of the summer, he rejoiced that Burr and Blennerhassett would be tried for treason.[21] As a testament to the continuing international flavor of New Orleans, Cox made a number of references to the Spanish in his letters but wrote that in English coffeehouses Americans outnumbered the French and Spanish by five to one and that the groups attended separate balls.[22]

In May of 1808, Cox wrote that the embargo was destroying his commercial career. In the fall of 1809, he listed the reasons for not realizing his dreams: failures in New Orleans, disputes with traders from the Chesapeake, the embargo, nonintercourse, Burr, Wilkinson, and the proclamation. "And in short," he wrote, "if the usual commercial arrangements had been continued between the United States and Europe my calculations might in some measure been realized."[23] One last letter from 1817 seems to indicate that he stayed in business—

he had suffered some kind of embarrassing loss, but he hoped to be successful again in the future. Originally, he had been a partner in the firm of Hart, Bartlet & Cox, and later just Bartlet & Cox.[24]

And what of Reed & Forde? By the late 1790s, the Philadelphia firm still had tens of thousands of acres of unsold land, and they engaged the services of William Croghan to help them sell it. At the age of sixteen, Dublin-born Croghan had moved to Philadelphia in 1768 to be mentored by his well-connected uncle, George. He apprenticed with a merchant in New York before serving in the Continental Army during the Revolution. He studied surveying at the College of William Mary, and the state of Virginia appointed him and George Rogers Clark as principal surveyors in charge of state boundary lands. He settled in Louisville and married Clark's sister, Lucy. In 1799, William Croghan wrote to John Reed and Standish Forde about their lands in Kentucky—including those in Christian County along the Pond River, Cumberland County along the Cumberland River, and Laird County along the Said River. Croghan indicated that he had the deed and conveyance for the land he had located for them but needed a power of attorney from William Pennock to legally hand over the military land warrants. Croghan had waited more than six months already and said that the warrants would lose value if they didn't act quickly. He had paid the taxes due to Kentucky covering the years 1792–98. By 1802, it seems that they had let their tax payments lapse once again: 70,000 acres of land had been advertised for sale for nonpayment of taxes. Croghan had lined up buyers for some of their military lands in 1803 but warned that the buyers were poor and could only afford a couple hundred acres, adding that they "must have independence for a year or two" before they could pay.[25]

Reed & Forde's correspondence spanning the months between 1801 and 1803 is filled with nothing but bad news. They spent much of their time trying to collect old debts, some of them more than a decade old, and often referred to those who owed them money as cruel and unjust. Reed traveled on business when Forde fell ill. David Ferguson, who had run their store in Natchez, failed to send remittances, and a letter to Daniel Clark Jr. indicated that they hadn't heard from him in two years. Despite their troubles, they still consigned cargoes to merchants in New Orleans.[26]

By chance, the year 1806 would be a momentous one for both George Morgan and the firm of Reed & Forde. George Morgan's biographer, Max Savelle, wrote that the old colonel knew the former vice president well and that when Aaron Burr wrote a letter from Pittsburgh that August asking to stop by for a visit, Morgan was pleased. As they ate dinner, Burr stated that westerners would not put up with the way easterners benefitted from western land sales and heavy taxes for long—they "would not allow themselves to become tributary." Later, Morgan testified at Burr's trial that Burr had stated that "the natural course of events seemed to indicate that the West should separate itself from the East," and the retired merchant replied, "God forbid." Burr mused that, because the federal government was so weak, a force of two hundred men could drive the president and Congress out of Washington, and a force of five hundred could capture New York. He then tried to recruit Morgan's sons for a military expedition down the Ohio River. Though he had sought the approval of the king of Spain just over a decade and a half before, George Morgan acted the only way a loyal citizen of a republic could: the next morning he wrote a letter to his president warning him of the danger.[27] Jefferson replied that Morgan's information "coincides with what has been learned from other quarters," and he went on to say that if Morgan could discover anything else about the plot, "whatever zeal you might think proper to use in this pursuit, would be used in fulfilment of the duties of a good citizen." The following spring, Jefferson confirmed that "your's was the very first intimation I had of this plot, for which it is but justice to say you have deserved well of your country."[28] Cleaving the continent in two had seemed possible in the years immediately following the Revolution, but such schemes were bound to fail after the Louisiana Purchase. The time for trading imperial loyalties had passed (see fig. E.1).

That same year Standish Forde signed a document ending his partnership with John Reed, probably to protect assets when he fell ill. Dated April 26, 1806, it read, "The partnership of Reed & Forde is dissolved this day of which all persons concerned are to take notice. This partnership has already continued 26 years and may hereafter be renewed in case the subscriber recovers from his present long indisposition." Unfortunately, he died two days later. John Reed went bankrupt and spent many years trying to pay off his debt, but he had enough influence in the end to gain "preferential treatment" for his son, who served as a midshipman in the navy after the War of 1812.[29]

Though not quite a full generation apart in age, George Morgan, John Reed, and Standish Forde pursued their businesses in different eras: one as the merchant of a colonial port, and the younger men as merchants of a national port. What they had in common was their pursuit of integrating the eastern half of the continent into the trade world of the Eastern Seaboard along western waters not fully under the control of any one empire. The year 1806 also saw the return of the Lewis and Clark Expedition. It only seemed natural to head up another river—the Missouri—to explore the Louisiana Purchase and beyond.

Figure E.1. Silhouette of George Morgan. Clarence Walworth Alvord, *The New Regime, 1765–1767*, 311. Courtesy of the Library of Congress

Though Lewis and Clark failed to find a northwest passage, they succeeded in focusing the new nation's attention on the trans-Mississippi West, ushering in a new century of settlement by overland journeys and railroads. Philadelphia merchants laid the groundwork for those continental ambitions by laying claim to the trans-Appalachian West through the creation of commercial networks that extended from Pittsburgh to New Orleans.

What shall we call this place during the critical half century between the eras of the ocean-going ships of the Atlantic World and the overland journeys of the trans-Mississippi West? US historiography recognizes the North, the South, the Mid-Atlantic, the Midwest, the West, and the Borderlands. Previous scholars of "the frontier in the formative years" simply called it "the trans-Appalachian West."[30] It's interesting that the history of the trans-Mississippi West doesn't have much to do with the Mississippi River and that the most salient geographical features of the trans-Appalachian West are in fact the Ohio and Mississippi Rivers rather than the Appalachian Mountains. Of course, both those terms were meant to trace frontier history from East to West, until Borderlands historians came along to shift the focus to the movement of peoples who started from the Southwest. But the Riverine West deserves a category of its own. It's all about moving downstream and moving between worlds along the most efficient route for goods to travel and having to share that journey with peoples of all nations, including Native American confederacies, because rivals claimed opposite banks. I don't know if the term will ever catch on, but it would not be for lack of trying on my part.

Abbreviations

BWMP	Baynton, Wharton, and Morgan Papers, Pennsylvania Historical and Museum Commission
CFP	Collins Family Papers, Tulane University Special Collections
DWCP	Daniel W. Coxe Papers, Historical Society of Pennsylvania
FHS	Filson Historical Society, Louisville
GFSP	Gratz-Franks-Simon Papers, Library Company of Philadelphia
GMP	George Morgan Papers, Illinois History and Lincoln Collections
HSP	Historical Society of Pennsylvania
KHS	Kentucky Historical Society
LSU	Louisiana State University, Special Collections
MDAH	Mississippi Department of Archives and History
NLP	Nicholas Low Papers, Tulane University Special Collections
PFP	Pile Family Papers, Historical Society of Pennsylvania
RFBC	Reed and Forde Business Collection, Seaport Museum
RFP	Reed and Forde Papers, Historical Society of Pennsylvania
TUSC	Tulane University Special Collections
WFP	Wharton Family Papers, Historical Society of Pennsylvania
WRC	Williams Research Center, New Orleans

Introduction

1. Thomas Hutchins to Thomas Jefferson, February 11, 1784, *Founders Online.*

2. Berg, "Economic Consequences"; Price, "Economic Function"; and Whitaker, "Reed and Forde."

3. Pitman, *Present State*, 1; Gruenwald, *River of Enterprise*; Salafia, *Slavery's Borderland.*

4. Adelman and Aron, "From Borderlands to Borders," 816. See also Narrett, *Adventurism and Empire.*

5. Turner, "Significance of the Frontier." For "accommodations," see Adelman and Aron, "From Borderlands to Borders," 814–16. For "zones of cultural interaction," see Lamar and Thompson, introduction to *Frontier in History*, 7. For the "new western history," see Limerick, *Legacy of Conquest*; Nobles, *American Frontiers.*

6. Mapp, *Elusive West.*

7. Furstenberg, "Significance."

8. Lee, *Masters*; Sleeper-Smith, *Indigenous Prosperity*; Stearns, *Empire of Commerce.*
9. Hinderaker, *Elusive Empires*; Mapp, *Elusive West.*
10. Wade, *Urban Frontier*, 1.
11. Hancock, *Oceans of Wine*, xvii; see also xvi–xxv, 144–45, 173.
12. Haggerty, *British-Atlantic Trading Community.*
13. James, *Oliver Pollock*; Clark, *New Orleans, 1718–1812*; DuVal, *Independence Lost*; Stern, *David Franks*; and Whitaker, "Reed and Forde."
14. Price, "What Did Merchants Do?" Studies of colonial merchants include Bailyn, *New England Merchants*; Doerflinger, *Vigorous Spirit of Enterprise*; Harrington, *New York Merchant*; Hunter, *Purchasing Identity*; Matson, *Merchants and Empire*; and Schlesinger, *Colonial Merchants.*
15. Price, "Economic Function," 123–86; Scheerer, "'For Ten Years Past,'" 12; Wilkinson, *Land Policy*, 64–65.
16. Marshall, "Lord Hillsborough"; Savelle, *George Morgan*, 200–228; Whitaker, "Reed and Forde."

Chapter 1 • An Imperial War

1. Jensen, *Maritime Commerce*, 41–106; Savelle, *George Morgan*; B&W Memo Book, Memo 1763–66, reel 10, BWMP.
2. Smith, "Account of the Journey," 75, 77, 85.
3. Usner, *Indians, Settlers, and Slaves*, 28–29.
4. Usner, *Indians, Settlers, and Slaves*, 65–72.
5. Cruzat, "Louisiana in 1724."
6. Hall, "Epilogue," 294–95; Usner, *Indians, Settlers, and Slaves*, 74–75.
7. Dart, "Gentleman of Pointe Coupee"; Anonymous Account Book, 1740, 1748, LSU.
8. Sturgill and Price, "On the Present State."
9. Sturgill and Price, "On the Present State," 38–39; Din, "First Spanish Instructions," 313–14; Vidal, "Antoine Bienvenu," 124.
10. Ekberg, "Flour Trade"; Vidal, "Antoine Bienvenu," 111–17.
11. Vidal, "Antoine Bienvenu," 113–23, 129.
12. Vidal, "Antoine Bienvenu," 119–23.
13. Dart, "Jamaica Pirates," 209.
14. Clark, *New Orleans*, 40–43.
15. Clark, *New Orleans*, 3–20.
16. Council of Trade and Plantations Letter Book, 1700–1721, LSU; Harrison, "Virginians on the Ohio"; Shelby, "Grenier's Journal"; Clark, *New Orleans*, 85, 90, 127; Mapp, *Elusive West*, 29–30.
17. Alvord, *Mississippi Valley*, 1:106–9.
18. Richard Carpenter to John Collins, March 4, 1744, CFP.
19. Salafia, *Slavery's Borderland*, 15–24.
20. Father Alexis F. De Guyenne to Pierre Vaudreuil, September 10, 1752, in Pease and Jenison, *Illinois on the Eve*, 717–18.
21. Payne, *French Encroachments Exposed*, 1–44.
22. Payne, *French Encroachments Exposed*, 22.
23. Berg, "Economic Consequences"; Price, "Economic Function," 155–57.
24. Daniel Clark Letter and Invoice Book, HSP.

25. Kingston, "Marine Insurance"; Price, "Economic Function," 151–53. For more on insurance, see Crothers, "Commercial Risk." For Philadelphia's more immediate hinterland, see Walzer, "Colonial Philadelphia."

26. Anderson, "Samuel Wharton," 121–22; Savelle, *George Morgan*, 4–10.

27. Journal B, 1754–60, reel 7, BWMP; Jensen, *Maritime Commerce*, 61–63.

28. Journal B, 1754–60, reel 7, BWMP.

29. Baynton & Wharton to Richard Neave, November 6, 1758, March 18, 1759; Baynton & Wharton to Christopher Rawson, December 10, 1758, in Baynton & Wharton Letter Book, 1758–60, vol. 4, WFP.

30. Baynton & Wharton to George Clark, December 11, 1758; Baynton & Wharton to John Dowel, November 18, 1758; and Baynton & Wharton to Gersham Williams, February 22, 1759, in Baynton & Wharton Letter Book, 1758–60, vol. 4, WFP.

31. Journal B, 1754–60, reel 7, BWMP.

32. John Noble to Baynton & Wharton, July 7 and 12 (quotation), August 12, September 17 and 27, 1760, in Correspondence of Baynton & Wharton, 1759–63, reel 2, BWMP.

33. John Noble to Baynton & Wharton, April 15 and July 7, 1763, in Correspondence of Baynton & Wharton, 1759–63, BWMP, reel 2. Baynton & Wharton to Robert Purviance, David Smith, John Fell, Lamar & Hill; Baynton & Wharton to Field & McLean, February 26, 1762 (quotations), and April 3, 1762, in Letter Books of Baynton & Wharton, 1762, reel 1, BWMP.

34. Baynton, Wharton & Morgan to Frederick Dansey, December 2, 1763, in Letter Books of Baynton, Wharton & Morgan, 1763–75, reel 1, BWMP.

35. Pitock, "Commerce and Community," 275–81.

36. Stern, *David Franks*, 7–21.

37. Dunn, *Opening New Markets*, 76–77; Savelle, *George Morgan*, 5; Stern, *David Franks*, 35–37.

38. Dunn, *Opening New Markets*, 79–80; Douds, "Merchants and Merchandising," 123–24.

39. Kenny and Jordan, "James Kenny's 'Journal.' "

40. Kenny and Jordan, "Journal of James Kenny," pts. 1 and 2.

41. Kimball and Quinn, "William Allen–Benjamin Chew," 207–10.

42. Savelle, *George Morgan*, 5–13.

43. Oaks, "Impact of British Western."

44. Jensen, *Maritime Commerce*, 154; Craig, "Grounds for Debate?"

45. Baynton, Wharton & Morgan to Nicholas Suite, October 16, 1763, in Letter Books of Baynton, Wharton & Morgan, 1763–66, reel 1, BWMP.

46. Baynton, Wharton & Morgan to Anthony Merry, October 22, 1763; and Baggon, Bacon & Company, October 21, 1763, in Letter Books of Baynton, Wharton & Morgan, 1763–66, BWMP, reel 1.

47. Benjamin Marshall to Hugh Forbes, November 12, 1763; Benjamin Marshall to James Tapscott, November 12, 1763, June 22 and October 22, 1764; Benjamin Marshall to John Townsend, May 2, 1764; Benjamin Marshall to James Brooks, July 28, 1764; Benjamin Marshall to Thomas Monkland, October 9, 1765; Benjamin Marshall to Barnaby Egan, November 9, 1765; Benjamin Marshall to Thomas Murphy, November 9, 1765, all in Stewardson, "Extracts from the Letter-Book," 205, 206, 208.

48. Jensen, *Maritime Commerce*, 154.
49. Jensen, *Maritime Commerce*, 154.
50. Savelle, *George Morgan*, 14–16.
51. Benjamin Marshall to Thomas Monkland, October 9, 1765; Benjamin Marshall to James Tapscott, October 22, 1765; Benjamin Marshall to Barnaby Egan, October 19, 1765; Benjamin Marshall to Thomas Murphy, November 9 and December 18, 1765, all in Stewardson, "Extracts from the Letter-Book," 205, 208.
52. Baynton, Wharton & Morgan to Benjamin Franklin, August 28, 1766, in Labaree, *Papers of Benjamin Franklin*, 13:396.
53. Baynton, Wharton & Morgan to Robert Callender, in Letter Books of Baynton, Wharton & Morgan, 1763–66, reel 1, BWMP; Dunn, *Opening New Markets*, 83.

Chapter 2 • Shifting Boundaries

1. Campbell, "Adverse Patron," 119–30.
2. Dunn, *Opening New Markets*, 3, 80–81.
3. Savelle, *George Morgan*, 18–23.
4. Contract for Hauling Merchandise, March 21, 1766, in Alvord and Carter, *New Regime*, 192–93.
5. Joseph Dobson to George Morgan, December 17, 1765; Joseph Dobson to Samuel Wharton, December 27, 1765; Joseph Dobson to Baynton, Wharton & Morgan, January 26, 1766, all in box 4, WFP. Joseph Dobson to Baynton, Wharton & Morgan, March 9, 1766; Joseph Dobson to George Morgan, April 5, 1766, all in box 5, WFP. See also George Morgan's Fort Pitt Trading Post Daybook, 1765–67, HSP.
6. Jennings, "Journal from Fort Pitt."
7. George Morgan to Molly Morgan, June 20–28, 1766; John Baynton to Mary (Molly) Morgan, July 11, 1766, all in Alvord and Carter, *New Regime*, 311–16.
8. "Journal of Captain H. Gordon, 1766," in Alvord and Carter, *New Regime*, 290–311, 300 (quotations).
9. "Journal of Captain H. Gordon, 1766," in Alvord and Carter, *New Regime*, 290–311.
10. Morgan, "Voyage Down the Mississippi, November 21, 1766–December 18, 1766," in Alvord and Carter, *New Regime*, 438–45. The next year, in a letter to his partners, Morgan mentions that French hunters, supplying meat to New Orleans and other settlements, had thinned out the buffalo along the Mississippi; see George Morgan to Dear Partners, December 10, 1767, George Morgan Letterbook, HSP.
11. Morgan, "Voyage Down the Mississippi, November 21, 1766–December 18, 1766," in Alvord and Carter, *New Regime*, 446–77.
12. Jennings, "Journal at Fort Chartres"; Marques de Grimaldi to Don Antonio de Ulloa, February 11, 1768; Instructions for the Locating of 29 Acadian Families; Instructions to Be Observed in Transporting the Acadians; Instructions for the Return; Distribution of the Lands for the Acadian Families, February 11, 1768; all in Chandler, "Odyssey Continued."
13. Jennings, "Journal at Fort Chartres."
14. Savelle, *George Morgan*, 39–41.
15. Morrissey, *Empire of Collaboration*, 204–5, 208.
16. Savelle, *George Morgan*, 31–36, 46–47; Lee, *Masters*, 149.

17. George Croghan to General Gage, January 12, 1767, in Alvord and Carter, *New Regime*, 479–81; see also Lee, *Masters*, 122–55, for discussion of French farmers crossing the river.

18. Lee, *Masters*, 150; Morrissey, *Empire of Collaboration*, 206–11.

19. Savelle, *George Morgan*, 42–44; Lee, *Masters*, 148–49; George Morgan to Dear partners, December 10, 1767, George Morgan Letterbook, HSP.

20. Samuel Wharton to John Baynton and George Morgan, August 12, 17, 21 (quotation), 25, and 28, 1767, in Correspondence of Baynton, Wharton & Morgan, 1763–83, reel 5, BWMP.

21. Lee, *Masters*, 148–49; for more on Morgan's troubles with his fellow residents, see Thomas, "Successful and Unsuccessful Merchants."

22. George Morgan to Dear partners, December 2, 1767, George Morgan Letterbook, HSP.

23. Samuel Wharton to John Baynton and George Morgan, February 17, 1766, in Correspondence of Baynton, Wharton & Morgan, 1763–83, reel 5, BWMP. George Morgan to John Fitzpatrick and C. Moore, October 25, 1769; George Morgan to John Baynton, November 1770, all in Letter Books of George Morgan, 1769–72, reel 1, BWMP. George Morgan to John R. Hanson, October 15, 1773, Letter Books of George Morgan, 1773–75, reel 1, BWMP. Samuel Young to George Morgan, February 18, 1768, GMP.

24. Samuel Wharton to John Baynton and George Morgan, August 12, 17, 28, 1767, in Correspondence of Baynton, Wharton & Morgan, 1763–83, reel 5, BWMP.

25. George Morgan to John Baynton and Samuel Wharton, December 2, 6, 11, 16, 1767; February, June 20, and July 11, 1768; April 5, 1768; John Baynton to James Rumsey, March 1, 1768, all in Alvord and Carter, *Trade and Politics*, 126, 128, 135, 140, 161–62, 181, 225, 331, and 348. Ledger December 9, 1767–October 27, 1768, in Ledgers, 1766–71, reel 10, BWMP.

26. Lee, *Masters*, 151; Morrissey, *Empire by Collaboration*, 214–15.

27. George Morgan to Dear Sir (McNamara), July 27, 1769, in Letter Books of George Morgan, 1768–70, reel 1, BWMP.

28. Memo, May 9, 1770, in Letter Books of George Morgan, 1769–72, reel 1, BWMP. See also Baynton & Wharton Memo Book, in Memo Books, reel 10, BWMP; Samuel Wharton to John Baynton and George Morgan, August 21, 1767, in Correspondence of Baynton, Wharton & Morgan, 1763–83, reel 5, BWMP.

29. George Morgan to Lieutenant Colonel Wilkins, September 16, 1770, Letter Books of George Morgan, 1769–72, reel 1, BWMP.

30. George Morgan affidavit, GMP; George Morgan to Molly Morgan, June 20–28, 1766, in Alvord and Carter, *New Regime*, 316.

31. Dunn, *Opening New Markets*, 132–36; Oaks, "Impact of British Western," 180.

32. Francis Poussett to Baynton and Wharton, April 2, May 14, and July 31, 1964, in Correspondence of Baynton, Wharton & Morgan, 1763–83, roll 5, BWMP.

33. Bemis, *Pinckney's Treaty*, 1–6; Clark, *New Orleans*, 158–65.

34. Clark, *New Orleans*, 161–65.

35. Francis Poussett to Baynton & Wharton, April 2, May 14, and July 31, 1964, in Correspondence of Baynton, Wharton & Morgan, 1763–83, roll 5, BWMP.

36. J. Marsh to Frederick Haldimand, November 20, 1767, in Alvord and Carter, *Trade and Politics*, 113–15.

37. Blackwell, "Contemporary English View," 221–22; Samuel Wharton to Benjamin Franklin, August 28, 1766, in Labaree, *Papers of Benjamin Franklin*, 13:395–402.

38. J. Marsh to Frederick Haldimand, November 20, 1767, in Alvord and Carter, *Trade and Politics*, 113–15.

39. Clark, *New Orleans*, 161–63.

40. James, *Oliver Pollock*, 1–3.

41. James, *Oliver Pollock*, 1–21, 53–56; Pollock, "Deposition of Oliver Pollock, June 8–10, 1808," in Wilkinson, *Memoirs*, vol. 2, appendix; DuVal, *Independence Lost*, 35–36.

42. Dalrymple, *Merchant of Manchac*, 62n52; Clark, *New Orleans*, 169–70; James, *Oliver Pollock*, 4–9.

43. Usner, *Indians, Settlers, and Slaves*, 116–18; Chandler, "Ulloa's Account," 407–10.

44. Leumas, "Ties That Bind," 202.

45. Chandler, "Ulloa's Account," 410–37.

46. Pollock, "Deposition of Oliver Pollock, June 8–10, 1808," in Wilkinson, *Memoirs*, vol. 2, appendix. See also DuVal, *Independence Lost*, 37–39.

47. Dalrymple, *Merchant of Manchac*, 9.

48. O'Reilly, "O'Reilly Proclamation."

49. James, *Oliver Pollock*, 1–21, 53–56; Rappleye, *Robert Morris*, 7–25, 76; DuVal, *Independence Lost*, 35–43.

50. Bjork, "Documents Relating."

51. Bayogoula leader quoted in Usner, *Indians, Settlers, and Slaves*, 131.

52. Usner, *Indians, Settlers, and Slaves*, 118; Peterson, *Colonial St. Louis*, 1–3; Ekberg, *French Roots*, 99–100.

53. Fabel, "Letter from West Florida."

54. James, *Oliver Pollock*, 53–56.

Chapter 3 • Land Grants

1. George Morgan to Samuel Wharton, January 13 and April 27, 1772, in Letter Books of Baynton, Wharton & Morgan, 1763–75, reel 1, BWMP. These two letters are out of order in the letter book, perhaps copied from elsewhere, grouped together with other correspondence from April and May of 1772. See also George Morgan affidavit, GMP.

2. Blaakman, *Speculation Nation*, 28–33.

3. Campbell, "Adverse Patron," 121–22; Livermore, *Early American Land Companies*, 75–93.

4. Livermore, *Early American Land Companies*, 102.

5. Blaakman, *Speculation Nation*, 32–34; Bailey, *Ohio Company of Virginia*; and Franklin, "Pennsylvania-Virginia Rivalry."

6. Alvord, *Mississippi Valley*, 2:87–93; Campbell, "Adverse Patron," 121–22; Hallock, "Between Accommodation and Usurpation," 121–43.

7. Campbell, "Adverse Patron," 119–30, 120.

8. Campbell, "Adverse Patron," 119–30.

9. Campbell, "Adverse Patron," 129–30, 138; Savelle, *George Morgan*, 75–78; Wainwright, *George Croghan*, 203–46; Livermore, *Early American Land Companies*, 111–19; Lee, *Masters*, 147, 151–52; Alvord, *Mississippi Valley*, 2:94–95; Blaakman, *Speculation Nation*, 46.

10. William Franklin, "Reasons to Colonize Illinois," in Alvord, *New Regime*, 251–57; Wainwright, *George Croghan*, 245–46, 260.

11. Wainwright, *George Croghan*, 245–46, 260; Savelle, *George Morgan*, 76–80.

12. Marshall, "Lord Hillsborough," 717–25; Blaakman, *Speculation Nation*, 47–48; William Trent to George Croghan, June 10, 1769, in Lingelbach and Trent, "William Trent Calls," 49.

13. Oaks, "Impact of British Western," 180–82.

14. John Baynton to George Morgan, March 1 and 20; April 4, 12, and 21 (quotation); and May 14, 27, and 31, 1770, in Letter Books of John Baynton Letterbook, 1769–70, reel 1, BWMP.

15. Lewis, *Indiana Company*.

16. George Morgan to Samuel Wharton, January 13 (quotation) and April 27, 1772, in Letter Books of Baynton, Wharton & Morgan, 1763–75, reel 1, BWMP.

17. George Morgan to Thomas Wharton, 6 May 1772, box 6, WFP.

18. George Morgan affidavit, GMP; Lewis, *Indiana Company*.

19. Marshall, "Lord Hillsborough," 733; Blaakman, *Speculation Nation*, 46–48.

20. Thomas to Samuel Wharton, November 30, 1773, in Wharton, "Selections from the Letter-Books," 320–21.

21. Wainwright, *George Croghan*, 281–87.

22. Wainwright, *George Croghan*, 281–87; Marshall, "Lord Hillsborough," 735–37.

23. Wharton, "Selections from the Letter-Books"; Alvord, *Illinois-Wabash Land Company*, 11–12; Emily Hager Kasecamp makes a similar argument in "Company, Colony, and Crown," characterizing the members of the Ohio Company of Virginia as active agents of empire.

24. Byars, "Gratz Papers," 1–9.

25. Michael Gratz to Barnard Gratz, July 6, 1770, box 1, folder 54, GFSP; Thomas, "Successful and Unsuccessful"; Fish, *Barnard and Michael Gratz*.

26. Livermore, *Early American Land Companies*, 106–11; Stern, *David Franks*, 100–101; David Franks to James Rumsey, October 19, 1770, Franks Family Papers.

27. Blaakman, *Speculation Nation*, 25.

28. For accounts of the opinion's spread, see Sosin, "Yorke-Camden Opinion"; and Blaakman, *Speculation Nation*, 332n2, 338–39n53. For Murray's account of his meeting with Croghan, see William Murray to Barnard and Michael Gratz, May 15, 1773, in Byars, *B. and M. Gratz*, 130–31. See also Livermore, *Early American Land Companies*, 106–11.

29. Sosin, "Yorke-Camden Opinion"; Blaakman, *Speculation Nation*, 49–50.

30. George Morgan to Samuel and Joseph Thomlinson, September 16, 1773; George Morgan to Richard Winston, October 1773, all in Letter Books of George Morgan, 1773–75, reel 1, BWMP. Thomas Hutchins to George Morgan, September 10, 1770, New Orleans Collection, box 1, New-York Historical Society.

31. Thomas Wharton to Thomas Walpole, May 2 and 31, 1774, in Wharton, "Selections from the Letter-Books," 330–32, 338–39; Oaks, "Impact of British Western," 183–85.

32. Potter, "Pennsylvania and Virginia Boundary," 407–14.

33. Thomas to Samuel Wharton, November 30, 1773, and May 17, 1774, in Wharton, "Selections from the Letter-Books," 319–21, 332–36.

34. Oaks, "Impact of British Western," 185–86; Marks, "William Murray," 41.

35. Oaks, "Impact of British Western," 185–86.

36. Alvord, *Mississippi Valley*, 2:241–51; see also Sosin, *Whitehall and the Wilderness*.

37. George Morgan to Dear Sir, November 29, 1770; George Morgan to Thomas

Hutchins, December 19, 1770, and February 18, February 27, and March 11, 1772; George Morgan to Samuel Wharton, December 21, 1771, all in Letter Books of George Morgan, 1769–72, reel 1, BWMP.

38. Byars, *B. and M. Gratz*, 177–79; Livermore, *Early American Land Companies*, 106–11.

39. Fabel and R, "Letters of R."

40. Cummins, "Oliver Pollock's Plantations," 37–43; James, *Oliver Pollock*, 44–45.

41. Din, "First Spanish Instructions," 317.

42. Fabel and R, "Letters of R."

43. Haynes, *Natchez District*, 4–6.

44. Haynes, *Natchez District*, 4–6; Dalrymple, *Merchant of Manchac*; Captain John Collins account with Davis, 1774, and Robert Bagnall receipt, May 15, 1755, CFP.

Chapter 4 • A Revolutionary War

1. Richard Checkley to John Reed, September 1, 1777, box 1, RFP.

2. Whitaker, "Reed and Forde," esp. 240 and 260; Doerflinger, *Vigorous Spirit of Enterprise*, 295–96. Thomas Doerflinger found that John Reed and Standish Forde were among ten new Philadelphia merchants who had been staff officers during the war. Adding five others to a list of what he deemed "upwardly mobile" men, Doerflinger estimated that one became an elite merchant and four others made modest profits—so he judged one-third of them to be successful. Three of the other men went bankrupt, and he ranked Reed and Forde just above them because they were deeply in debt to British creditors. Others had left trade, died, or moved, thus placing Reed and Forde solidly in the middle, but not successful by Doerflinger's standards; see Doerflinger, *Vigorous Spirit of Enterprise*, 222–23, 247.

3. Erwin, "Philadelphia Merchant"; Luskey, "'What Is My Prospects?,'" 669–75; Hart and Matson, "Situating Merchants," 670–77.

4. John Reed to John Irvine, April 15, 1778; Thomas Lawrence to John Reed, May 5, 1778; Thomas Lawrence to Nathaniel Barret, May 5, 1778; Thomas Bend to John Reed, May 19, 1778; Anthony Butler to John Reed, May 31, 1778; Richard Checkley to John Reed, March 9, 1779; Dan Taylor to John Reed, June 2 1781, all in, box 1, RFP. Doerflinger, *Vigorous Spirit of Enterprise*, 216.

5. Richard Checkley to John Reed, August 31, 1777, box 1, RFP.

6. Checkley and Checkley, "Five Gossipy Letters." Richard Checkley to John Reed, September 1, 1777; Peter Anspach to John Reed, April 24, 1778, both in box 1, RFP.

7. Standish Forde to Peter Anspach, September 11, 1780, box 1, RFP.

8. Standish Forde Will, box 1, RFBC.

9. Jacob Garrigues to Standish Forde, August 21, 1780, box 1, RFP.

10. Reed & Forde Daybook, 1785–91, vol. 10, RFP.

11. Doerflinger, *Vigorous Spirit of Enterprise.*

12. Savelle, *George Morgan*, 131–40.

13. Savelle, *George Morgan*, 141–51.

14. Haynes, *Natchez District*, 51–54; Narrett, *Adventurism and Empire*, 74–77.

15. DuVal, *Independence Lost*, 40.

16. Clark, *New Orleans*, 203–5; James, *Oliver Pollock*, 61–64; Oliver Pollock, "Deposition of Oliver Pollock, June 8–10, 1808," in Wilkinson, *Memoirs*, vol. 2, appendix.

17. James, *Oliver Pollock*, 74–75; Clark, *New Orleans*, 203–5; Oliver Pollock, "Deposition of Oliver Pollock, June 8–10, 1808," in Wilkinson, *Memoirs*, vol. 2, appendix.

18. James, *Oliver Pollock*, 79–80.

19. Haynes, *Natchez District*, 14–18; Alexander McIntosh Journal, MDAH.

20. Heerman, *Alchemy of Slavery*, 59–64; James, *Oliver Pollock*, 81; Oliver Pollock, "Deposition of Oliver Pollock, June 8–10, 1808," in Wilkinson, *Memoirs*, vol. 2, appendix.

21. Gitlin, *Bourgeois Frontier*, 26–45, 37. Gitlin's emphasis on kinship networks between the French and Native Americans throughout the book is echoed in Morrissey's *Empire by Collaboration* and Lee's *Masters of the Middle Waters*, which also take as their focus the Upper Mississippi River. David Franks and the Gratz brothers utilized kinship networks among Jewish colonists in the East. In contrast, such networks played a minimal role in the commercial connections of George Morgan, John Reed, and Standish Forde.

22. James, *Oliver Pollock*, 81; Oliver Pollock, "Deposition of Oliver Pollock, June 8–10, 1808," in Wilkinson, *Memoirs*, vol. 2, appendix.

23. James, *Oliver Pollock*, 77–78; Stearns, *Empire of Commerce*, 48–51.

24. Stearns, *Empire of Commerce*, 50.

25. Haynes, *Natchez District*, 32–33.

26. Haynes, *Natchez District*, 43–46.

27. Haynes, *Natchez District*, 56–75; Narrett, *Adventurism and Empire*, 78–88.

28. Haynes, *Natchez District*, 72–90.

29. Haynes, *Natchez District*, 90–94.

30. Haynes, *Natchez District*, 95–100.

31. Haynes, *Natchez District*, 111–23.

32. Oliver Pollock to George Washington, January 3, 1782, *Founders Online*.

33. For land speculation in the late eighteenth and early nineteenth centuries, see Abernethy, *Western Lands*; Billington, "Origin of the Land"; Blaakman, *Speculation Nation*; Sakolski, *Great American Land Bubble*; and Van Atta, *Securing the West*.

34. Dater, "Albert Gallatin," 25–26.

35. Wilkinson, *Land Policy*, 10–13, 19–44; Chernow, "Robert Morris," 195.

36. Blaakman, *Speculation Nation*, 7–19, 15 (quotation); for a discussion of how the new federal government developed the doctrine of preemption to dispossess Native Americans, see chap. 6.

37. Stearns, *Empire of Commerce*, 59–60; Baron Carondelet to the Duke of Alcudia, November 24, 1794, in Turner, "Carondelet," 477–78.

38. Michael Connor to Nicholas Low, November 25, 1783; J. B. MaCarty to McIntire, August 23, 1783, all in NLP; Whitaker, *Spanish-American Frontier*, 63–67.

39. Whitaker, *Spanish-American Frontier*, 16, 70–80; Reeder, "Diego de Gardoqui," 234–35; Stearns, *Empire of Commerce*, 67–68; Furstenberg, "Significance," 663–68.

40. Whitaker, *Spanish-American Frontier*, 16, 70–80; Reeder, "Diego de Gardoqui," 234–35; Stearns, *Empire of Commerce*, 67–81; Furstenberg, "Significance," 663–68.

41. Reeder, "Diego de Gardoqui," 237–40, 237; Whitaker, *Spanish-American Frontier*, 119–220.

42. Scheerer, "'For Ten Years Past,'" 7, 12–17; Tyler, "Mississippi River Trade," 260–61.

43. Doerflinger, *Vigorous Spirit of Enterprise*, 263–65.

44. Wilkinson, *Land Policy*, 64–65.

45. Jonathan Wilkins Jr. to John Clifford, February 8, 1790, vol. 9, Clifford Family Papers, HSP.

46. Reed & Forde Daybook, 1785–91, vol. 10, RFP; James Elliot to Reed & Forde, December 8, 1783, box 2, RFP.

47. Reed & Forde Daybook, 1785–91, vol. 10, RFP.

48. Standish Forde to John Reed, December 1, 1785, box 2, RFP.

49. Reed & Forde to Major Samuel Hanway, September 10, 1789; Reed & Forde to Mr. Davidson, September 10, 1789; Reed & Forde to William Haymond, October 10, 1789, all in vol. 2, RFP. John Davis to Reed & Forde, October 3, 1790, box 3, RFP.

50. Reed & Forde to Ephraim Grant, June 3, 1787; Reed & Forde to Halie & Leroy, June 7, 1787; Reed & Forde to C. L. Mullett, June 8, 1787, all in vol. 1, RFP.

51. Reed & Forde to Ephraim Grant, June 3, 1787; Reed & Forde to Charles Steward, June 3, 1787, all in vol. 1, RFP. Reed & Forde to James Groome, September 8, 1788; Reed & Forde to Joseph Thompson, September 14, 1788, all in vol. 2, RFP.

52. Reed & Forde to Cruger, Leyard & Mullett, March 3, April 19, and June 14, 1787, all in vol. 1, RFP; Chernow, "Robert Morris," 195–202.

Chapter 5 • Maneuvering in the Riverine West

1. Reed & Forde Daybook, 1785–91, vol. 10, RFP.

2. Stearns, *Empire of Commerce*, 32–48; Whitaker, *Spanish-American Frontier*, 8–9. Susan Gaunt Stearns comes to a conclusion similar to my own: "settlement and trade would expand in lockstep"; Stearns, *Empire of Commerce*, 62.

3. On the 24th Instant Resolved, May 28, 1784, Durrett Collection, Broadsides, Broadsheets, and Circulars, University of Chicago.

4. Oliver Pollock to George Washington, January 2, 1782, *Founders Online*.

5. Whitaker, *Spanish-American Frontier*, 15–23; Tyler, "Mississippi River Trade."

6. Whitaker, *Spanish-American Frontier*, 35–36; Din, "Immigration Policy"; Hilton, "Loyalty and Patriotism."

7. Whitaker, *Spanish-American Frontier*, 7–13; Reeder, "Diego de Garodoqui," 228–34.

8. Baron Carondelet to the Duke of Alcudia, November 24, 1794, in Turner, "Carondelet," 477–78; Haynes, *Natchez District*, 147–57; Din, "Immigration Policy."

9. Kolodny, "Travel Diary," 217, 220, 222.

10. Kolodny, "Travel Diary," 222, 223.

11. Kolodny, "Travel Diary," 226, 229, 230.

12. Eliza House Trist to Thomas Jefferson, May 4, 1785, *Founders Online*.

13. Eliza House Trist to Thomas Jefferson, May 4, 1785, *Founders Online*.

14. Richard Carpenter to John Collins, June 1, 1784, CFP; John Collins to Richard Carpenter, April 5 and 6, 1785, CFP; David Wood Meriwether to William Meriwether, September 14, 1785, Short File, FHS.

15. David Wood Meriwether to Wm Meriwether, September 14, 1785, Short File FHS.

16. L. Butler to Dear Madam, November 20, 1786, Durrett Collection, Codex 32.

17. Stearns, *Empire of Commerce*, 95.

18. Doerflinger, *Vigorous Spirit of Enterprise*, 293; Stearns, *Empire of Commerce*, 98–101. For a different take on Wilkinson's career, see Watson, "James Wilkinson."

19. Harry Innes to John Brown, December 7, 1787, KHS.

20. Whitaker, *Spanish-American Frontier*, 78–82.

21. Whitaker, *Spanish-American Frontier*, 90.

22. Whitaker, *Spanish-American Frontier*, 90–107; Whitaker, "Harry Innes."

23. Whitaker, *Spanish-American Frontier*, 96–106.

24. Whitaker, "Letters of James Robertson."

25. Whitaker, "Letters of James Robertson," 410–11.

26. Whitaker, *Spanish-American Frontier*, 159–60.

27. Oliver Pollock, "Deposition of Oliver Pollock, June 8–10, 1808," in Wilkinson, *Memoirs*, vol. 2, appendix.

28. Whitaker, *Spanish-American Frontier*, 163–70.

29. Whitaker, *Spanish-American Frontier*, 171–85; Furstenberg, "Significance," 665–68.

30. Whitaker, *Spanish-American Frontier*, 185–200; Stearns, *Empire of Commerce*, 123–24.

31. Smith, *A Short Description*, 1–16, 16.

32. Savelle, *George Morgan*, 76–199.

33. George Morgan to George Washington, July 31–August 5, 1788; George Washington to George Morgan, August 25, 1788, all in *Founders Online*.

34. Savelle, *George Morgan*, 200–228; Narrett, *Adventurism and Empire*, 180–82; Tyler, "Mississippi River Trade"; Miro's Offer to Western Americans, April 26, 1789, in Kinnaird, *Annual Report*, 269–71.

35. Savelle, *George Morgan*. M. Scott Heerman echoed Savelle's observation that Morgan wished for a functioning government in the West to protect his ventures in his analysis of Clark's takeover of Vincennes. Clark supported the establishment of a slave code to control their behavior—masters in the region had long complained that far-off imperial governments were no help when it came to controlling slaves. See Heerman, *Alchemy of Slavery*.

36. George Morgan, handbill, October 3, 1788, in Savelle, *George Morgan*, facsimile opposite 206.

37. Savelle, *George Morgan*, 209–10.

38. George Morgan, handbill, October 3, 1788, in Savelle, *George Morgan*, facsimile opposite 206.

39. Savelle, *George Morgan*, 218–20; Narrett, *Adventurism and Empire*, 182–86; Thomas Hutchins to Daniel Clark, December 20, 1788, in Kinnaird, *Annual Report*, 263–64.

40. Swem, "Letter from New Madrid."

41. John Halley Journal, 1789, 1791, Durrett Collection, Codex 83.

42. "Memorial by Barthelemi Tardiveau," in Alvord, *Kaskaskia Records*, 487–88.

43. Wade, *Urban Frontier*, 7–13, 44–45; Stearns, *Empire of Commerce*, 67–68.

44. Standish Forde to John Lewis, August 28, 1788, vol. 1, RFP; Caleb Copeland to Reed & Forde, November 19, 1788, May 3, 1789, box 2, RFP; Standish Forde to John Reed, undated November 1789, vol. 2, RFP.

45. Reed & Forde to Caleb Copeland, November 19, 1788, vol. 2, RFP; Caleb Copeland to Reed & Forde, November 19, 1788, May 3, 1789 (quotation), September 12, 1789, October 20, 1789, box 2, RFP; Caleb Copeland to Reed & Forde, April 21, 1790, February 25, 1792, box 3, RFP.

46. John Reed to Standish Forde, June 11, 1789, July 6, 1789; Standish Forde to John Reed, undated November 1789, November 25, 1789, December 7, 1789, December 10, 1789, box 2, RFP; Standish Forde to John Reed, January 7, 1790, October 28, 1791, December 5, 1791, box 3, RFP; Standish Forde to John Reed, June 7, 1793, June 19, 1793, vol. 3, RFP.

47. For this paragraph and the two that follow: Standish Forde to John Reed, undated November 1789, November 25, 1789, vol. 2, RFP.

48. Standish Forde to Jonathan Arnold, December 5, 1791; and Reed & Forde to John Lewis, January 20, 1793, Letter Book, RFBC.

49. Jordan, "Notes of a Journey," 209–12.

50. Wade, *Urban Frontier*, 13–18, 64–66.

51. Jordan, "Notes of a Journey," 212–16; Horsman, *Frontier*, 64; Woodward, "Spanish Commercial Policy," 151–52. One of their partners in a venture to New Orleans, John Lewis, had similar troubles with cold weather and ice the year before; see John Lewis to Reed & Forde, February 8, 1789, box 2, RFP.

52. John Reed to William Shannon, January 22, 1792; David Ferguson to Reed & Forde, August 5, 1791, box 3, RFP. For more on trade for provisions from Pittsburgh along the Ohio, see Downes, "Trade in Frontier Ohio," 473.

53. Agreement between Reed & Forde and James Wilkinson, February 9, 1790; John Reed to Standish Forde, February 10, 1790, box 21, RFP.

54. Woodward, "Spanish Commercial Policy," 145–46 (quotation), 151–53; Horsman, *Frontier*, 56–58.

55. Louis Tarascon Journal, translated from the French, entries of November 5–8, 1799, FHS.

56. Copy of John Lewis letter to Diego de Gardoqui, August 1, 1788; Standish Forde to John Lewis, August 28, 1788, vol. 1, RFP; Whitaker, "Reed and Forde," 243–44, 246–47. Diego de Gardoqui and James Gardoqui are one and the same; Gardoqui used either name to sign correspondence.

57. Reed & Forde to John Lewis, October 10, 1788, vol. 2, RFP.

58. Reed & Forde to John Lewis, September 17, 1788, vol. 2, RFP.

59. Reed & Forde to John Lewis, September 4, 1788, vol. 2, RFP; John Lewis to Reed & Forde, January 1791, box 3, RFP; Whitaker, "Reed and Forde," 243–44, 246–47; Horsman, *Frontier*, 15–16.

60. David Ferguson to Reed & Forde, June 10, 1790, July 4, 1790, August 5, 1791 (first quotation), November 20, 1791, March 28, 1792 (second quotation), April 3, 1792, box 3, RFP.

Chapter 6 • Completing the Circuit

1. Daniel W. Coxe and Daniel Clark Jr. to Reed & Ford, March 6, 1793; Daniel Clark Jr. to Reed & Ford, March 16, 1793, all in box 3, RFP. Whitaker, "Reed and Forde," 237–62.

2. Marzagalli, "Establishing Transatlantic Trade Networks"; Hancock, "Organizing Our Thoughts," 319.

3. Reed & Forde Daybook, vol. 10, RFP.

4. Whitaker, "Reed and Forde," 245–48.

5. Whitaker, "Reed and Forde," 251.

6. Daniel Hodge to Reed & Forde, May 29, 1789, June 11, 1789, August 7, 1789, September 10, 1789; James Jones to Reed & Forde, October 5, 1789, all in box 2, RFP. Thomas Dunsford to Reed & Forde, July 19, 1790, box 3, RFP.

7. Standish Forde to John Reed, December 5, 1791, box 3, RFP.

8. Reed & Forde Daybook, vol. 10, RFP.

9. Jonathan Arnold to Thomas Arnold, 1792, no. 4806, LSU.

10. Reed & Forde Daybook, vol. 10, RFP.

11. Reed & Forde to Joseph Graisbury, July 16, 1791; John Reed to Charles White, August 27, 1791; Standish Forde to John Lewis, July 25, mid-August 1791; Standish Forde to Richard S. Blackburn, September 26, 1791; Standish Forde to Captain Thomas Porteu, September 1791; Standish Forde to John Reed, October 15 and 28, 1791, all in Letter Book, RFBC.

12. Standish Forde to John Reed, November 4 and 17, 1791; Standish Forde to Daniel W. Coxe, November 13, 1791, January 6, 1792, and March 15, 1792; Reed & Forde to Daniel Clark Jr., February 20, 1795, all in Letter Book, RFBC.

13. Standish Forde to John Reed, January and March 15, 1792; Standish Forde to Daniel W. Coxe, January 6 and March 15, 1792, all in Letter Book, RFBC.

14. Standish Forde to John James Maund, March 21, 1792; Standish Forde to Thomas Garnet, May 9, 1792; Standish Forde to John O'Bannon, May 24, 1792; Standish Forde to Daniel Clark Jr., June 8, 1792, all in Letter Book, RFBC. Standish Forde to Peter Anspach in New York, various dates between January and April 1792, Anspach & Rogers Papers, box 1, folder 2, New-York Historical Society.

15. John Reed to James Wilkinson, June 8, 1792; John Reed to William Lintok, June 19, 1792; John Reed to John Lewis, June 19, 1792; John Reed to Daniel Clark Jr., June 28, 1792; John Reed to Captain James Graisbury, June 28, 1792; John Reed to Gilber Leonard, July 10, 1792; John Reed to Don Joseph Antonio de Hoa, July 20, 1792, all in Letter Book, RFBC. Whitaker, "Reed and Forde," 251.

16. Reed & Forde to Thomas Porteu, September 4, 1792; Reed & Forde to Robert Cochran, October 2, 1792; Reed & Forde to Daniel Clark Jr., November 14 and December 17, 1792; Reed & Forde to William Lamb, December 17, 1792, all in Letter Book, RFBC.

17. Reed & Forde to Charles Ewing, June 4, 1793, vol. 3, RFP; Whitaker, "Reed and Forde," 252–53.

18. Reed & Forde to Daniel Clark Jr., November 14, 1792; Reed & Forde to Captain Graisbury, November 17, 1792; Reed & Forde to Captain Jonas Keen, December 17, 1792, all in Letter Book, RFBC.

19. Standish Forde to John Reed, June 19, 1793, vol. 3; ship records, Ulali, box 17; Reed & Forde to John Wheeler, vol. 3; Coxe & Clark to Reed & Forde, October 29, November 9, and December 23, 1793; Daniel W. Coxe to Reed & Forde, September 16 and 30, 1794, all in box 3, RFP.

20. Whitaker, "Reed and Forde," 254–60; Samuel Jackson to John Reed, March 31, 1794, box 3, RFP.

21. Alexander, "Daniel Clark"; Coxe & Clark to Reed & Forde, March 6, 1793; Daniel Clark Jr. to Reed & Forde, March 16, 1793, all in box 3, RFP.

22. Letters from various merchants to Juan Baptiste McCarty, NLP.

23. Salvucci, "Atlantic Intersections." Philadelphia lagged behind Charleston and

New York in the volume of goods shipped to St. Augustine in Florida; see Cusick, "Across the Border," 287.

24. Pollock, "Memorandum on New Orleans," Library of Congress.

25. Cruzat, "Letters in Journal Form."

26. Alexander, "Daniel Clark." Coxe & Clark to Reed & Forde, March 6, 1793; Daniel Clark Jr. to Reed & Forde, March 16, 1793, all in box 3, RFP.

27. Daniel Clark Jr. to Daniel W. Coxe, July 15, September 24, and October 12, 1793, DWCP.

28. John Reed to James Wilkinson, June 8, 1792, Letter Book, RFBC; Whitaker, *Spanish-American Frontier*, 153–70, 174–77, 191–97.

29. Coxe & Clark to Reed & Forde, March 17, March 21, March 25, April 16, April 20, April 30, May 26, June 9, July 10, July 25, August 10, August 12, August 15, and September 22, 1793, box 3, RFP. See also Daniel Clark Jr. to Daniel W. Coxe, September 24, October 3, and October 16, 1793, DWCP.

30. Marzagalli, "Establishing Transatlantic Trade Networks"; Daniel W. Coxe to Reed & Forde, January 7, January 16, January 27, March 12, March 22, March 30, April 7, April 23, April 29, May 4, May 9, May 12, May 16, and May 17, 1794, box 3, RFP.

31. Daniel W. Coxe to Reed & Forde, August 15, August 27, August 28, September 16, September 21, September 30, and October 24, 1794, box 4, RFP; Reed & Forde to Samuel Byard, March 6, 1795, Letter Book, RFBC.

32. For this paragraph and the one that follows, see correspondence between Daniel Clark Jr. and Reed & Forde between 1792 and 1795, boxes 3–5, RFP; Daniel Clark Jr. to Daniel W. Coxe, October 16, 1793, DWCP.

33. Whitaker, "Reed and Forde," 254–55, 255.

34. Daniel Clark Jr. to Reed & Forde, February 12, 1796, box 4, RFP.

35. Whitaker, "Reed and Forde," 237–62.

36. Quoted in Sterns, *Empire of Commerce*, 123.

37. Clark, *New Orleans*, 208–10; Stearns, *Empire of Commerce*, 123–24.

38. Stearns, *Empire of Commerce*, 113–28.

39. Account Book (day book), Hunt (Abijah and David) Papers, MDAH.

40. Louis Tarascon Journal, translated from the French, FHS.

41. Louis Tarascon Journal, translated from the French, FHS.

42. Account Book (day book), Hunt (Abijah and David) Papers, MDAH.

43. Louis Tarascon Journal, translated from the French, FHS.

44. Stearns, *Empire of Commerce*, 136–42.

45. Account Book (day book), Hunt (Abijah and David) Papers, MDAH.

46. Louis Tarascon Journal, translated from the French, FHS.

47. Ermus, "Reduced to Ashes," 331; Cummins, "Oliver Pollock's Plantations," 44.

48. Thomas Morgan Jr. to Thomas Morgan, May 3, 1793; George W. Morgan to Rebecca Morgan Pile, March 4, undated March, September 29, October 20, 1794; undated 1795; January 14, 1798, August 17, 1799; April 28, June 28, 1800; George W. Morgan to Thomas Morgan, May 18 and 23, 1795, all in PFP. George W. Morgan also mentions the impact of the fire in 1794; see George W. Morgan to Rebecca Pile, March 14 and 31, 1794, PFP.

49. Thomas Morgan Jr. to George W. Morgan, April 11, 1795; George W. Morgan to Rebecca Morgan Pile, January 14, 1798, August 17, 1799, April 28 and June 28, 1800; George W. Morgan to Thomas Morgan, May 18 and 23, 1795, all in PFP.

50. Atherton, "John McDonogh," 457–60.

51. Sterling, "New Orleans, 1801," 217–33; John Foley to William Wallace, May 11, 1804, NLP.

52. Pollock, "Memorandum on New Orleans," Library of Congress.

53. Furstenberg, "Significance"; Furstenberg, *When the United States.*

54. Holmes, "Abortive Slave Revolt," 343–44. See also Furstenberg, "Significance," 656–67.

55. Clark, *New Orleans*, 220.

56. Clark, *New Orleans*, 219–20, 248–49, 272–74, 220.

57. Whitaker, "Reed and Forde," 262. Though he focused on Reed & Forde, Whitaker did not specifically highlight Philadelphia's role in general, but he did note that New Yorkers began taking the lead in trade in New Orleans in the late 1790s; Whitaker, "Reed and Forde," 260. For a more recent examination of the Louisiana Purchase, see Kukla, *Wilderness So Immense.*

Epilogue

1. Reed & Forde Daybook, 1785–91, vol. 10, RFP.

2. Truman Mayberry to John A. Collins, February 5, 1803, CFP.

3. John Leslie to John Forbes, December 4, 1802, Kuntz Collection, TUSC.

4. John Leslie to John Forbes, April 12, 1803, Kuntz Collection, TUSC.

5. Benjamin Morgan to John A. Collins, October 9, 1802, CFP.

6. George W. Morgan to Samuel Pile, June 19, 1802, PFP.

7. George W. Morgan to Rebecca Pile, August 5, 1803, PFP; Atherton, "John McDonogh," 471.

8. Handbill, Washington City, March 27, 1804 by John Fowler, Calk Family Collection, KHS.

9. David Bradford to David Redick, March 10, 1803, David Bradford Letters, LSU.

10. David Bradford to David Redick, September 1, 1804, July 1, 1805, David Bradford Letters, LSU.

11. Robert McShane to Abijah Hunt, May 17, 1804, Hunt (David and Family) Papers, 1803–38, LSU.

12. Kolodny, "Travel Diary"; George W. Morgan to Rebecca Pile, August 17, 1799, PFP.

13. Philander Chase to John Reade, December 12, 1805, WRC.

14. Strormann and Ludeling Circular Letter, March 1, 1805, LSU.

15. Hemmis, "American Scoundrel on Trial."

16. Elizabeth House Trist Letter, June 15, 1807, WRC.

17. Elizabeth House Trist to Thomas Jefferson, October 27, 1807, *Founders Online.*

18. Nathaniel Cox to Gabriel Lewis, November 23, 1806, "Letters of Nathaniel Cox," 181.

19. Nathaniel Cox to Gabriel Lewis, June 15, 1807, and July 1807, "Letters of Nathaniel Cox," 185–86.

20. Nathaniel Cox to Gabriel Lewis, December 16, 1806, "Letters of Nathaniel Cox," 181–82.

21. Nathaniel Cox to Gabriel Lewis, February 13, 1807, and February 27, 1807, "Letters of Nathaniel Cox," 183–84.

22. Nathaniel Cox to Gabriel Lewis, September 17, 1807, "Letters of Nathaniel Cox," 187.

OK as edited?

23. Nathaniel Cox to Gabriel Lewis, September 15, 1809, "Letters of Nathaniel Cox," 191.

24. Nathaniel Cox to Gabriel Lewis, April 5, 1817, "Letters of Nathaniel Cox," 192.

25. William Croghan to Reed & Forde, July 1, 1799, August 23, 1802, and August 23, 1803, boxes 7, 8, and 9, RFP.

26. Reed & Forde to Samuel Forman, April 10, 1801; Reed & Forde to John Holmes, April 14, 1801; Reed & Forde to David Ferguson, April 16, 1801; Reed & Forde to Daniel Clark, April 16, 1801, all in vol. 12, RFP.

27. Savelle, *George Morgan*, 234–35, 234; Lewis, *Burr Conspiracy*, 46; Hemmis, "American Scoundrel on Trial."

28. Thomas Jefferson to George Morgan, September 19, 1806, and March 26, 1807, *Founders Online*; for Burr's denial, see Aaron Burr to Jonathan Rhea, July 25, 1807, in Vroom, "Interesting Letters," 372–74.

29. Standish Forde Memo, April 26, 1806, box 10, RFP; Whitaker, "Reed and Forde," 261.

30. Horsman, *Frontier*; Rohrbough, *Trans-Appalachian Frontier*.

Primary Sources

MANUSCRIPT COLLECTIONS

Center for Jewish History, New York, New York
Franks Family Papers, 1711–1821

Filson Historical Society, Louisville, Kentucky
Louis Tarascon Journal
Meriwether, David Wood

Historical Society of Pennsylvania, Philadelphia
Clifford Family Papers
Daniel Clark Letter and Invoice Book
Daniel W. Coxe Papers
Fort Pitt Trading Post Journal, 1765–72
George Morgan Letterbook
Pile Family Papers
Reed and Forde Papers
Wharton Family Papers

Illinois History and Lincoln Collections, University of Illinois at Urbana-Champaign
George Morgan Papers, 1766–1826, 1907–57

Independence Seaport Museum, Philadelphia, Pennsylvania
Reed and Forde Business Collection, 1735–1886

Kentucky Historical Society, Frankfort
Calk Family Collection, 1744–1978
Harry Innes Letter to John Brown, 1787

Library Company of Philadelphia, Pennsylvania
Gratz-Franks-Simon Papers

Louisiana State University, Special Collections, Baton Rouge
Anonymous Account Book, 1740, 1748, Mss. 519
Council of Trade and Plantations Letter Book, Mss. 680
David Bradford Letters, Mss. 855
David Hunt and Family Papers, Mss. 4943
Jonathan Arnold to Thomas Arnold, Mss. 4806
Strormann and Ludeling Circular Letter, Mss. 4943

Mississippi Department of Archives and History, Jackson
Alexander McIntosh Journal
Hunt (Abijah and David) Papers

New-York Historical Society Museum and Library, New York City
Anspach & Rogers
New Orleans Collection

Pennsylvania Historical and Museum Commission, Pennsylvania State Archives, Harrisburg
Manuscript Group 19, II. Baynton, Wharton, and Morgan Papers, 1746–87, microfilm

Tulane University Special Collections, New Orleans
Collins Family Papers
Kuntz Collection
Nicholas Low Papers, 1781–1811, 1857

University of Chicago Library, Chicago
Reuben T. Durrett Collection

University of Pittsburgh, Special Collections
Pittsburgh Waste Book and Fort Pitt Trading Post Papers, 1757–65

Williams Research Center, New Orleans
Elizabeth House Trist Letter
Morgan-Wetherill Letters

Online Sources

Bernard, Jean Frederic. *Le cours du fleuve Missisipi selon les relations les plus modernes.* Library of Congress. https://www.loc.gov/item/gm71000980.

Filson, John. "A Map of Kentucky." Library of Congress. https://www.loc.gov/item/99441724.

Hutchins, Thomas, to Thomas Jefferson. February 11, 1784. *Founders Online*, National Archives. https://founders.archives.gov/documents/Jefferson/01-06-02-0392.

Jefferson, Thomas, to George Morgan. March 26, 1807. *Founders Online*, National Archives. https://founders.archives.gov/documents/Jefferson/99-01-02-5358.

Jefferson, Thomas, to George Morgan. September 19, 1806. *Founders Online*, National Archives. https://founders.archives.gov/documents/Jefferson/99-01-02-4294.
McMurray, William, and Robert Scot. "The United States According to the Definitive Treaty of Peace Signed at Paris Sept. 3d. 1783." Library of Congress. https://www.loc.gov/item/gm71005423.
Morgan, George, to George Washington. July 31–August 5, 1788. *Founders Online*, National Archives. https://founders.archives.gov/documents/Washington/04-06-02-0375.
O'Reilly, Alejandro. "O'Reilly Proclamation, 1769, New Orleans." Louisiana Public Documents Digital Archive. http://cdm16313.contentdm.oclc.org/cdm/ref/collection/LPC/id/281.
Pollock, Oliver. "Memorandum on New Orleans Vicinity." Library of Congress. www.loc.gov/resource/mtj1.015_0836_0837.
Pollock, Oliver, to George Washington. January 3, 1782. *Founders Online*, National Archives. https://founders.archives.gov/documents/Washington/99-01-02-07643.
Ross, Lieut., and Robert Sayer. *Course of the River Mississipi from Balise to Fort Chartres; Taken on an Expedition to the Illinois, in the Latter End of the Year 1765*. Library of Congress. https://www.loc.gov/item/74693015.
Scull, Nicholas, Matthew Clarkson, and Mary Biddle. "To the Mayor, Recorder, Aldermen, Common Council, and Freemen of Philadelphia This Plan of the Improved Part of the City Surveyed and Laid Down by the Late Nicholas Scull." Library of Congress. https://www.loc.gov/item/74692589.
Trist, Eliza House, to Thomas Jefferson. March 12, 1785. *Founders Online*, National Archives. https://founders.archives.gov/documents/Jefferson/01-08-02-0014.
Trist, Eliza House, to Thomas Jefferson. May 5, 1785. *Founders Online*, National Archives. https://founders.archives.gov/documents/Jefferson/01-08-02-0080.
Trist, Eliza House, to Thomas Jefferson. October, 27, 1807. *Founders Online*, National Archives. https://founders.archives.gov/documents/Jefferson/99-01-02-6667.
Washington, George, to George Morgan. August 25, 1788. *Founders Online*, National Archives. https://founders.archives.gov/documents/Washington/04-06-02-0427.

Printed Primary Sources

Alvord, Clarence Walworth. *The Critical Period, 1763–1765*. Springfield: Illinois State Historical Library, 1915.
Alvord, Clarence Walworth. *The Illinois-Wabash Land Company Transcript*. Cyrus H. McCormick, 1915.
Alvord, Clarence Walworth. *Kaskaskia Records, 1778–1790*. Springfield: Illinois State Historical Library, 1909.
Alvord, Clarence Walworth, and Clarence Edwin Carter, eds. *The New Regime, 1765–1767*. Springfield: Illinois State Historical Library, 1916.
Alvord, Clarence Walworth, and Clarence Edwin Carter, eds. *Trade and Politics, 1767–1769*. Springfield: Illinois State Historical Library, 1921.
Bjork, David K. "Documents Relating to Alexandro O'Reilly and an Expedition Sent Out by Him from New Orleans to Natchitoches, 1769–1770." *Louisiana Historical Quarterly* 7 (1924): 20–39.

Blackwell, Jacob. "A Contemporary English View of Trade and Prospects of New Orleans at the Close of the French Dominion." *Louisiana Historical Quarterly* 6 (1923): 221–22.

Byars, William Vincent, ed. *B. and M. Gratz: Merchants in Philadelphia, 1754–1798.* Jefferson City, MO: Hugh Stephens, 1916.

Chandler, R. E. "Ulloa's Account of the 1768 Revolt." *Louisiana History* 27 (1986): 407–37.

Checkley, J. W., and Richard Checkley. "Five Gossipy Letters." *Pennsylvania Magazine of History and Biography* 36 (1912): 222–25.

Cox, Nathaniel. "Letters of Nathaniel Cox to Gabriel Lewis." *Louisiana Historical Quarterly* 2 (1919): 179–92.

Croghan, George, and Nicholas B. Wainwright. "George Croghan's Journal. April 3, 1759–April [30], 1763." *Pennsylvania Magazine of History and Biography* 71, no. 4 (1947): 313–444.

Cruzat, Heloise H., trans. "Letters in Journal Form, Written to Don Estevan Miro, Ex-Governor of Louisiana, by Don Joseph Xavier de Pontalba, in 1792." *Louisiana Historical Quarterly* 2 (1919): 393–417.

Cruzat, Heloise H., trans. "Louisiana in 1724: Banet's Report to the Company of the Indies, Dated Paris, December 20, 1724." *Louisiana Historical Quarterly* 12 (1929): 122–33.

Dalrymple, Margaret Fisher. *The Merchant of Manchac: The Letterbooks of John Fitzpatrick, 1768–1790.* Baton Rouge: Louisiana State University Press, 1978.

Dart, Harry P. "A Gentleman of Pointe Coupee, 1743." *Louisiana Historical Quarterly* 5 (1922): 462–65.

Dart, Sally, and Edith Dart Price. "The Jamaica Pirates and Louisiana Commerce, 1739: Seizure of the Ship 'Le Comte De Maurepas' by Pirates off Cape San Antoine, Cuba, 1739." *Louisiana Historical Quarterly* 16 (1933): 209–20.

Din, Gilbert C. "The First Spanish Instructions for Arkansas Post November 15, 1769." *Arkansas Historical Quarterly* 53 (1994): 312–19.

Erwin, Joseph. "A Philadelphia Merchant, 1768–1791." *Pennsylvania Magazine of History and Biography* 19, no. 3 (1895): 397–402.

Fabel, Robin, and R. "The Letters of R: The Lower Mississippi in the Early 1770s." *Louisiana History* 24 (1983): 402–27.

Fabel, Robin F. A. "A Letter from West Florida in 1768." *Florida Historical Quarterly* 74 (1996): 461–63.

Gordon, Harry. "Extracts from the Journal of Captain Harry Gordon [. . .]." *Journal of the Illinois State Historical Society* 2 (1909): 55–64.

Harrison, Fairfax. "The Virginians on the Ohio and Mississippi in 1742." *Louisiana Historical Quarterly* 3 (1922): 316–32.

Jennings, John. "John Jennings 'Journal from Fort Pitt to Fort Chartres in the Illinois Country,' March–April, 1766." *Pennsylvania Magazine of History and Biography* 31, no. 2 (1907): 145–56.

Jennings, John. "John Jennings' Journal at Fort Chartres, and Trip to New Orleans, 1768." *Pennsylvania Magazine of History and Biography* 31, no. 3 (1907): 304–10.

Jordan, John W. "Notes of a Journey from Philadelphia to New Madrid, Tennessee, 1790." *Pennsylvania Magazine of History and Biography* 36, no. 2 (1912): 209–16.

Kenny, James, and John W. Jordan. "James Kenny's 'Journal to Ye West-Ward,' 1758–59." *Pennsylvania Magazine of History and Biography* 37, no. 4 (1913): 395–449.

Kenny, James, and John W. Jordan. "Journal of James Kenny, 1761–1763." *Pennsylvania Magazine of History and Biography* 37, no. 1 (1913): 1–47.

Kenny, James, and John W. Jordan. "Journal of James Kenny, 1761–1763 (continued)." *Pennsylvania Magazine of History and Biography* 37, no. 2 (1913): 152–201.

Kimball, David A., and Miriam Quinn. "William Allen–Benjamin Chew Correspondence, 1763–1764." *Pennsylvania Magazine of History and Biography* 90 (1966): 202–26.

Kinnaird, Lawrence, ed. *Annual Report of the American Historical Association for the Year 1945*. Vol. 3, *Spain in the Mississippi Valley, 1765–1794*. Pt. 2, *Post War Decade, 1782–1791*. Washington, DC: US Government Printing Office, 1946.

Kolodny, Annette, ed. "The Travel Diary of Elizabeth House Trist: Philadelphia to Natchez, 1783–84." In *Journeys in New Worlds: Early National Women's Narratives*, ed. William L. Andrews (Madison: University of Wisconsin Press, 1990), 181–231.

Labaree, Leonard W., ed. *The Papers of Benjamin Franklin*. 42 vols. New Haven, CT: Yale University Press, 1969.

Lingelbach, William E., and William Trent. "William Trent Calls on Benjamin Franklin." *Pennsylvania Magazine of History and Biography* 74, no. 1 (1950): 43–50.

Oaks, Robert F. "George Morgan's 'Memorandums': A Journey to the Illinois Country, 1770." *Journal of the Illinois State Historical Society* 69 (1976): 185–200.

Payne, J. *The French Encroachments Exposed or, Britain's Original Right to all that Part of the American Continent claimed by France* [. . .]. London: George Keith, 1756.

Pease, Theodore Calvin, and Ernestine Jenison, eds. *Illinois on the Eve of the Seven Years' War, 1747–1755*. Springfield: Illinois State Historical Library, 1940.

Perry, William. "New Orleans in 1758." *Louisiana Historical Quarterly* 5 (1922): 53–57.

Pitman, Philip. *The Present State of the European Settlements on the Mississippi*. London: J. Nourse, 1770.

Shelby, Charmion Clair. "Grenier's Journal of His Voyage to Vera Cruz, 1745." *Louisiana Historical Quarterly* 21 (1938): 631–55.

Smith, Daniel. *A Short Description of the Tennassee Government [. . .]*. Philadelphia: M. Carey, 1793.

Smith, Ralph A. "Account of the Journey of Bernard de la Harpe: Discovery Made by Him by Several Nations Situated in the West." *Southwestern Historical Quarterly* 62 (1958): 75–86.

Sterling, David Lee. "New Orleans, 1801: An Account by John Pintard." *Louisiana Historical Quarterly* 34 (1951): 217–33.

Stewardson, Thomas. "Extracts from the Letter-Book of Benjamin Marshall, 1763–1766." *Pennsylvania Magazine of History and Biography* 20, no. 2 (1896): 204–12.

Sturgill, Claude C., and Charles L. Price. "On the Present State of the Province of Louisiana in the Year 1720, by Jean Baptiste Bernard de la Harpe." *Louisiana Historical Quarterly* 54 (1971): 28–48.

Swem, E. G. "A Letter from New Madrid, 1789." *Mississippi Valley Historical Review* 5 (1918): 342–46.

Turner, Frederick J. "Carondelet on the Defense of Louisiana, 1794." *American Historical Review* 2, no. 3 (1897): 474–505.

Vroom, G. D. W. "Interesting Letters of George Morgan and Aaron Burr." *Pennsylvania Magazine of History and Biography* 26, no. 3 (1902): 370–74.

Wharton, S., et al. "Some Letters of Franklin's Correspondents." *Pennsylvania Magazine of History and Biography* 27, no. 2 (1903): 151–75.

Wharton, Samuel. *View of the Title to Indiana.* 1775.

Wharton, Samuel, et al. *Report of the Lords Commissioners for Trade and Plantations on the Petition of* [. . .] *for a Grant of Lands on the River of Ohio* [. . .]. London: J. Almon, 1772.

Wharton, Thomas. "Selections from the Letter-Books of Thomas Wharton, 1773–1783." *Pennsylvania Magazine of History and Biography* 33, no. 3 (1909): 319–39.

Wharton, Thomas. "Selections from the Letter-Books of Thomas Wharton, 1773–1783." *Pennsylvania Magazine of History and Biography* 33, no. 4 (1909): 432–53.

Wharton, Thomas. "Selections from the Letter-Books of Thomas Wharton, 1773–1783." *Pennsylvania Magazine of History and Biography* 34, no. 1 (1910): 41–61.

Whitaker, Arthur Preston. "Harry Innes and the Spanish Intrigue: 1794–1795." *Mississippi Valley Historical Review* 2 (1928): 236–48.

Whitaker, Arthur Preston. "Letters of James Robertson and Daniel Smith." *Mississippi Valley Historical Review* 3 (1925): 409–12.

Wilkinson, James. *Memoirs of My Own Times.* 3 vols. Philadelphia: Abraham Small, 1816.

Secondary Sources

BOOKS, ESSAYS, AND ARTICLES

Abernethy, Thomas Perkins. *Western Lands and the American Revolution.* New York: D. Appleton-Century, 1937.

Adelman, Jeremy, and Stephen Aron. "From Borderlands to Borders: Empires, Nation-States, and the Peoples in between in North American History." *American Historical Review* 104 (1999): 814–41.

Alexander, Elizabeth Urban. "Daniel Clark: Merchant Prince of New Orleans." In *Nexus of Empire: Negotiating Identity in the Revolutionary Borderland, 1760s–1820s*, ed. Gene Allen Smith and Sylvia L. Hilton, 241–67. Gainesville: University Press of Florida, 2010.

Alvord, Clarence Walworth. *The Mississippi Valley in British Politics: A Study in Trade, Land Speculation, and Experiments in Imperialism Culminating in the American Revolution.* 2 vols. Cleveland: Arthur C. Clark, 1917.

Anderson, James D. "Samuel Wharton and the Indians' Rights to Sell Their Land: An Eighteenth-Century View." *Western Pennsylvania Historical Magazine* 63 (1980): 121–40.

Arena, C. Richard. "Philadelphia-Spanish New Orleans Trade in the 1790s." *Louisiana History* 2 (1961): 429–45.

Atherton, Lewis E. "John McDonogh—New Orleans Mercantile Capitalist." *Journal of Southern History* 7 (1941): 451–81.

Bailey, Kenneth P. *The Ohio Company of Virginia and the Westward Movement, 1748–1792: A Chapter in the History of the Colonial Frontier.* Glendale, CA: Arthur H. Clark, 1939.

Bailyn, Bernard. *The New England Merchants in the Seventeenth Century.* New York: Harper & Row, 1955.

Bemis, Samuel Flagg. *Pinckney's Treaty: America's Advantage from Europe's Distress.* New Haven, CT: Yale University Press, 1960.

Berg, Harry D. "Economic Consequences of the French and Indian War for Philadelphia Merchants." *Pennsylvania History* 13 (1946): 185–93.
Berg, Harry D. "The Organization of Business in Colonial Philadelphia." *Pennsylvania History* 10 (1943): 157–77.
Billington, Ray Allen. "The Origin of the Land Speculator as a Frontier Type." *Agricultural History* 19 (1945): 204–12.
Blaakman, Michael A. *Speculation Nation: Land Mania in the Revolutionary American Republic.* Philadelphia: University of Pennsylvania Press, 2023.
Byars, William Vincent. "The Gratz Papers." *Publications of the American Jewish Historical Society*, no. 23 (1915): 1–23.
Campbell, William J. "An Adverse Patron: Land, Trade, and George Croghan." *Pennsylvania History* 76 (2009): 117–40.
Carson, W. Wallace. "Transportation and Traffic on the Ohio and Mississippi before the Steamboat." *Mississippi Valley Historical Review* 7 (1920): 26–38.
Caughey, John. "Bernardo de Galvez and the English Smugglers on the Mississippi, 1777." *Hispanic American Historical Review* 12 (1932): 46–58.
Chandler, Richard E. "Odyssey Continued: Acadians Arrive in Natchez." *Louisiana History* 19 (1978): 446–63.
Chernow, Barbara A. "Robert Morris: Genesee Land Speculator." *New York History* 58 (1977): 194–220.
Clark, John G. *New Orleans, 1718–1812: An Economic History.* Baton Rouge: Louisiana State University Press, 1970.
Cole, Arthur H. "The Tempo of Mercantile Life in Colonial America." *Business History Review* 33 (1959): 277–99.
Craig, Michelle L. "Grounds for Debate? The Place of the Caribbean Provisions Trade in Philadelphia's Prerevolutionary Economy." *Pennsylvania Magazine of History and Biography* 128 (2004): 149–77.
Crothers, A. Glenn. "Commercial Risk and Capital Formation in Early America: Virginia Merchants and the Rise of American Marine Insurance, 1750–1815." *Business History Review* 78 (2004): 607–33.
Cummins, Light T. "Oliver Pollock's Plantations: An Early American Anglo Landowner on the Lower Mississippi, 1769–1824." *Louisiana History* 29 (1988): 35–48.
Cusick, James. "Across the Border: Commodity Flow and Merchants in Spanish St. Augustine." *Florida Historical Quarterly* 69 (1991): 277–99.
Dater, Henry M. "Albert Gallatin—Land Speculator." *Mississippi Valley Historical Review* 1 (1939): 21–38.
Din, Gilbert C. "Empires Too Far: The Demographic Limitations of Three Imperial Powers in the Eighteenth-Century Mississippi Valley." *Louisiana History* 50 (2009): 261–92.
Din, Gilbert C. "The Immigration Policy of Governor Esteban Miro in Spanish Louisiana." *Southwestern Historical Quarterly* 73 (1969): 155–75.
Din, Gilbert C. "The Offices and Functions of the New Orleans Cabildo." *Louisiana History* 37 (1996): 5–30.
Doerflinger, Thomas M. A *Vigorous Spirit of Enterprise: Merchants and Economic Development in Revolutionary Philadelphia.* New York: W. W. Norton, 1986.
Douds, Howard C. "Merchants and Merchandising in Pittsburgh, 1759–1800." *Western Pennsylvania Historical Magazine* 20 (1937): 121–32.

Downes, Randolph C. "George Morgan, Indian Agent Extraordinary, 1776–1779." *Pennsylvania History* 1 (1934): 202–16.

Downes, Randolph C. "Trade in Frontier Ohio." *Mississippi Valley Historical Review* 16 (1930): 467–94.

Dunn, Walter S., Jr. *Frontier Profit and Loss: The British Army and the Fur Traders, 1760–1764*. Westport, CT: Greenwood, 1998.

Dunn, Walter S., Jr. *Opening New Markets: The British Army and the Old Northwest*. Westport, CT: Praeger, 2002.

DuVal, Kathleen. *Independence Lost: Lives on the Edge of the American Revolution*. New York: Random House, 2015.

Ekberg, Carl J. *Colonial St. Genevieve: An Adventure on the Mississippi Frontier*. Gerald, MO: Patrice, 1985.

Ekberg, Carl J. "The Flour Trade in French Colonial Louisiana." *Louisiana History* 37 (1996): 262–82.

Ekberg, Carl J. *French Roots in the Illinois Country: The Mississippi Frontier in Colonial Times*. Urbana: University of Illinois Press, 1998.

Ermus, Cindy. "Reduced to Ashes: The Good Friday Fire of 1788 in Spanish Colonial New Orleans." *Louisiana History* 54 (2013): 292–331.

Fabel, Robin F.A. "An Eighteenth Colony: Dreams for Mississippi on the Eve of the Revolution." *Journal of Southern History* 59 (1993): 647–72.

Fish, Sidney M. *Barnard and Michael Gratz: Their Lives and Times*. Lanham, MD: University Press of America, 1994.

Franklin, W. Neil. "Pennsylvania-Virginia Rivalry for the Indian Trade of the Ohio Valley." *Mississippi Valley Historical Review* 20 (1934): 463–80.

Frederick, Julia. "In Defense of Crown and Colony: Luis de Unzaga and Spanish Louisiana." *Louisiana History* 49 (2008): 389–422.

Furstenberg, François. "The Significance of the Trans-Appalachian Frontier in Atlantic History." *American Historical Review* 113 (2008): 647–77.

Furstenberg, François. *When the United States Spoke French: Five Refugees Who Shaped a Nation*. New York: Penguin, 2014.

Gitlin, Jay. *The Bourgeois Frontier: French Towns, French Traders and American Expansion*. New Haven, CT: Yale University Press, 2010.

Gruenwald, Kim M. *River of Enterprise: The Commercial Origins of Regional Identity in the Ohio Valley, 1790–1850*. Bloomington: Indiana University Press, 2002.

Haggerty, John, and Sheryllynne Haggerty. "The Life Cycle of a Metropolitan Business Network: Liverpool, 1750–1810." *Explorations in Economic History* 48 (2011): 189–206.

Haggerty, Sheryllynne. *The British-Atlantic Trading Community, 1760–1810: Men, Women, and the Distribution of Goods*. Leiden: Brill, 2006.

Hall, Gwendolyn Midlo. "Epilogue: Historical Memory, Consciousness, and Conscience in the New Millennium." In *French Colonial Louisiana and the Atlantic World*, ed. Bradley G. Bond, 291–310. Baton Rouge: Louisiana State University Press, 2005.

Hallock, Thomas. "Between Accommodation and Usurpation: Lewis Evans, Geography, and the Iroquois-British Frontier, 1743–1784." *American Studies* 44 (2003): 121–46.

Hancock, David. *Citizens of the World: London Merchants and the Integration of the British Atlantic Community, 1735–1785*. Cambridge: Cambridge University Press, 1995.

Hancock, David. *Oceans of Wine: Madeira and the Emergence of American Trade and Taste.* New Haven, CT: Yale University Press, 2009.

Hancock, David. "Organizing Our Thoughts: 'Global Systems' and the Challenge of Writing a More Complex History." *Journal of the Historical Society* 10 (2010): 319–35.

Hancock, David. "The Trouble with Networks: Managing the Scots' Early-Modern Madeira Trade." *Business History Review* 79 (2005): 467–91.

Harrington, Virginia. *The New York Merchant on the Eve of the Revolution.* New York: Columbia University Press, 1935.

Hart, Emma, and Cathy Matson. "Situating Merchants in Late Eighteenth-Century British Atlantic Port Cities." *Early American Studies* 15 (2017): 660–82.

Haynes, Robert V. *The Natchez District and the American Revolution.* Jackson: University Press of Mississippi, 2008.

Heerman, M. Scott. *The Alchemy of Slavery: Human Bondage and Emancipation in the Illinois Country, 1730–1865.* Philadelphia: University of Pennsylvania Press, 2018.

Hemmis, Timothy C. "An American Scoundrel on Trial: Aaron Burr and His Failed Insurrection, 1805–1807." In *A Republic of Scoundrels: The Schemers, Intriguers and Adventurers Who Created a New American Nation*, ed. David Head and Timothy C. Hemmis, 243–61. New York: Pegasus Books, 2023.

Henderson, Elizabeth K. "The Northwestern Lands of Pennsylvania, 1790–1812." *Pennsylvania Magazine of History and Biography* 60 (1936): 131–60.

Hilton, Sylvia L. "Loyalty and Patriotism on North American Frontiers: Being and Becoming Spanish in the Mississippi Valley, 1776–1803." In *Nexus of Empire: Negotiating Identity in the Revolutionary Borderland, 1760s–1820s*, ed. Gene Allen Smith and Sylvia L. Hilton, 8–36. Gainesville: University Press of Florida, 2010.

Hinderaker, Eric. *Elusive Empires: Constructing Colonialism in the Ohio Valley, 1673–1800.* New York: Cambridge University Press, 1997.

Holmes, Jack D. L. "The Abortive Slave Revolt at Pointe Coupee, Louisiana, 1795." *Louisiana History* 11 (1970): 341–62.

Horsman, Reginald. *The Frontier in the Formative Years, 1783–1815.* New York: Holt, Rinehart & Winston, 1970.

Hunter, Phyllis Whitman. *Purchasing Identity in the Atlantic World: Massachusetts Merchants, 1670–1780.* Ithaca, NY: Cornell University Press, 2001.

James, James A. "Oliver Pollock and the Free Navigation of the Mississippi River." *Mississippi Valley Historical Review* 19 (1932): 331–47.

James, James Alton. *Oliver Pollock: The Life and Times of an Unknown Patriot.* New York: D. Appleton-Century, 1937.

Jensen, Arthur L. *The Maritime Commerce of Colonial Philadelphia.* Madison: University of Wisconsin Press, 1963.

Kingston, Christopher. "Marine Insurance in Britain and America, 1720–1844: A Comparative Institution Analysis." *Journal of Economic History* 67 (2007): 379–409.

Kukla, Jon. *A Wilderness So Immense: The Louisiana Purchase and the Destiny of America.* New York: Alfred A. Knopf, 2003.

Lamar, Howard, and Leonard Thompson. Introduction to *The Frontier in History: North America and Southern Africa Compared*, ed. Howard Lamar and Leonard Thompson. New Haven, CT: Yale University Press, 1981.

Lee, Jacob F. *Masters of the Middle Waters: Indian Nations and Colonial Ambitions along the Mississippi*. Cambridge, MA: Harvard University Press, 2019.

Leumas, Emilie. "Ties That Bind: The Family, Social, and Business Associations of the Insurrectionists of 1768." *Louisiana History* 47 (2006): 183–202.

Lewis, George E. *The Indiana Company, 1763–1798: A Study in Eighteenth Century Frontier Land Speculation and Business Venture*. Glendale, CA: Arthur H. Clark, 1941.

Lewis, James E., Jr. *The Burr Conspiracy: Uncovering the Story of an Early American Crisis*. Princeton, NJ: Princeton University Press, 2017.

Limerick, Patricia Nelson. *The Legacy of Conquest: The Unbroken Past of the American West*. New York: Norton, 1988.

Livermore, Shaw. *Early American Land Companies: Their Influence on Corporate Development*. New York: Commonwealth Fund, 1939.

Luskey, Brian P. "'What Is My Propects?': The Contours of Mercantile Apprenticeship, Ambition, and Advancement in the Early American Economy." *Business History Review* 78 (2004): 665–702.

Mapp, Paul W. *The Elusive West and the Contest for Empire, 1713–1763*. Chapel Hill: University of North Carolina Press, 2011.

Marshall, Peter. "Lord Hillsborough, Samuel Wharton and the Ohio Grant, 1769–1775." *English Historical Review* 80 (1965): 717–39.

Marzagalli, Silvia. "Establishing Transatlantic Trade Networks in Time of War: Bordeaux and the United States, 1793–1815." *Business History Review* 79 (2005): 811–44.

Matson, Cathy. *Merchants and Empire: Trading in Colonial New York*. Baltimore: Johns Hopkins University Press, 1998.

Morrissey, Robert Michael. *Empire by Collaboration: Indians, Colonists and Governments in Colonial Illinois Country*. Philadelphia: University of Pennsylvania Press, 2015.

Narrett, David E. *Adventurism and Empire: The Struggle for Mastery in the Louisiana-Florida Borderlands, 1762–1803*. Chapel Hill: University of North Carolina Press, 2015.

Nobles, Gregory H. *American Frontiers: Cultural Encounters and Continental Conquest*. New York: Hill & Wang, 1997.

Oaks, Robert F. "The Impact of British Western Policy on the Coming of the American Revolution in Pennsylvania." *Pennsylvania Magazine of History and Biography* 101 (1977): 171–89.

Oaks, Robert F. "Philadelphia Merchants and the Origins of American Independence." *Society Proceedings of the American Philosophical* 121 (1977): 407–36.

Peterson, Charles E. *Colonial St. Louis: Building a Creole Capital*. St. Louis: Missouri Historical Society, 1949.

Pitock, Toni. "Commerce and Community: Philadelphia's Early Jewish Settlers, 1736–1776." *Pennsylvania Magazine of History and Biography* 140 (2016): 271–304.

Potter, John E. "The Pennsylvania and Virginia Boundary Controversy," *Pennsylvania Magazine of History and Biography* 38 (1914): 407–26.

Price, Jacob M. "Economic Function and the Growth of American Port Towns in the Eighteenth Century." *Perspectives in American History* 8 (1974): 123–86.

Price, Jacob M. "What Did Merchants Do? Reflections on British Overseas Trade, 1660–1790." *Journal of Economic History* 49 (1989): 267–84.

Rao, Gautham, "Thomas Worthington and the Great Transformation: Land Markets and Federal Power in the Ohio Valley, 1790–1805." *Ohio Valley History* 3 (2003): 21–34.

Rappleye, Charles. *Robert Morris: Financier of the American Revolution*. New York: Simon & Schuster, 2010.

Reeder, Tyson. "Diego de Gardoqui: From Hero of the Revolution to Scoundrel of the Early Republic." In *A Republic of Scoundrels: The Schemers, Intriguers and Adventurers Who Created a New American Nation*, ed. David Head and Timothy C. Hemmis, 225–41. New York: Pegasus Books, 2023.

Rohrbough, Malcolm J. *The Land Office Business: The Settlement and Administration of American Public Lands, 1789–1837*. New York: Oxford University Press, 1968.

Rohrbough, Malcolm J. *The Trans-Appalachian Frontier: Peoples, Societies, and Institutions, 1775–1850*. New York: Oxford University Press, 1978.

Sakolski, Aaron M. *The Great American Land Bubble: The Amazing Story of Land-Grabbing, Speculations, and Booms from Colonial Days to the Present Time*. New York: Harper & Brothers, 1932.

Salafia, Matthew. *Slavery's Borderland: Freedom and Bondage along the Ohio River*. Philadelphia: University of Pennsylvania Press, 2013.

Salvucci, Linda K. "Atlantic Intersections: Early American Commerce and the Rise of the Spanish West Indies (Cuba)." *Business History Review* 79 (2005): 781–809.

Savelle, Max. "The Founding of New Madrid, Missouri." *Mississippi Valley Historical Review* 19 (1932): 30–56.

Savelle, Max. *George Morgan, Colony Builder*. New York: Columbia University Press, 1932.

Scheerer, Hanno. "'For Ten Years Past I Have Constantly Wished to Turn My Western Lands into Money': Speculator Frustration and Settlers' Bargaining in Ohio's Virginia Military District, 1795–1810." *Ohio Valley History* 14 (2014): 3–27.

Schlesinger, Arthur M., Sr. *The Colonial Merchants and the American Revolution, 1763–1776*. New York: Columbia University Press, 1918.

Sleeper-Smith, Susan. *Indigenous Prosperity and American Conquest: Indian Women of the Ohio River Valley, 1690–1792*. Chapel Hill: University of North Carolina Press, 2018.

Sosin, Jack M. *Whitehall and the Wilderness: The Middle West in British Colonial Policy, 1760–1775*. Lincoln: University of Nebraska Press, 1961.

Sosin, Jack M. "The Yorke-Camden Opinion and American Land Speculators." *Pennsylvania Magazine of History and Biography* 85 (1961): 38–49.

Stearns, Susan Gaunt. *Empire of Commerce: The Closing of the Mississippi and the Opening of the Atlantic Trade*. Charlottesville: University of Virginia Press, 2024.

Stern, Mark Abbott. *David Franks: Colonial Merchant*. University Park: Pennsylvania State University Press, 2010.

Sutton, Robert M. "George Morgan, Early Illinois Businessman: A Case of Premature Enterprise." *Journal of the Illinois State Historical Society* 69 (1976): 173–84.

Thomas, Charles M. "Successful and Unsuccessful Merchants in the Illinois Country." *Journal of the Illinois State Historical Society* 30 (1938): 429–40.

Turner, Frederick Jackson. "The Significance of the Frontier in American History." In *The Frontier in American History*, ed. Frederick Jackson Turner, 1–38. New York: Henry Holt, 1920.

Turner, Morris K. "The Baynton, Wharton, and Morgan Manuscripts." *Mississippi Valley Historical Review* 9 (1922): 236–41.

Tyler, Bruce. "The Mississippi River Trade, 1784–1788." *Louisiana History* 12 (1971): 255–67.

Usner, Daniel H. *Indians, Settlers, and Slaves in a Frontier Exchange Economy: The Lower Mississippi Valley before 1783*. Chapel Hill: University of North Carolina Press, 1992.

Van Atta, John R. *Securing the West: Politics, Public Lands, and the Fate of the Old Republic, 1785–1850*. Baltimore: Johns Hopkins University Press, 2014.

Vidal, Cecile. "Antoine Bienvenu, Illinois Planter and Mississippi Trader: The Structure of Exchange between Lower and Upper Louisiana under French Rule." In *French Colonial Louisiana and the Atlantic World*, ed. Bradley G. Bond, 111–33. Baton Rouge: Louisiana State University Press, 2005.

Volwiler, Albert T. *George Croghan and the Westward Movement, 1741–1782*. Cleveland: Arthur H. Clark, 1926.

Wade, Richard. *The Urban Frontier: Pioneer Life in Early Pittsburgh, Cincinnati, Lexington, Louisville, and St. Louis*. Chicago: University of Chicago Press, 1964.

Wainwright, Nicholas B. *George Croghan: Wilderness Diplomat*. Chapel Hill: University of North Carolina Press, 1958.

Walzer, John F. "Colonial Philadelphia and Its Backcountry." *Winterthur Portfolio* 7 (1972): 161–73.

Watson, Samuel. "James Wilkinson: Schemer, Scoundrel, Solider, Spy . . . Success?" In *A Republic of Scoundrels: The Schemers, Intriguers and Adventurers Who Created a New American Nation*, ed. David Head and Timothy C. Hemmis, 109–32. New York: Pegasus Books, 2023.

Whitaker, Arthur P. "Reed and Forde, Merchant Adventurers of Philadelphia: Their Trade with Spanish New Orleans." *Pennsylvania Magazine of History and Biography* 61 (1937): 237–62.

Whitaker, Arthur P. *The Spanish-American Frontier: 1783–1795; the Westward Movement and the Spanish Retreat in the Mississippi Valley*. Boston: Houghton Mifflin, 1927.

Whitaker, Arthur Preston. "James Wilkinson's First Descent to New Orleans in 1787." *Hispanic American Historical Review* 8 (1928): 82–97.

Whitaker, Arthur Preston. *The Mississippi Question, 1795–1803: A Study in Trade, Politics, and Diplomacy*. Gloucester, MA: Peter Smith, 1962.

Wilkinson, Norman B. *Land Policy and Speculation in Pennsylvania, 1779–1800: A Test of the New Democracy*. New York: Arno, 1979.

Wohl, Michael. "Nor Yet Saint nor Sinner: A Further Note on Daniel Clark." *Louisiana History* 24 (1983): 195–205.

Woodward, Ralph Lee, Jr. "Spanish Commercial Policy in Louisiana, 1763–1803." *Louisiana History* 44 (2003): 133–64.

Wright, Robert E. "Thomas Willing (1731–1821): Philadelphia Financier and Forgotten Founding Father." *Pennsylvania History* 63 (1996): 525–60.

THESES AND DISSERTATIONS

Kasecamp, Emily Hager. "Company, Colony, and Crown: The Ohio Company of Virginia, Empire-Building, and the Seven Years' War, 1747–1763." PhD diss., Kent State University, 2019.

Marks, Anna Edith. "William Murray, Trader and Land Speculator in the Illinois County." BA thesis, University of Illinois, 1919.

INDEX